APHA MISSION STATEMENT

The American Public Health Association is an association of individuals and organizations working to improve the public's health. It promotes the scientific and professional foundation of public health practice and policy, advocates the conditions for a healthy global society, emphasizes prevention, and enhances the ability of members to promote and protect environmental and community health.

American Public Health Association
800 I Street, NW
Washington, DC 20001
www.apha.org

Mohammad N. Akhter, MD, MPH
Executive Director

Printed and bound in the United States of America

Cover Design: Orin Buck and Marianne Irmler

Cover Photo: © Lannis Waters/The Palm Beach Post

Typesetting: Joseph R. Loehle and Edward A. Tureen

Set in: New Baskerville and Gill Sans

Printing and Binding: Kirby Lithographic

ISBN: 0-87553-025-7

1.5 M 10/01, 1.5 M 3/02, 2.5 M 5/02

Library of Congress card catalog number: 2001096511

PUBLIC HEALTH MANAGEMENT OF DISASTERS

THE PRACTICE GUIDE

Linda Young Landesman, DrPH, MSW

Table of Contents

Publisher's Note

People throughout the world are sharing common feelings of outrage, frustration, sadness and concern in the wake of the tragic events of September 11, 2001, when hijacked commercial airliners, filled with passengers, were deliberately crashed into both the World Trade Center towers in New York City, into the Pentagon in Washington, DC, and a fourth crashed in Pennsylvania. Thousands of lives were lost, with countless more people maimed and injured, and millions of people across the country and around the world emotionally shaken. These events have forever redefined our lives as individuals and as a nation. No longer do we have the luxury of feeling invulnerable as we walk along our streets, go to work or school each day, or fly off on spur–of–the–moment holidays.

Our spirit is not broken. However, emergency response and public health preparedness has gained a heightened awareness in our consciousness. For the first time ever, the Secretary of Health and Human Services(HHS), Tommy Thompson, made the decision to launch the National Disaster Medical System (NDMS). HHS is the primary agency for coordinating health, medical and health–related social services under the federal emergency response plan, and its Office of Emergency Preparedness (OEP) is the "medical 911" for all national and catastrophic disasters, both natural and manmade.

CDC activated its Health Alert Network which provides rapid information nationally to all health departments. The agency issued a precautionary advisory to state and local health departments to be alert to any unusual disease symptoms; however, as of the writing of this Note, no reports had resulted from this alert. The CDC Health Alert Network also was used to provide information on safe handling of bodies to ensure against the spread of disease, and CDC provided information regarding dust hazards arising from the collapse of the World Trade Center towers.

The NDMS activation placed 80 disaster medical assistance teams (DMATs) nationwide, ready for deployment if necessary. In total, OEP deployed 328 medical personnel from disaster readiness teams to assist health providers in both New York City and Washington, DC. OEP also deployed mortuary services personnel to assist in retrieval, identification and preparation for burial of those killed at both disaster sites. The Public Health Service Commissioned Corps was put on readiness alert the evening of September 11, making over 5,700 corps personnel available for deployment where needed.

The American Public Health Association (APHA), also acted quickly, in response to numerous inquiries from members. Our initial action was to send letters to Mayor Giuliani of New York City, Mayor Williams of Washington, DC, and HHS Secretary Thompson, offering support and help. As it became increasingly clear that the number of injured needing medical attention was much lower than anticipated and was overwhelmed by the numbers of dead, the need for mental health services and grief counseling became especially acute. Mental health experts from our membership have generously come forth and APHA is now working with the Public Health Association of New York, federal and state agencies and private organizations to develop a plan of action. Our goal is to develop a sustained effort to help people cope with their loss and to rebuild their lives.

In addition, APHA has created a website: www.apha.org/united with information and resources on the public health response to this tragedy.

For the long term, APHA is working with its partners in the public health community on strategies to strengthen the public health infrastructure to address unpredictable and unprecedented attacks in the future. At the same time, we must address the root causes that breed terrorism: poverty and injustice in too many corners of the globe.

This publication, Public Health Management of Disasters: The Practice Guide, was nearing completion as this tragedy occurred. This book is the first comprehensive public health text for public health practitioners and public safety personnel on emergency management response. The book acts as a resource to guide practitioners in this relatively new practice area as public health leaders begin the comprehensive nationwide integration of health departments into the emergency management response of communities. An epilogue addressing the disaster has been added. As more is learned from this national tragedy, this book will be updated and expanded.

Mohammad N. Akhter, MD, MPH
Executive Director
American Public Health Association

ACKNOWLEDGEMENTS

The completion of a book requires love of the work, time and space from your family, and the assistance of many people. I thank the colleagues who participated in the development of the disaster curriculum through the Association of Schools of Public Health and Centers for Disease Control and Prevention (CDC). These public health leaders, Michael Ascher, Erik Auf der Heide, Scott Becker, Steve Becker, Rick Bissell, Paul Bolton, Rick Brennan, Skip Burkle, Gil Burnham, Debbie Guha-Sapir, Ehren Ngo, Josephine Malilay, Ernie Pretto, Ed Ricci, Les Roberts, and Paul Spiegel, helped establish the direction for the model disaster curriculum. Material for this book was derived from that project supported under a cooperative agreement from the Centers for Disease Control and Prevention (CDC) through the Association of Schools of Public Health. Don Mattison provided the early encouragement that led to this book, for which I am very grateful.

My colleagues in the public health and emergency management communities, Sam Benson, Peter Cann, Gilberto Cardona, Ed Gabriel, Wilfredo Lopez, Maryann Marrocolo, Marci Layton, Eric Noji, and Joe Stevens generously gave of their time to provide me with the latest information in their domains. I am indebted for their contribution to the content of this book and to my thinking. In addition to their great cover design, working with Marianne Irmler and Orin Buck allowed me to add my mark, and I thank them for the opportunity.

The process of completing this book afforded me the luck of working closely with colleagues at APHA. Burt Wilcke had a vision that fostered the creation of a more comprehensive manual than I had originally drafted. Ellen T. Meyer, Edward A. Tureen, and Joseph R. Loehle cheerfully provided the technical assistance that made production enjoyable. The completion of this project depended on their dedicated help.

Finally, a project this time consuming is not possible without personal support. This book is dedicated to the two best men in the world – my husband, Paul, and my son, Andy. Hopefully, with the wake up call of the World Trade Center attack, this book will help strengthen public health preparedness across the country.

Foreword

BY

ERIC K. NOJI, M.D., M.P.H.

CENTERS FOR DISEASE CONTROL & PREVENTION (CDC)

With both disasters and the number of people affected by such events on the increase, the importance of disasters as a public health problem is now widely recognized. The last quarter century has witnessed a heightened recognition of the role of the health professional in managing disasters. For example, in the early 1970s, health personnel working in disaster situations observed that the effects of disasters on the health of populations were amenable to study by epidemiological methods and that certain common patterns of morbidity and mortality following certain disasters could be identified. Subsequently, post-disaster evaluations of the effectiveness of the health management of disasters have provided critical lessons for improving preparedness and mitigating the human impact of these events. Furthermore, government officials and other decision-makers have increasingly acknowledged the importance of collecting relevant health data that can be used as a scientific basis for taking action on a myriad of problems facing a disaster-affected community (i.e., recovery and reconstruction).

During the past 15 years, the medical and public health impact of disasters have been reviewed in a number of publications with periodic updates on the "state of the art" appearing every few years. As a result, a considerable body of knowledge and experience related to the adverse health effects of disasters is now accumulating that requires regular updating so that we can apply the lessons learned during one disaster to the management of the next. This book, Public Health Management of Disasters: The Practice Guide, does exactly that and more. With years of experience, Dr. Landesman gives the reader ample technical descriptions of each kind of disaster, the structural and organizational makeup of emergency management particularly those related to the role and responsibilities of health professionals, and copious information useful for management practices in the disaster setting (e.g., risk assessment, surveillance, communications and environmental issues). In addition, always emphasizing the use of proven management methods and practices, Dr. Landesman challenges public health professions with questions that must still be answered to respond effectively in emergency situations.

All disasters are unique because each affected region of the world has different social, economic, and baseline health conditions. Public Health Management of Disasters: The Practice Guide will serve as the essential desk reference not only for health professionals responsible for preparing for and responding to disasters, but for emergency managers, government officials and other decision-makers charged with ensuring that limited resources of the affected community are well managed.

Chapter *1*

Types of Disasters and Their Consequences

Disasters are emergencies of a severity and magnitude resulting in deaths, injuries, illness and/or property damage that cannot be effectively managed by the application of routine procedures or resources. These events are caused by nature, the result of technological or manmade error, or from emerging diseases. The public health community should be concerned about disasters because there is a ubiquitous risk, there has been an increase in natural disasters across the U.S., disasters have negative impacts on the public's health, and the actual and potential effects of manmade and human disasters will likely increase.

A significant proportion of Americans are at risk from only three classes of natural disasters: floods, earthquakes, and hurricanes. Twenty-five to fifty million people live in floodplains that have been highly developed as living and working environments. Another 110 million people live in coastal areas of the United States, including the Great Lakes region. By the year 2010, 60% of the US population may be living within 50 miles of the East or West Coast. A category 4 hurricane has an 80% chance of hitting the coastal area from Maine to Texas.

Disasters pose a number of unique problems not encountered in the routine practice of emergency health care. Examples include the need for warning and evacuation, widespread urban search and rescue, triage and casualty distribution, and coordination among multiple jurisdictions, levels of government offices, and private sector organizations in dealing with a damaged, disabled health care infrastructure. The effective management of these concerns requires special expertise.

Further, hospitals and other health care agencies must be able to address these situations quickly and effectively to meet the standards of the Joint Commission on Accreditation of Healthcare Organizations and the regulations of the Occupational and Safety Health Administration.

NATURAL AND TECHNOLOGICAL DISASTERS

Natural disasters can be categorized as "acute" or "slow" in their onset. They are predictable because they cluster in geographic areas. Natural hazards are unpreventable and, for the most part, uncontrollable. Even if quick recovery occurs, natural disasters can have long-term effects. Natural disasters with acute onsets include events such as earthquake; flood; hurricane, cyclone or typhoon; tornado; fire; tsunami or storm surge; avalanche; volcanic eruption; extreme cold or blizzard; and heatwave. Natural hazards with a slow or gradual onset include drought, famine, desertification, deforestation, and pest infestation. The most important natural disasters and examples of their environmental effects are listed in Table 1.

Technological or manmade disasters include nuclear accidents, bombings, and bioterrorism. Increasingly, agencies involved in disasters and their management are concerned with the interactions between man and nature, which can be complex and can aggravate disasters.

TABLE 1—NATURAL DISASTERS AND THEIR ENVIRONMENTAL IMPACT

Natural Disaster	Environmental Effects
Blizzard/Heavy Snowfall	Avalanche, erosion, snow melt (flooding)
Coldwave	Loss of plants and animals, river ice jams (flooding)
Cyclone	Flooding, landslide, erosion, loss of plant and animal life
Drought	Fire, depletion of water resources, deterioration of soil, loss of plant and animal life
Earthquake	Landslide, rock fall, avalanche
Heatwave	Fire, loss of plants and animals, depletion of water resources, deterioration of soil, snow melt (flooding)
Lightning	Fire
Thunderstorm/Heavy Rainfall	Flooding, fire, landslide, erosion, destruction of plant life
Tornado	Loss of plant and animal life, erosion, water disturbance
Tsunami	Flooding, erosion, loss of plant and animal life
Volcanic Eruption	Loss of plant and animal life, deterioration of soil, air and water polution

The severity of damage caused by natural or technological disasters is affected by population density in disaster-prone areas, local building codes, community preparedness, and the use of public safety announcements and education on how to respond correctly at the first signs of danger. Recovery following a disaster varies according to the public's access to pertinent information (eg, sources of government and private aid), pre-existing conditions that increase or reduce vulnerability (ie, economic or biological factors), prior experience with stressful situations, and availability of sufficient savings and insurance.

CYCLONES, HURRICANES & TYPHOONS

Cyclones are large-scale storms characterized by low pressure in the center surrounded by circular wind motion (counter clockwise in the Northern Hemisphere, clockwise in the Southern Hemisphere). Severe storms arising in the Atlantic waters are known as hurricanes, while those developing in the Pacific Ocean and the China seas are called typhoons. The precise classification (eg, tropical depression, tropical storm, hurricane) depends on the wind force (Beaufort scale), wind speed, and manner of creation.

Hurricanes are powerful storms that form at sea with wind speeds of 74 miles per hour or greater. They are tracked by satellites from the moment they begin to form, so warnings can be issued three to four days before a storm strikes. A hurricane covers a circular area between 200 and 480 miles in diameter. In the storm, strong winds and rain surround a central, calm "eye," which is about 15 miles across. Winds in a hurricane can sometimes reach 200 miles per hour. However, the greatest damage to life and property is not from the wind but from tidal surges and flash flooding. Owing to its violent nature, its potentially prolonged duration, and the extensive area that could be affected, the hurricane or cyclone is potentially the most devastating of all storms due to violent winds, excessive rainfall and an increase in see level. Scientists have developed a relatively good understanding of the nature of hurricanes through observation, radar, weather satellites, and computer models.

A distinctive characteristic of hurricanes is the increase in sea level, often referred to as the storm surge. This increase in sea level is the result of the low-pressure central area of the storm creating suction, the storm winds piling up water, and the tremendous speed of the storm. Rare storm surges have risen as much as 14 meters above normal sea level. This phenomenon can be experienced as a large mass of sea water pushed along by the storm with great force. When it reaches land, the impact of the storm surge can be exacerbated by high tide, a low-lying coastal area with a gently sloping seabed, or a semi-enclosed bay facing the ocean.

The severity of a storm's impact on humans is exacerbated by deforestation, which often occurs as the result of population pressure. When trees disappear along the coastlines, the winds and the storm surges can enter the land with greater force. Deforestation on the slopes of hills and mountains increases the risk of violent flash floods and landslides caused by the heavy rain associated with tropical cyclones. At the same time, the beneficial effects of the rainfall—replenishment of the water resources—may be negated due to the inability of a forest ecosystem to absorb and retain water.

Risk of Morbidity and Mortality

Deaths and injuries from hurricanes occur because victims fail to evacuate or take shelter, do not take precautions in securing their property despite adequate warning, and do not follow guidelines on food and water safety or injury prevention during recovery. Morbidity during and after the storm itself results from drowning, electrocution, lacerations or punctures from flying debris, and blunt trauma or bone fractures from falling trees or other objects. Heart attacks and stress-related disorders can arise during the storm or its aftermath. Gastrointestinal, respiratory, vector-borne, and skin disease as well as accidental pediatric poisoning can all occur during the period immediately following the cyclone. Injuries from improper use of chain saws or other power equipment, disrupted wildlife (eg, bites from animals, snakes, or insects), and fires are common. Fortunately, the ability to detect and track storms has helped reduce morbidity and mortality in many countries.

Injury Prevention

Public health professionals work with local emergency management agencies to prepare people to evacuate and to turn off their utilities. To avoid injury, residents should be advised to use common sense and wear proper clothing, including long sleeved shirts, pants, and safety shoes or boots. Further, they should learn proper safety precautions and operating instructions before operating gas-powered or electric chainsaws. People should use extreme caution when using electric chainsaws to avoid electrical shock and should always wear gloves and a safety face shield or eyeglasses when using any chainsaw. Evacuees should be advised against wading in water as there may be downed power lines, broken glass, metal fragments, or other debris beneath the surface.

When returning to their dwellings after a disaster, residents should check for structural damage and electrical or natural gas or propane tank hazards. They should return to homes during the daytime and only use battery-powered flashlights and lanterns to provide light rather than candles, gas lanterns, or torches.

During the recovery period, public health and local emergency management officials must ensure an adequate supply of safe water and food for the displaced population. In addition to offering acute emergency care, community plans should provide for the continuity of care for homeless residents with chronic conditions.

Public Health Interventions

- Conduct needs assessment for affected communities, including a review of public health infrastructure.

- Establish active and passive surveillance systems for deaths, illness, and injuries.

- Educate the public about maintaining safe and adequate supplies of food and water.

- Establish environmental controls.

- Monitor infectious disease and make determinations about needed immunizations (eg tetanus).

- Institute multifaceted injury control programs.

- Establish protective measures against potential disease vectors.

- Monitor potential release of hazardous materials.

- Assure evacuation plans for people with special needs in nursing homes, hospitals, and home care.

- Work with local communities to improve building codes (eg, developing improved designs for wind safety).

DROUGHT

Drought affects more people than any other environmental hazard, yet it is perhaps the most complex and least understood type of all environmental hazards. Drought is often seen as the result of too little rain and used synonymously with famine. However, fluctuation in rainfall alone does not cause a famine. Drought often triggers a crisis in the arid and semi-arid areas, since rain is sparse and irregular, but alone does not cause desertification. The ecosystem changes leading to desertification are all attributed to human activities, such as overcultivation, deforestation, overgrazing, and unskilled irrigation. Each of these activities is exacerbated by increasing human populations. The first three activities strip the soil of vegetation and deplete its organic and nutrient content. This leaves the soil exposed to the eroding forces of the sun and the wind. The subsoil that is left can become so hard that it no longer absorbs rain, and the water flows over the surface, carrying away the little topsoil that might have remained.

Risk of Morbidity and Mortality

Displaced populations suffer high rates of disease due to stress of migration, crowding, and unsanitary conditions of relocation sites. Morbidity and mortality can result from diarrheal disease, respiratory disease, and malnutrition. Mortality exceeding a baseline rate of one death per 10,000 people per day is the index of concern. Low weight to height is identified through the percentage of children two or more standard deviations (z-score) from the reference median compared with mean z-scores; children with edema are severely malnourished.

Public Health Interventions

- Monitor health and nutritional status by assessing weights and heights.

- Assess and ensure food security, including availability, accessibility, and consumption patterns.

- Monitor death rate.

- Ensure safe water, sanitation, and disease control.

EARTHQUAKE

Earthquakes are sudden slippages or movements in a portion of the earth's crust accompanied and followed by a series of vibrations. Aftershocks of similar or lesser intensity can follow the main quake. An earthquake is generally considered to be the most destructive and frightening of all forces of nature. Earthquake losses, like those of other disasters, tend to cause more financial losses in industrialized countries and more injuries and deaths in undeveloped countries.

The Richter magnitude, used as an indication of the force of an earthquake, measures the magnitude and intensity or energy released by the quake. This value is calculated based on data recordings from a single observation point for events anywhere on earth, but it does not address the possible damaging effects of the earthquake. According to global observations, an average of two earthquakes of a Richter magnitude 8 or slightly more occur every year. A one digit drop in magnitude equates with a tenfold increase in frequency. In other words, earthquakes of magnitude 7 or more generally occur 20 times in a year, while those with a magnitude 6 or more occur approximately 200 times.

Earthquakes can result in a secondary disaster, catastrophic tsunami. Tsunami, a series of waves of very great length and period, are usually generated by large earthquakes under or near the oceans, close to the edges of the tectonic plates. These waves may travel long distances, increase in height abruptly when they reach shallow water, and cause great devastation far away from the source. Submarine landslides and volcanic eruptions beneath the sea or on small islands can also be responsible for tsunami, but their effects are usually limited to smaller areas. Volcanic tsunami are usually of greater magnitude than seismic ones; waves of more than 40 meters in height have been witnessed.

Geologists have identified regions where earthquakes are likely to occur. With the increasing population worldwide and urban migration trends, higher death tolls and greater property losses are more likely in many areas prone to earthquakes. At least 70 million people face significant risk of death or injury from earthquakes because they live in the 39 states that are seismically active. In addition to the significant risks in California, the Pacific Northwest, Utah, and Idaho, six major cities with populations greater than 100,000 are located within the seismic area of the New Madrid fault. Major Third World cities in which large numbers are forced to live on earthquake-prone land in structures unable to withstand damage include Lima, Peru; Santiago, Chile; Quito, Ecuador; and Caracas, Venezuela.

Risk of Morbidity and Mortality

Deaths and injuries from earthquakes vary according to the type of housing available, time of day of occurrence, and population density. Common injuries include cuts, broken bones, crush injuries, and dehydration from being trapped in rubble. Stress reactions are also common. Morbidity and mortality can occur during the actual quake, the delayed collapse of unsound structures, or clean-up activity.

Injury Prevention

Public health officials can intervene both in advance of and after earthquakes to prevent post-earthquake injuries. The safety of homes and the work environment can be improved by building standards that require stricter codes and use of safer materials. Measures to prevent injuries include securing appliances, securing hanging items on walls or overhead, turning off utilities, storing hazardous materials in safe, well-ventilated areas, and checking homes for hazards such as windows and glass that might shatter.

Public health workers should follow the recommendations listed previously for Cyclone.

Public Health Interventions

- Encourage earthquake drills to practice emergency procedures.

- Recommend items for inclusion in an extensive first aid kit and a survival kit for home and automobile, and encourage maintenance of those kits.

- Teach basic precautions regarding safe water and safe food.

- Ensure the provision of emergency medical care to those who seek acute care in first three to five days after an earthquake.

- Ensure continuity of care for those who have lost access to prescriptions, home care, and other medical necessities.

- Conduct surveillance for communicable disease and injuries, including location and severity of injury, disposition of patient, and follow-up contact information.

- Prepare media advisories with appropriate warnings and advice for injury prevention.

- Establish environmental controls.

- Facilitate use of surveillance forms by search and rescue teams to record type of building, address of site, type of collapse, amount of dust, fire or toxic hazards, location of victims, and nature and severity of injuries.

FLOOD

Global statistics show that floods are the most frequently recorded destructive events, accounting for about 30% of the world's disasters each year. The frequency of floods is increasing faster than in any type of disaster. Much of this rise in incidence can be attributed to uncontrolled urbanization, deforestation, and, more recently, the effects of El Niño. Floods may also accompany other natural disasters, such as sea surges during hurricanes and tsunamis following earthquakes.

Except for flash floods, flooding causes few deaths. Instead, widespread and long-lasting detrimental effects include mass homelessness, disruption of communications and health care systems, and heavy loss of business, livestock, crops, and grain, particularly in densely-populated, low lying areas. The frequent repetition of flooding means a constant, or even increasing, drain on the economy for rural populations.

Risk of Morbidity and Mortality

Flood-related mortality varies from country to country. Flash flooding, such as from excessive rainfall or sudden release of water from a dam, is the cause of most flood-related deaths. Most flood-related death victims become trapped in their cars and drown when attempting to drive through rising or swiftly moving water. Other deaths have been caused by wading, bicycling, or other recreational activities in flooded areas.

The stress and exertion required for clean up following a flood also cause significant morbidity (mental and physical) and mortality (eg, myocardial infarction). Fires, explosions from gas leaks, downed live wires, and debris can all cause significant injury. Water-borne diseases (eg enterotoxigenic *Escherichia* coli, *Shigella*, hepatitis A, leptospirosis, giardiasis) become a significant hazard, as do other vector-borne disease and skin disorders. Injured and frightened animals, hazardous waste contamination, molds and mildew, and dislodging of graves pose additional risks in the period following a flood. Food shortages due to water-damaged stocks may occur due to flooding and sea surges.

Injury Prevention

Educating the public about the dangers of floods and about avoiding risky behaviors may prevent deaths. Since most flood-related deaths are due to drowning in motor vehicles, educational campaigns can discuss how cars do not provide protection from moving water and that as little as two feet of water is capable of carrying vehicles away.

Even more important to injury and disease prevention is education regarding clean up procedures and precautions. Rubber boots and waterproof gloves should be worn during cleanup. Walls, hard-surfaced floors, and many other household surfaces should be cleaned with soap and water and disinfected with a solution of one cup of bleach to five gallons of water. Surfaces on which food may be stored or prepared and areas in which small children play must be thoroughly disinfected.

Children's toys must be disinfected prior to use or discarded. All linens and clothing must be washed in hot water or dry cleaned. Items that cannot be washed or dry cleaned, such as mattresses and upholstered furniture, should be air dried in the sun and then sprayed thoroughly with a disinfectant. All carpeting must be steam cleaned. Household materials that cannot be disinfected should be discarded.

Residents must understand that flood water may contain fecal material from overflowing sewage systems as well as agricultural and industrial byproducts. Although skin contact with flood water does not by itself pose a serious health risk, there is some risk of disease from eating or drinking anything contaminated with flood water. Anyone with open cuts or sores that could be exposed to flood water must keep these areas as clean as possible by washing with soap to control infection. Wounds that develop redness, swelling, or drainage require immediate medical attention.

Routine sanitary procedures are essential for disease prevention. Hands must be washed with soap and water that has been boiled or disinfected before preparing or eating food, after toilet use, after participating in flood clean up activities, and after handling articles contaminated with flood water or sewage. Children's hands should be washed frequently, and children should not be allowed to play in previously flooded areas.

Public Health Interventions

- Conduct needs assessment to determine the status of public health infrastructure, utilities (eg, water, sewage, electricity), and health, medical, and pharmaceutical needs.

- Conduct surveillance of drinking water sources, injuries, increases in vector populations, and endemic, water-borne, and vector borne disease.

- Organize delivery of health care services and supplies and continuity of care.

- Educate public regarding proper sanitation and hygiene.

- Educate public regarding proper clean up.

HEAT WAVE

Over time, populations can acclimatize to hot weather. However, mortality and morbidity rise when daytime temperatures remain unusually high several days in a row and nighttime temperatures do not drop significantly. Because populations acclimatize to summer temperatures, heat waves in June and July have more of an impact than those in August and September. There is often a delay between the onset of a heat wave and adverse health effects. Deaths occur more commonly during heat waves where there is little cooling at night and taper off to baseline levels if a heat wave is sustained.

Risk of Morbidity and Mortality

Heat waves result in adverse health effects in cities more than in rural areas. Those at greatest risk of adverse health outcomes include older adults, infants, those with a history of prior heatstroke, and those who are obese. Drugs that may predispose users to heatstroke include neurolepics and anticholinergics. Heat-related morbidity and mortality come from heat cramps, heatstroke, heat exhaustion, heat syncope, myocardial infarction, loss of consciousness, dizziness, cramps, and stroke.

Injury Prevention

Residents at greatest risk must be moved to air-conditioned buildings for at least a few hours each day. All residents must maintain adequate hydration and reduce outdoor activity levels. Education campaigns should concentrate on protecting older adults and helping parents of children under five years of age understand how to protect their children from heat and prevent heat disorders.

Public Health Interventions

- Develop an early warning surveillance system that triggers the mobilization of prevention and intervention activities.

- Identify the location of residents who might be at risk due to age, pre-existing conditions, lack of air conditioning, and other environmental or health factors.

- Work with utilities to educate the public about preventive actions when energy blackouts might be anticipated.

TORNADO

Tornados are rapidly whirling, funnel-shaped air spirals that emerge from a violent thunderstorm and reach the ground. Tornados can have a wind velocity of up to 200 miles per hour and generate sufficient force to destroy even massive buildings. The average circumference of a tornado is a few hundred meters, and it is usually exhausted before it has travelled as far as 20 kilometers. Severity is rated on the Fujita Scale according to wind speed. The Fujita Scale uses a scoring system of F0 (no damage) to F5 (total destruction). The extent of damage depends on updrafts within the tornado funnel, the tornado's atmospheric pressure (which is often lower than the surrounding barometric pressure), and the effects of flying debris.

Risk of Morbidity and Mortality

Approximately 1,000 tornadoes occur annually in the United States, and none of the lower 48 states is immune. Certain geographic areas are at greater risk due to their recurrent weather patterns; tornados most frequently occur in the midwestern and southeastern states. Although tornadoes often develop in the late afternoon and more often from March through May, they can arise at any hour of the day and during any month of the year.

Injuries from tornados occur due to flying debris or people being thrown by the high winds (eg. head injuries, soft tissue injury, secondary wound infection). Stress-related disorders are more common, as is disease related to loss of utilities, potable water, or shelter.

Injury Prevention

Because tornadoes can occur so quickly, communities should develop redundant warning systems (eg, media alerts and automated telephone warnings), establish protective shelter to reduce tornado-related injuries, and practice tornado-shelter drills. In the event of a tornado, the residents should take shelter in a basement if possible, away from windows, while protecting their heads. Special outreach should be made to people with special needs who can make a list of their limitations, capabilities, and medications and have ready an emergency box of needed supplies. People with special needs should have a "buddy" who has a copy of the list and who knows of the emergency box. Other precautions include those listed under Cyclone.

Public Health Interventions

- Work with emergency management on tornado shelter drills for vulnerable communities.

- Conduct needs assessment using maps that detail pre-existing neighborhoods, including landmarks, and aerial reconnaissance.

- Ensure the provision of medical care, shelter, food, and water.

- Establish environmental controls.

- Establish a surveillance system based at both clinical sites and shelters.

TECHNOLOGICAL DISASTER

Technological or manmade disasters are unpredictable, can spread across geographic areas, may be unpreventable, and may have limited physical damage but long-term effects. Technological disasters occur because industrial sites are located in communities affected by natural disasters, equipment failures occur, process and procedural failures happen or workers have inadequate training or fatigue and make errors. The threat of terrorism is categorized as a potential technological disaster and includes bioterrorism, bombings, civil and political disorders, riots, and economic emergency.

Technological disasters include a broad range of incidents. Hazardous material (eg, chemical, biological, or radioactive) can be released into the environment at a fixed facility or during transport. Fires, explosions, building or bridge collapse, transportation crashes, dam or levee failure, nuclear reactor accidents, and breaks in water, gas, or sewer lines are all examples of technological disasters.

Risk of Morbidity and Mortality

Communities in which industrial sites are located or through which hazardous materials pass via highway, rail, or pipeline are at risk for technological disasters. Injuries can occur to workers at the site, to responders bringing the incident under control and providing emergency medical care, and to residents in the community. Those with pre-existing medical conditions, such as lung or heat disease, could be at increased risk for negative health outcomes if exposed to toxic releases. Burns, skin disorders, and lung damage can result from exposure to specific agents. Table 2 lists the health consequences of several classes of toxins.

Injury Prevention

Ensuring that local industry implements basic safety procedures can significantly reduce negative health outcomes from accidental releases of toxins. Emergency preparedness—including the ability of prehospital and hospital systems to care for patients exposed to industrial agents, the training of medical personnel to work in contaminated environments, and the stockpiling of personal protective equipment for

TABLE 2. HEALTH EFFECTS OF CHEMICAL AGENTS

Chemical Agent	Health Effects
Nerve agents	Miosis, rhinorrhea, dyspnea
Vesicants	Erythema, blisters, eye irritation, cough, dyspnea
Cyanide	Loss of consciousness, seizures, apnea
Pulmonary CG (phosgene)	Dyspnea, coughing

responders—is key to providing care following industrial accidents.

Government agencies should conduct computer simulations or field exercises to test their ability to evacuate those at risk and the ability of the health sector to provide care to those exposed to accidental releases. Information about the clinical management of exposure to toxins can be provided by poison control centers, CHEMTREC, and industry databases.

Public Health Interventions

- Take a visible role in community planning.

- Conduct hazard assessments.

- Review Material Safety Data Sheets for agents produced, stored, or used locally and regionally to evaluate range of potential adverse health effects.

- Conduct vulnerability analyses to identify target populations and potential adverse public health consequences.

- Conduct risk assessment to determine if specific agents will reach toxic levels in the vicinity of vulnerable populations.

- Determine minimal thresholds of exposure for specific agents that would trigger evacuation.

- Gather information on chemical neutralization, estimation models of plume-dispersion, and appropriate antidotes.

- Work with local hospitals to stockpile appropriate antidotes, medications, and supplies.

- Stockpile two pills per person of potassium iodide in communities located within ten miles of nuclear reactor sites.

- Provide emergency services and medical care to victims.

- Activate the Health Alert Network.

EPIDEMICS

The spread of infectious disease depends upon preexisting levels of the disease, ecological changes resulting from disaster, population displacement, changes in density of population, disruption of public utilities, interruption of basic public health services, and compromises to sanitation and hygiene. The risk that epidemics of infectious diseases will occur is proportional to the population density and displacement. A true epidemic can occur in susceptible populations in the presence or impending introduction of a disease agent compounded by the presence of a mechanism that facilitates large-scale transmission (eg, contaminated water supply or vector population).

Quick response is essential because epidemics, which result in human and economic losses and political difficulties, often arise rapidly. An epidemic or threatened epidemic can become an emergency when the following characteristics of the events are present. Not all of these characteristics need be present and each must be assessed with regard to relative importance locally:

- risk of introduction to and spread of the disease in the population

- large number of cases may reasonably be expected to occur

- disease involved is of such severity as to lead to serious disability or death

- risk of social or economic disruption resulting from the presence of the disease

- authorities are unable to cope adequately with the situation due to insufficient technical or professional personnel, organizational experience, and necessary supplies or equipment (eg, drugs, vaccines, laboratory diagnostic materials, vector-control materials)

- risk of international transmission

The categorization of "emergency" differs from country to country, depending on two local factors: whether the disease is endemic and a means of transmitting the agent exists. Table 3 describes epidemic emergencies for particular diseases listed in nonendemic areas.

TABLE 3. EPIDEMIC EMERGENCIES DEFINED

Disease	Nonendemic areas	Endemic areas
Cholera	One confirmed indigenous case	Significant increase in incidence over and above what is normal for the season, particularly if multifocal and accompanied by deaths in children less than 10 years old
Giardiasis	A cluster of cases in a group of tourists returning from an endemic area	A discrete increase in incidence linked to a specific endemic place
Malaria	A cluster of cases, with an increase in incidence in a defined geographical area	Rarely an emergency; increased incidence requires program strengthening
Meningococcal meningitis	An incidence rate of 1 per 1000 in one week in a defined geographical area	The same rate for two consecutive weeks is an emergency
Plague	One confirmed case apparently linked by domestic rodent or respiratory transmission or by a rodent epizootic	A cluster of cases
Rabies	One confirmed case of animal rabies in a previously rabies-free locale	Significant increases in animal and human cases
Salmonellosis	A large cluster of cases in a limited area, with a single or predominant stereotype (eg, specific event or restaurant), or a significant number of cases occurring in multiple foci, apparently related by a common source (eg, specific food product)	
Smallpox (a)	Any strongly suspected case	Not applicable
Typhus fever/ rickettsia	One confirmed case in a louse-infested, nonimmune population	Significant increase in number of cases in a limited period of time
Viral Encephalitis	Cluster of time- and space-related cases in a nonimmune population (a single case should be regarded as a warning)	Significant increase in the number of cases with a mosquito-borne single, identified etiological agent in a limited period
Viral haemorhragic fever	One confirmed indigenous or imported case with an etiological single agent with which person-to-person transmission may occur in a limited period of time	Significant increase in the number of cases with an identified etiological agent
Yellow fever	One confirmed case in a community	Significant increase in the number of cases in a population and an adequate/limited period of time for vector population to increase

Public Health Interventions

- Control or prevent epidemic situations.

- Conduct surveillance to identify when an epidemic is likely to occur.

- Ensure that items requiring refrigeration, such as vaccines, are kept refrigerated throughout the chain of distribution.

- Monitor the maintenance of immunization programs against childhood infectious disease (eg, measles, mumps, polio).

TABLE 4 NATURAL DISASTER EFFECTS MATRIX – MOST COMMON EFFECTS OF SPECIFIC EVENTS ON ENVIRONMENTAL HEALTH

1- Severe possible effect;

2 -Less severe possible effect;

3- Least or no possible effect

	Earthquake	Hurricane	Flood	Tsunami	Volcanic Eruption
WATER SUPPLY AND WASTE DISPOSAL					
Damage to civil engineering structures	1	1	1	3	1
Broken mains	1	2	2	1	1
Damage to water sources	1	2	2	3	1
Power outages	1	1	2	2	1
Contamination (biological or chemical)	2	1	1	1	1
Transportation failures	1	1	1	2	1
Personnel shortages	1	2	2	2	1
System overload (due to population shifts)	3	1	1	2	1
Equipment, parts, and supply shortages	1	1	1	2	1
SOLID WASTE HANDLING					
Damage to civil engineering structures	1	2	2	3	1
Transportation failures	1	1	1	2	1
Equipment shortage	1	1	1	2	1
Personnel shortage	1	1	1	3	1
Water, soil, and air pollution	1	1	1	2	1
FOOD HANDLING					
Spoilage of refrigerated foods	1	1	2	2	1
Damage to food preparation facilities	1	1	2	3	1
Transportation failures	1	1	1	2	1
Power outages	1	1	1	3	1
Flooding of facilities	3	1	1	1	2
Contamination/degradation of relief supplies	2	1	1	2	1
VECTOR CONTROL					
Proliferation of vector breeding sites	1	1	1	1	3
Increase in human/vector contacts	1	1	1	2	1
Disruption of vector-borne disease control programs	1	1	1	1	1
HOME SANITATION					
Destruction or damage to structures	1	1	1	1	1
Contamination of water and food	2	2	1	2	1
Disruption of power, heating, fuel, water or supply waste disposal services	1	1	1	2	1
Overcrowding	3	3	3	3	2

REPRINTED FROM NATURAL DISASTERS- PROTECTING THE PUBLIC'S HEALTH, SCIENTIFIC PUBLICATION #575, PAN AMERICAN HEALTH ORGANIZATION, 2000, PAHO PUBLICATIONS (WWW.PAHO..ORG) 525 23RD ST., NW, WASHINGTON DC 20037

Chapter 2

Role and Responsibility of Public Health

Public health professionals must take responsibility for community health in both disaster preparedness and response. This chapter outlines in detail action plans, personnel requirements, applicable laws, and the functional model of public health response.

PUBLIC HEALTH ROLE

- Identify community resources applicable to the physical, social, and psychosocial effects of disaster.

- Identify groups most at risk from disaster (ie, children, older adults, homeless, chronically ill, homebound, physically or mentally disabled).

- Provide disaster education both in advance of (ie, what to expect in a disaster) and after (ie, how to deal with effects) event.

- Take responsibility for the health of a community following a disaster.

- Use such resources as assessment, epidemiology, and data analysis to make and implement recommendations for limiting morbidity and mortality following disaster.

- Cooperate and collaborate with colleagues in the health sector to ensure that primary health, public health, mental health, and social impacts are adequately addressed in disaster planning.

- Prevent disease by providing health advisories on injury prevention, food and water safety, and vector control.

- Assure that health services continue post impact, including acute, continuity of care, primary care and emergency care.

- Inspect Red Cross shelters and feeding operations.

- Request volunteers from the American Red Cross to supplement medical and nursing needs.

- Communicate with government officials about the public health effects of potential disasters and provide expert assistance during and after disasters.

- Develop and advocate public policies designed to reduce the public health impact of potential disasters.

- Collaborate with other health and human service professionals to rigorously evaluate intervention outcome.

Local public health authorities have the primary responsibility for the health of a community following a disaster. These professionals bring unique resources to the emergency management community that can limit morbidity and mortality caused by both natural and technological disasters. In fact, the contributions of public health authorities to community disaster preparations and response represent an extension of their normal activities. Public health officials are knowledgeable about the prevention of infectious disease and injury, routinely conduct surveillance for infectious disease, maintain working relationships with other agencies within the health sector, have governmental jurisdiction for overseeing the public's health, can draw from the expertise of multidisciplinary members, and use triage skills that can easily be adapted for use following a disaster.

The responsibilities of public health agencies in disaster preparedness and response are more complicated than in a typical public health activity. In preparedness activities, public health professionals must participate as part of a multiagency team, some members of which have little or no knowledge of public health. Further, public health practitioners must work with multiple bureaucratic layers of infrastructure in a condensed time frame and interact with personnel with whom they normally do not have contact and whose lexicon and methods may be different. Since the sectors involved in the Incident Command System have already trained together, public health must integrate itself into this established response, particularly where there is a Unified Command.

Public health workers can conduct assessments and epidemiological studies and can make and implement appropriate recommendations based on data analysis. Such data collection is critical before disaster occurs so as to ensure that potential social impacts are adequately addressed in disaster planning and that emergency, public, and mental health needs are met in the community. Maintenance of continuity of care is especially important for older adults, those with chronic disease, and those in long-term care facilities. Health advisories on injury prevention, food and water safety, and disaster-specific precautions should be developed in advance and available for immediate distribution when needed. Public health officials should regularly communicate with elected officials about the likely impact of potential disasters for which the community is at risk and help develop policies and regulations that can prevent or reduce morbidity and mortality following disaster.

ACTION PLAN

The health sector is responsible for ensuring the continuity of health care services. Resource problems following disasters in the United States have resulted from poor planning in the use or distribution of assets rather than a deficiency of those assets. Public health works with health sector agencies in the community to coordinate planning for the continued delivery of services both during and after the disaster. This interagency coordination includes the development of an action plan to address community health needs. Components of the plan include:

- ensuring continuity of health care services (acute emergency care, continuity of care, primary care, and preventive care)

- monitoring environmental infrastructure (water, sanitation, and vector control)

- assessing the needs of the elderly and other special populations

- initiating injury prevention programs and surveillance

- ensuring that essential public health sector facilities will be able to function post-impact (hospitals, health departments, physicians' offices, storage sites for health care supplies, dispatch centers, paging services, and ambulance stations)

- allocating resources to ensure that the above responsibilities can be accomplished

PERSONNEL

The responsibility of disaster preparedness should be assigned to someone who has the organizational authority to ensure an adequate level of preparation. Otherwise, the effort may be less than optimal because the designated individual lacks authority to delegate tasks to the proper offices and personnel. In addition, such a decision creates the false impression that an effective program exists because someone has been assigned to disaster preparedness.

Both the lead individual and all those involved in disaster preparedness and response must have a well-grounded understanding of the public health consequences of disaster and human response to disaster on the part of both victims and responders. Public health practitioners must recognize how the health sector fits in the emergency management model of disaster preparedness and response, including components of a typical response and team-based, interdisciplinary problem solving. Those involved in disaster response must have both the expertise and ability to access state-of-the-art resources to provide technical assistance to communities and to collect and analyze data as quickly as possible. Through such data collection, epidemiological methods can be applied to develop the best disaster response both to prevent morbidity and mortality and to mitigate medical or public health problems. Public health officials also help blend public health approaches with clinical practice. Likewise, they provide direction to the American Red Cross to ensure the provision of appropriate care and resources and inspect Red Cross shelters and feeding operations.

PUBLIC HEALTH LAW AND EMERGENCIES

As part of public health disaster preparedness, health departments must review state and local laws to understand the nuances of their authority in these circumstances and to prepare a legal plan of action for times of emergency. While universal generalities form the underpinnings of emergency authority, operational authority will vary among jurisdictions. Indeed, the Centers for Disease Control and Prevention have developed a public health law program whose mission is to articulate the connection between law and public health for public health practitioners, including emergencies. As of this writing, local health department heads do not have the necessary authority to declare a health emergency, an issue of national concern.

The authority to protect the health of the public in emergencies is not assigned in a single law, but generally requires a chain of events. For example, a Board of Health could declare an emergency, allowing the Commissioner of Health to modify requirements set forth in the health code. A mayor could declare an emergency, which would in turn allow the mayor's office to modify provisions of local laws and regulations or the health code. Similarly, if a governor declares an emergency, the governor can modify applicable provisions of state and local laws and regulations, including the health code. However, again, each public health department must research in advance which procedures for declaring emergencies and altering health codes apply to each jurisdiction.

FUNCTIONAL MODEL OF PUBLIC HEALTH RESPONSE

The functional model summarizes a typical disaster response within the public health field and categorizes the cycle of activities. The model identifies tasks assigned to each of the core areas of public health in the context of emergency management activities. The functional model expands traditional public health partnerships with other disciplines and agencies and emphasizes collaboration to ensure competence in disaster preparedness and response.

The functional model outlined below and on the pages following comprises six phases that correspond to the type of activities involved in preparing for and responding to a disaster: planning, prevention, assessment, response, surveillance, and recovery. The model additionally delineates the responsibilities of the various disciplines of public health.

Planning

- Apply basic concepts of local public health to disaster management

- Conduct hospital disaster planning and coordinate with hospitals

- Help community develop plan with public health focus

- Develop health promotion and disease prevention protocols and motivate use through education campaign

- Conduct needs assessments and analyze hazards and vulnerability

- Work with other health professionals to write a disaster plan specifically for public health and health concerns

- Train workforce on public health responsibilities

- Inventory supplies, equipment, communications, and people available for response

- Develop mutual aid agreements in advance

- Conduct facility-wide/agency-wide exercises to stress organizational mobilization, coordination, and communication

Prevention

Primary Prevention (before event)

- Immunization

- Control/prevent outbreaks

- Protect against risks identified in hazards, vulnerability, and needs assessments

- Conduct community education in first aid, personal hygiene, and injury prevention

- Protect and distribute safe food and water

- Protect or reestablish sanitation systems

Secondary Prevention (response to event)

- Detect and extricate victims

- Provide emergency medical care

- Organize services and treatment

- Conduct case identification and surveillance

- Establish infectious disease control

- Conduct short-term counseling/intervention

- Manage bystander response

Tertiary Prevention (recovery from event)

- Provide long-term counseling and mental health intervention

- Manage emergency services

- Manage injuries and clean-up behavior

- Reestablish health services

- Use records from response to update action plan

Assessment

- Identify potential outbreaks

- Identify potential medical, behavioral, social, and political effects of event

- Assess potential effect of loss of infrastructure on health and mental health

- Identify potential hazards and levels of acceptable exposure

- Determine incidence of disease and causal factors

- Understand mechanics of hazardous agents (ie, radiation, toxins, thermal and water pollution, landmines, weapons)

- Determine vulnerability, level of risk, and requirement for rapid needs assessment

- Identify appropriate data to collect for decision making

- Summarize damage to health care infrastructure

- Establish continuous data monitoring

Response

Service

- Conduct "quick and dirty" assessments on which to base initial decisions

- Administer logistics

- Organize services (casualty management and behavioral health)

- Communicate plans and needs (internal and external)

- Identify need for and provide emergency treatment, resources, and equipment

- Institute unified command and control

- Continue provision of primary care

- Coordinate with emergency management response structures (incident command, federal response plan, international disaster relief, UN agencies, International Committee of the Red Cross, Non-Governmental Organizations)

Education

- How long foods can be stored in a refrigerator or freezer after the power goes off

- When the water is or is not safe to drink

- How long water should be boiled before drinking

- Whether mass immunizations are needed

- When it is safe to reenter homes or eat food after a toxic cloud has dissipated

- What is risk of delayed effects (ie, cancer, birth defects) from the chemical or nuclear mishap to the average citizen and to those who are pregnant

Management

- Dispose of waste, debris, human and animal bodies, and biologic hazards

- Control disease vectors

- Monitor water, sanitation, food, and shelter

- Control infection

- Control clean-up injuries (ie, chainsaw accidents, electrocution, fire, unsafe structures)

- Coordinate delivery of mental health services

- Communicate health information and risks via media outlets

- Control disease and issue quarantines where necessary

- Provide interventions to large groups

Surveillance

- Establish syndromic information systems for disaster

- Conduct sentinel surveillance, using active or passive systems, of disease and public health conditions

- Use data to recognize acute disease states and high risk groups

Recovery

- Determine present level and extent of patient care capability

- Interpret data to influence deployment of resources

- Work with community agencies to mitigate long-term impact on public health

- Conduct evaluations (structured, semi-structured, qualitative)

- Plan and direct field studies

- Manage media

- Use principles of capacity building

- Mobilize resources

- Use techniques for supplemental and therapeutic food distribution and feeding

- Organize and conduct large-scale immunization and primary health care

- Ensure maintenance of mental health program

- Establish and operate special needs shelters

Chapter 3

Structure and Organization of Health Management in Disaster Response

Local response to disaster situations requires extensive planning, organization, and coordination with other regional, state, and federal officials. This chapter reviews the responsibilities of local responders and health providers, the importance of an incident command system, interactions with state and federal agencies, and costs and reimbursement sources for disaster response and relief.

PUBLIC HEALTH ROLE

- Participate with other professionals who engage in emergency preparedness and response.

- Assess medical, public health, and mental health needs and assure provision of services.

- Assess viability of health care infrastructure.

- Conduct health surveillance, identify and verify individual cases, and institute measures to control infectious disease.

- Provide expert assistance in responding to chemical, radiological, or biological hazards.

- Assure potable water supply, food safety, and sanitation.

- Educate about vector control and implement appropriate measures.

- Provide public health information.

- Work with American Red Cross to provide emergency shelter.

- Identify victims and manage corpses.

- Be able to respond 24 hours a day, 7 days a week.

STRUCTURE AND OPERATION OF THE LOCAL RESPONSE

Emergency Medical Services

Throughout most of the United States, Emergency Medical Services (EMS) are provided by local agencies with oversight at the regional or state level. In most states, EMS is not provided directly by the state health department but is under its authority. The health department or other duly appointed governmental agency has training and regulation jurisdiction over all EMS personnel regardless of their organizational affiliation. Some EMS systems are based in local fire departments, with ambulance and fire services operated side by side. Medics based in fire departments are often cross-trained in both fire fighting and victim extrication. Some cities and counties operate independent EMS systems. In some parts of the United States, particularly the east coast and in many rural areas, EMS is provided by volunteer independent rescue squads or volunteer ambulance squads, which may be connected with a volunteer fire department. Finally, some EMS services are operated from local hospitals.

The EMS system includes both pre-hospital and in-hospital components. The pre-hospital components start with a public access system through which a resident notifies authorities that a medical emergency exists. Where available, the 911 emergency telephone system is used for this access. A dispatch communications system is then used to dispatch ambulance personnel or other emergency first responders to respond to the person(s) in need.

Emergency medical technicians (EMTs) and paramedics (EMT-Ps), who are trained to identify and treat medical emergencies and injuries, provide medical support while transporting patients to hospitals or other source of definitive care. The medical care delivered by EMS is classified as basic or advanced life support. Most EMS providers are trained to provide care at the basic life support level (ie, noninvasive first aid, stabilization for a broad variety of emergency conditions, and defibrillation for cardiac arrest victims). Paramedics provide more sophisticated diagnosis through advanced life support, with treatment following medical protocols both in the field and while being transferred to the hospital. Ground ambulances are the vehicle of choice for most transports, but helicopters, boats, or snow cats may be used under specific circumstances.

When planning for the delivery of disaster care through EMS, officials must consider response patterns that commonly occur. Initially, units can be dispatched in an atypical fashion. Often they will hear about the disaster on police scanners or via the news media rather than through normal dispatch. Assuming that too much help is better than too little, emergency units may respond on an unsolicited basis, sometimes from tens or even hundreds of miles away. In widespread disasters such as earthquakes, floods, tornadoes, and hurricanes, there may be no single site to which trained emergency units can be sent. Similarly, hospitals may obtain their initial information about what has happened, in an unplanned way, from the first arriving casualties or the news media.

Hospital Preparedness

The in-hospital system components include definitive care, usually delivered in the emergency department of a hospital, often by emergency physicians and certified emergency nurses who specialize in emergency medical care. As of 2001, hospitals must meet expanded standards for comprehensive emergency management as part of their accreditation by the Joint Commission on Accreditation of Healthcare Organizations (JCAHO). JCAHO standards mandate that hospitals marry the range of activities regularly conducted by the emergency management community with the traditional tasks of providing health care.

Hospitals are required to establish a hospital emergency incident command system (HEICS). HEICS establishes a chain of command with one person in charge. Hospital disaster plans must be applicable to all hazards. HEICS requires that hospitals conduct a hazard analysis (as discussed in Chapter 5 and Appendix H); establish mutual aid; coordinate with the local office of emergency management; and maintain comprehensive documentation on how decisions were made, where patients went, how patients were tracked, and how reimbursement was obtained.

The new standards help to protect hospitals from claims of liability after a disaster. Further, the National Fire Protection Association, NFPA 99 and 1600 establish minimum criteria for health care facilities and standardize the coordination of disaster management and business continuity within communities. Hospitals must follow federal procedures to be reimbursed for disaster-related response, and administrators should review the requirements of the Stafford Act, JCAHO, and NFPA 1600. The 2001 JCAHO standards are provided in full in Appendix G.

INCIDENT COMMAND SYSTEM

In the United States, the response to disasters is organized though multiple jurisdictions, agencies, and authorities. The term "comprehensive emergency management" is used to refer to these activities. The emergency management field organizes its activities by sectors, such as fire, police, and emergency medical services. Because disasters, regardless of magnitude, require a coordinated response from a number of different agencies, the emergency management community uses standard methodology referred to as the Incident Command System (ICS)—alternatively called Incident Management System (IMS)—for organizing the delivery of services in disaster response. While the ICS was originally developed in the 1970s as a way of responding to fires in Southern California, this methodology now applies to all disaster situations. The ICS organizes its responses with a single person in charge and divides the tasks, functions, and resources into manageable components. Table 5 identifies some of the agencies involved in the incident command system and the resources that they bring.

The ICS organization is constructed with five major components: command, planning, operations, logistics, and finance/administration. Whether there is a routine emergency, a major event, or a catastrophic disaster, the management system employs all five components. The management system expands or contracts depending on the size of the event. An incident commander is responsible for on-scene management, regardless of the size or complexity or the event. Incident management encompasses:

- Establishing command

- Ensuring responder safety

- Assessing incident priorities

- Determining operational objectives

- Developing and implementing an Incident Action Plan (IAP)

- Developing an appropriate organizational structure

- Maintaining a manageable span of control

- Managing incident resources

- Coordinating overall emergency activities

- Coordinating the activities of outside agencies

- Authorizing the release of information to the media

- Monitoring and recording costs

ICS is used to respond to all types of incidents, including hazardous material incidents, fires, transportation accidents, mass casualty incidents, search and rescue operations, and natural or technological disasters. The sector responsible for public health services (including non-EMS health care providers, such as hospitals, urgent care centers, and health departments) faces several challenges when integrating their efforts into this coordinated response. First, the ICS is a pre-existing management structure that may have planned and practiced for incidents without any input from the broader public health community. Public health agencies must find a "fit" with this pre-existing response structure. Second, since health care systems draw patients from broader geographic areas than the political jurisdiction in which they are located, coordination is required between the prehospital system, which uses the ICS, and the public health delivery system, which may have a broader authority.

TABLE 5. AGENCIES INVOLVED IN THE INCIDENT COMMAND SYSTEM

Agency	Resources
American Red Cross	Shelter personnel Road signs, blockades Communications equipment
Electric company	Repair personnel Trucks Repair equipment Communications equipment
Emergency management	Emergency Operations Center (EOC) Equipment
Fire	Fire fighters Fire apparatus
Law enforcement	Police officers Flares, blockades Communications equipment
Public Health	Surveillance systems Public health personnel
Public works/ Highway department	Repair personnel Trucks Repair equipment Communications equipment

SOURCE: BASIC INCIDENT COMMAND SYSTEM (ICS) INDEPENDENT STUDY COURSE, FEDERAL EMERGENCY MANAGEMENT AGENCY, EMERGENCY MANAGEMENT INSTITUTE, IS-195/JAN 1998.

ICS CONCEPTS AND PRINCIPLES

Many jurisdictions establish and maintain an emergency operations center as part of their community's emergency preparedness program. The ICS and emergency operations center function together but at different levels of responsibility. The ICS is responsible for on-scene activities, while the operations center is responsible for the community-wide response.

The organization of ICS response is modular and develops from the top-down structure at any incident. Several communications networks may be established, depending on the size of the incident, but all communication is integrated. ICS employs a unified command whereby all agencies with responsibility for the incident, including public health, establish a common set of objectives and strategies. All involved agencies help to determine overall objectives, plan for joint operational

TABLE 6. THE INCIDENT COMMAND ORGANIZATION

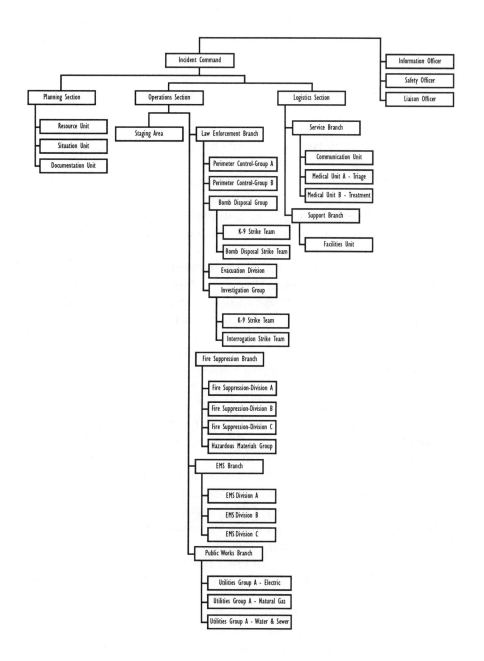

activities, and maximize the use of assigned resources. Under unified command, the incident functions under a single, coordinated plan. Effective response depends on all personnel using common terminology, as defined by the ICS. The Incident Commander will give a specific name to the incident (ie, Ground Zero for the bombing at this location). All response personnel use the same name for all personnel, equipment, and facilities. Radio transmissions should not use agency specific codes or terms but rather the language that everyone will understand.

EMERGENCY AND DISASTER RESPONSE COMPONENTS

While public safety agencies (ie, emergency management, sheriff's office/police department, fire department) are usually the local lead for the overall disaster response, optimally local health departments coordinate the many health related agencies. The health department plans in advance how personnel will carry out their emergency response functions and assigns tasks to appropriate divisions within each department. One division should be designated as the emergency coordinator. Health departments work with the emergency management sectors, local hospitals, and other health care providers to develop an emergency response plan. Those designing the public health plan should coordinate with their other health sector colleagues (ie, EMS and hospitals), with the community's emergency management and public safety communities, and the ICS. A well-designed preparedness program will include a hazard and vulnerability analysis, a risk assessment, a forecast of the probable health effects, a list of the resources needed, an analysis of resource availability, and the identification of vulnerable individuals in the community who will require additional assistance (ie, elderly, homebound, disabled).

Public health professionals work with many community agencies in a multidisciplinary effort. In a local operation, the American Red Cross has a credentialing system for those who respond in the field. The Red Cross also provides sheltering, feeding, emergency first aid, family reunification, and distribution of emergency relief supplies to disaster victims. Faith-based affiliated groups provide meals, clothing, or assistance during recovery and reconstruction efforts. Public works departments manage the water supply and clean up. Social services agencies work with the displaced, deliver psychosocial services, and assure that special needs populations (ie, elderly, children, disabled) receive needed care.

State Disaster Response

Every state has an emergency management agency, alternately called an office of emergency preparedness. Under the authority of the governor's office, the emergency management agency coordinates the deployment of state resources used in an emergency or disaster. This includes the resources of the many agencies of state government, such as health, public safety, and social services.

Mutual Aid

When the resources of the local jurisdiction are insufficient to respond to a given disaster, additional resources are requested from surrounding jurisdictions, a process commonly referred to as mutual aid. Additional resources may also be requested from the state, regional, or federal level. This is called "escalating a response." States can receive aid from neighbors through regional mutual aid compacts, or they can request federal resources, as described below. States in many regions of the country have formed regional agreements. Due to geographic closeness to disaster sites, these regional consortia enable neighboring states to respond rapidly.

Disaster Declarations and Federal Assistance

In the event of a natural disaster, the Stafford Act (PL 92-388 amended by Disaster Mitigation Act 2000 PL 106-340) provides for "an orderly and continuing means of assistance by the Federal government to state and local governments in carrying out their responsibilities to alleviate the suffering and damage which result from major disasters and emergencies."[1] Under the Stafford Act, the President may provide federal resources, financial assistance, services, and medicine, food, and other consumables through what is known as a presidential declaration.

Federal assistance is initiated in one of three ways: states request federal assistance in advance of the disaster to activate a declaration when the threat is imminent and warrants limited predeployment actions to lessen or avert a catastrophe; governors submit requests after the disaster has struck; or the President exercises primary authority, as was done following the bombing at Oklahoma City. As of this writing, the Presidential Decision Directives for disaster response are being examined, and this chapter reviews general principles. Public health

---

[1] Robert T. Stafford Disaster Relief and Emergency Assistance Act; 42 USC, §5121 (2000).

agencies should periodically confer with their local office of emergency management to ascertain if there have been changes to the procedures.

Federal Response Plan

In national disasters, the lead agency coordinating the operation of the federal response plan is the Federal Emergency Management Agency (FEMA). The federal response plan provides guidance for the coordination of federal assistance following natural disasters. FEMA performs many of the same functions as a local emergency management agency but can also directly utilize federal resources and money toward the preparation for, response to, and recovery from larger emergencies and disasters. A core principle of the federal response plan is that the local or state jurisdiction is in charge of managing the disaster response and that the responding federal resources work in support of local groups.

In disasters of the magnitude requiring a presidential declaration, public health resources may be deployed through the US Public Health Service's Office of Emergency Preparedness, which is responsible for managing and coordinating public health and medical services postimpact. Federal assistance may be provided to the states by the Epidemic Intelligence Service officers from the Centers for Disease Control and Prevention or by experts from the Agency for Toxic Substances Disease Registry, among others. These federal public health personnel, stationed at regional offices of the US Department of Health and Human Services, can quickly get into the field to conduct surveillance and rapid needs assessments.

In incidents involving weapons of mass destruction, Health and Human Services officials provide both technical and operational support. The agency assists with identification of agents, sample collection and analysis, on-site safety and protection, and medical management. Operational activities may include mass immunizations, mass prophylaxis, mass fatality management, pharmaceutical stockpiling, patient tracking, contingency medical records, patient evaluation, and provision of definitive medical care. The Substance Abuse and Mental Health Services Administration (including the Center for Mental Health Services and the Emergency Services and Disaster Relief Branch) also plays a key role in responding to the social and psychosocial impacts of disaster.

Once there has been a presidential declaration, FEMA contacts the agencies that take lead roles, including as many as 28 other federal agencies and the American Red Cross. These agencies provide person-

TABLE 7. THE 12 EMERGENCY SUPPORT FUNCTIONS

Emergency Support Function	Responsibility	Lead Agency
ESF 1: Transportation	Providing civilian and military transportation	Department of Transportation
ESF 2: Communications	Providing telecommunications support	National Communications System
ESF 3: Public Works and Engineering	Restoring essential public services and facilities	US Army Corps of Engineers, Department of Defense
ESF 4: Fire Fighting	Detecting and suppressing wilderness, rural, and urban fires	US Forest Service, Department of Agriculture
ESF 5: Information and Planning	Collecting, analyzing, and disseminating critical information to facilitate the overall federal response and recovery operations	Federal Emergency Management Agency
ESF 6: Mass Care	Managing and coordinating food, shelter, and first aid for victims; providing bulk distribution of relief supplies; operating a system to assist family reunification	American Red Cross
ESF 7: Resource Support	Providing equipment, materials, supplies, and personnel to federal entities during response operations	General Services Administration
ESF 8: Health and Medical Services	Providing assistance for public health and medical care needs	US Public Health Service, Department of Health and Human Services
ESF 9: Urban Search and Rescue	Locating, extricating and providing initial medical treatment to victims	Federal Emergency Management Agency
ESF 10: Hazardous Materials	Supporting federal response to actual or potential releases of oil and hazardous materials	Environmental Protection Agency
ESF 11: Service, Food	Identifying food needs; ensuring that food gets to areas affected by disaster	Food and Nutrition US Department of Agriculture
ESF 12: Energy	Restoring power systems and fuel supplies	US Department of Energy

nel, technical expertise, equipment, and other resources to state and local governments, and they assume an active role in managing the response. To coordinate the federal efforts, FEMA recommends and the President appoints a Federal Coordinating Officer for each state that is affected by a disaster. The Federal Coordinating Officer and the state response team set up a Disaster Field Office or Regional Operations Center near the disaster scene. There federal and state personnel work together to carry out their response and recovery responsibilities. The emergency management community uses the term "function" to describe each of twelve responsibilities. These responsibilities are grouped into 12 Emergency Support Functions (ESFs), each headed by an agency with the support of the others.

In addition to their Washington, DC headquarters, FEMA operates a number of regional offices (see Appendix F for list). Other agencies, such as US Department of Health and Human Services and the National Disaster Medical System (NDMS) described below, use the same geographic zones to organize personnel and resources throughout the nation.

All of the ESFs directly or indirectly affect efforts to protect the health and welfare of disaster victims. However, federal response to the specific health needs of disaster victims is primarily contained in ESF 8: Health and Medical Services. Roles maintained through this function include:

• Assessment of health and medical needs

• Health surveillance

• Medical care personnel

• Medical equipment and supplies

• Patient evacuation

• In-hospital care

• Food/drug/medical device safety

• Worker health/safety

• Radiological, chemical, and biological hazards

- Mental health

- Public health information

- Vector control

- Potable water/wastewater & solid waste disposal

- Victim identification/mortuary services

- Veterinary services

The lead agency for ESF 8: Health and Medical Services is the Office of Emergency Preparedness in the US Public Health Service. This office works in close coordination with local authorities to avoid duplication of services. Operating within the Office of Emergency Preparedness, the NDMS is a federally coordinated, multiagency system representing the Departments of Defense, Health and Human Services, and Veterans Affairs as well as FEMA that augments the US emergency medical response capability. The NDMS establishes a single integrated national medical response capability for assisting state and local authorities in addressing the medical and health effects of major peacetime disasters and providing support to the military and Department of Veterans Affairs medical systems in caring for casualties evacuated back to the United States from overseas armed conflicts.

To carry out its functions, the NDMS supports the following components:

Disaster Medical Assistance Teams

Disaster Medical Assistance Teams (DMAT) are self-sustaining squads of licensed, actively practicing professional and paraprofessional medical personnel who provide emergency medical care at the site of a disaster or other event. These teams include a cadre of logistical and administrative staff and all the equipment needed to set up ambulatory clinics and remain self-sustaining for 72 hours. DMATs are sent to augment local capacity, not to supplant or replace it. In mass casualty incidents, their responsibilities include triaging patients, providing austere medical care, and preparing patients for evacuation. In other situations, they may provide primary health care or assist overloaded medical staffs. Additionally, they are prepared to provide patient care during evacuation to definitive care sites.

Once a DMAT is activated, the professionals on that team are federalized, allowing them to practice with their professional license in any jurisdiction in the United States, so that additional credentialing is not necessary. Further, federalized providers are protected from malpractice liability when providing care in times of disaster through the Federal Torts Claims Act. The Commission Core Response Force is another group of volunteer clinicians who can be activated to practice as federal providers to augment federal assets. They are pulled from their regular jobs for a two-week course of duty.

Where the need for hospital beds exceeds local capacity, patients will be stabilized by Disaster Medical Assistance Teams or other specialty teams and then evacuated to hospitals that are part of the NDMS system, either by the Department of Defense aeromedical system or contracts with reconfigured commercial carriers. At the airport of the NDMS reception area, patients will be met by a local medical team who will assess patients and transport them to participating hospitals according to procedures developed by local authorities and the local area's NDMS federal coordinating center. Patients will be transported to participating hospitals using locally organized ground and air transport.

Hospitals become part of the NDMS by signing a Memorandum of Agreement between the Chief Executive of the hospital and the Director of the Federal Coordinating Center in their locale. As of this printing, NDMS reimburses those hospitals up to 110% of the Medicare rate and is secondary to the primary carrier. Hospitals should assume that comprehensive and complete documentation will be required to receive reimbursement and must establish information systems necessary to comply.

Management Support Units

Management Support Units provide field command and control for federal medical assets that are deployed post-impact. These units can provide and coordinate communications, transportation, a medical cache, and other logistical support to disaster medical assistance and other specialty teams.

Federal Coordinating Centers

Federal coordinating centers recruit hospitals and maintain local nonfederal hospital participation in the NDMS; assist in the recruitment, training, and support of Disaster Medical Assistance Teams; coordinate exercises and emergency plans with participating hospitals and other local authorities to develop patient reception, transportation, and communication plans; and coordinate the reception and distribution of patients being evacuated to the area.

Disaster Mortuary Teams

Disaster Mortuary Teams (DMORT) are comprised of mortuary specialists and experienced forensics experts whose function is to augment the capacity of the coroner. The team members are skilled in identifying victims and working with relatives of victims. They bring their own equipment and are self-contained.

COSTS AND REIMBURSEMENT FOR DISASTER RESPONSE

For public and nonprofit entities, the Stafford Act provides for federal reimbursement of some expenses associated with the effects of the disaster and disaster response. This funding is known as public assistance. Title 44 of the Code of Federal Regulations (Emergency Management and Assistance) contains the rules, policies, and procedures regarding the administration of federal disaster assistance programs by FEMA. Part 206 of the 44 CFR, Subparts G, H, and I contain most of the regulations applicable to FEMA's disaster assistance program. FEMA coordinates that process and provides the forms that must be submitted for reimbursement. When local governments receive the support of any federal assets, the federal government absorbs the costs in the initial hours of the response. However, local governments are expected to reimburse the federal government for assets provided thereafter through a cost-sharing formula.

Public assistance will reimburse for damage to infrastructure, for equipment, and for overtime for personnel. It will not reimburse for providing patient care as part of the normal course of doing business. The usual cost sharing formula provides for the federal government to reimburse 50.0% of the costs, for states to provide 12.5% to 25.0% of the costs, and for the local entity to absorb the remaining expenses. Public assistance will not reimburse for service eligible for funding under another federal program, such as the Veterans Administration. All public health agencies should obtain a copy of the rules, including the details of documentation necessary for reimbursement.

Local agencies should identify what aid is available through their state. Some have a state-funded reimbursement mechanism, similar to the federal assistance program, that may reimburse local health departments for a percentage of costs for medical emergencies through public health law. However, total reimbursement from state and federal sources cannot exceed 100%. Finally, if an event is declared a terrorist attack, localities should realize that commercial insurance policies may deny reimbursement because care was required due to "an act of war."

Chapter **4**

Disaster-Related Surveillance and Emergency Information Systems

Surveillance and exchange of gathered information guides emergency response as well as long-term planning. This chapter examines disaster epidemiology, emergency information systems throughout the disaster event, and public health surveillance in response to disaster.

PUBLIC HEALTH ROLE

- Determine needs and match resources in affected communities.

- Provide information about probable adverse health effects for decision making.

- Describe and monitor medical, public health, and psychosocial effects of disaster.

- Detect illness or injuries, including sudden changes in disease occurrence.

- Monitor long-term disease trends.

• Identify changes in agents and host factors.

• Detect changes in health practices.

• Investigate rumors.

• Evaluate the effectiveness of response activities.

DISASTER EPIDEMIOLOGY

Epidemiology can be used to investigate the public health and medical consequences of disasters. The aim of disaster epidemiology is to ascertain strategies for the prevention of both acute and chronic health events due to the occurrence of natural or technological hazards. Primary prevention seeks to prevent disaster-related deaths, injuries, or illness before they occur (ie, evacuate residents prior to landfall of a hurricane). With secondary prevention, the goal is to mitigate the health consequences of a disaster by providing education about injury control during the clean-up and recovery period. Tertiary prevention minimizes the effects of disease and disability among those already ill by setting up evaluation units where the chronically ill can obtain access to short-term pharmaceuticals when their usual source of care has been disrupted.

Disaster epidemiology includes rapid needs assessment, disease control strategies, assessment of the availability and use of health services, surveillance systems for both descriptive and analytic investigations of disease and injury, and research on risk factors contributing to disease, injury, or death.

EMERGENCY INFORMATION SYSTEMS

Emergency Information Systems (EIS) collect data about the effects of a disaster during the impact phase, the response phase, and the early stages of recovery. EIS consist of integrated sets of files, procedures, and equipment for the storage, manipulation, and retrieval of information. Data must be collected rapidly, sometimes under adverse circumstances, and the analysis must be processed and interpreted cohesively yet ensure a timely flow of information to inform an appropriate response.

The data collected through EIS are used to make decisions about the services that are needed post-impact. EIS personnel examine how the everyday relationship between people and their physical and social environments has been disrupted by disasters, such as lost productivity, as well as emerging problems or problems under control. Surveillance concentrates on the incidence, prevalence, and severity of illness or injury due to ecological changes, changes in endemic levels of disease, population displacement, loss of usual source of health care, overcrowding, breakdowns in sanitation, and disruption of public utilities. Surveillance also monitors increases in communicable diseases, including vector-borne, waterborne, and person-to-person transmission. EIS data provides accurate and reliable information needed to make decisions about emergency and short-term relief as well as long-term planning for recovery and reconstruction. Table 8 summarizes the types and uses of data collected through EIS.

TABLE 8. EIS DATA COLLECTION

Type of Data	Uses for Data
Deaths	Assess the magnitude of disaster
	Evaluate effectiveness of disaster preparedness
	Evaluate adequacy of warning system
	Identify high-risk groups for contingency planning
Casualties	Estimate needs for emergency care
	Evaluate pre-impact planning and preparedness
	Evaluate adequacy of warning systems
Morbidity	Estimate type and volume of immediate medical relief needed
	Evaluate appropriateness of relief
	Identify populations at risk
	Assess needs for further planning
Health needs	Prioritize services delivered
	Prioritize groups most affected
	Evaluate adequacy of resources
Public health resources	Estimate the type and volume of needed supplies, equipment, and services
	Evaluate appropriateness of relief
	Assess needs for further planning
Donated goods	Estimate type and volume of supplies, equipment, and services needed
	Evaluate appropriateness of relief[1]
	Assess needs for further planning
Hazards	Monitor health events, disease, injuries, hazards, exposures, or risk factors
	Support early warning system to forecast occurrence of a disaster event by monitoring conditions that may signal the event[2]

[1] For example, the Pan American Health Organization's supply management program (SUMA) facilitates the sorting, classifying, and inventorying of the supplies sent to a disaster-stricken area.

[2] An example is the Famine Early Warning System, which predicts the occurrence of famine by monitoring meteorological data, availability of food, and morbidity related to nutrition.

PUBLIC HEALTH SURVEILLANCE

Before initiating an EIS, managers assess concern about public health issues and the necessity of monitoring disaster-related morbidity and mortality to determine actions important for a public health response. Considerations include whether existing systems could be used (preferable due to the level of resources required for active surveillance); sufficient personnel are available, including volunteers such as medical, nursing, or public health students; the data are needed to influence the public health response; and data collection can be funded, either by the participating institutions or externally, such as funding through the Stafford Act.

When using existing systems, such as those established to track reportable diseases, EIS personnel must ensure they have the capacity to provide information that is both adequate and timely. Existing hospital-based data may provide an accurate representation of morbidity related to the disaster. Data can be obtained from mobile care sites and clinics. All health care facilities may be asked to participate in a syndromic surveillance system, or, given finite resources, selected sites may be chosen to provide a reasonable representation of the health effects being monitored. An existing surveillance system that measures morbidity and mortality is the American Red Cross–Centers for Disease Control and Prevention (CDC) Health Impact Surveillance System for Disasters. Through a joint agreement, the American Red Cross collects morbidity and mortality information from all disasters to which it responds in the United States. The CDC analyzes the information and reports findings annually. In addition, many developing countries have surveillance systems that routinely monitor acute diarrheal and respiratory illness and can track changes in incidence before and after a disaster event, such as a flood.

If existing systems do not meet the adequate and timely standard, temporary systems can be organized for the duration of the emergency period or at any point before, during, or after the disaster. To initiate an EIS, epidemiologists need portable computers with access to other data reporting systems, such as the Health Alert Network, and existing electronic disease reporting. Data should be collected using standardized protocols, including veterinary inputs. The information should be presented in a simple format, in a manner easily understood by both public and emergency management officials.

ESTABLISHING A POST-IMPACT SURVEILLANCE SYSTEM

Outcomes appropriate for the specific disaster must be identified (ie crush injuries from earthquakes, diarrheal diseases from floods). The incidence of diseases endemic to an area prior to the disaster event would be expected to rise due to population displacement, increased population density, the interruption of existing public health programs, and breakdown in sanitation and hygiene. From a sample of the disaster-affected population, epidemiologists determine associations between exposure and outcome (disease variables) by identifying demographic, biological, chemical, physical, or behavioral factors associated with outcomes of death, illness, or injury. Examples of exposure-outcome relationships in disaster settings are included in Table 9.

TABLE 9. EXPOSURE-OUTCOME RELATIONSHIPS

Timing	Disaster	Exposure	Outcome
Pre-impact	Cyclone Tornado	High winds Presence of functioning warning system	Injury Evacuate or not, injury, death
Impact	Flash flood Volcanic eruption	Motor vehicle occupancy Ash particulate of respirable size	Death by drowning Silicosis
Post-impact	Earthquake Cyclone	Building type, floor level, age Outdoor cleanup activity	Injury, death Injury during cleanup act- ivity, death by electrocution

To ensure uniformity, case definitions must be established in advance for the outcomes that will be measured. Criteria for evaluating morbidity include clinical signs and symptoms, results from laboratory tests that confirm a diagnosis, and epidemiological limits on person, place, and time. Four case classifications are used: confirmed, probable, suspect, or not a case because it failed to fulfill the criteria for confirmed, probable, or suspect cases. In addition, sources of comparison data, such as incidence of a disease in the same month or time period during prior years, should be identified for use in analysis.

Appropriate methods for analysis must be considered and applied. Examples include descriptive (age, gender, ethnic group), geographic location, rates of disease or death, secular trends, and an analytic time series defining the total number of cases and trends over time.

Possible reporting units for data collection include all the institutions that provide information for the surveillance system (ie, hospital, clinic, health post, mobile health unit, Non-Governmental Organizations, health care facility, temporary shelters, first responder logs).

DATA COLLECTION USED FOR DECISION MAKING

Since response activities and planning for relief and recovery are based on the data collected, the information should reflect as accurate and reliable a picture of the public health needs as possible. Hazard mapping and vulnerability assessments can provide useful background information about the disaster event that can be used for planning disaster preparedness programs, response activities, and evacuation plans. Usually this information is available from the local emergency management office, geological institutions, or ministries related to natural resources and the environment.

Information about the incident itself includes:

• Demographic characteristics of affected areas

• Assessment of casualties, injuries, and selected illness

• Numbers of displaced populations

• Coordination of volunteers

• Management of healthcare infrastructure

• Storage and distribution of relief materials, including food, water, medical supplies

• Public information and rumor control

Information can often be obtained from existing data sets (census, state hospitalization data), hospitals and clinics (emergency departments, patient medical records, e-codes), health maintenance organizations and insurance companies, private providers, temporary shelters (daily shelter census, logs at medical facility in shelter), first responders (Disaster Medical Assistance Team patient logs), and mobile health clinics, such as those run by the military, Non-Governmental organizations, and volunteer medical groups (patient logs, records of prescription medications dispensed).

Due to time constraints and adverse environmental conditions, use of rigorous epidemiological methods may not be feasible in the post-impact phase. In disaster situations, assessment teams members often use "quick and dirty" methods. "Quick" in that they are simple, flexible, and can be used under difficult circumstances. "Dirty" in that numerator and denominator data may be rough estimates that are subject to bias, although they serve to answer immediate questions whose answers are needed for the response.

EVALUATING DISASTER SURVEILLANCE

Finally, EIS must be evaluated in the disaster setting to know when the system is no longer needed. This endpoint is often determined by both the resources and personnel available to run the system and the ability to merge the emergency system into routine surveillance. In addition to describing the attributes, usefulness, and cost of EIS, evaluations can lead to recommendations on the initiation and conclusion of future surveillance related to disasters. See Chapter 12 for more information on such evaluation methods.

Chapter **5**

Hazard Assessment, Vulnerability Analysis, Risk Assessment, and Rapid Health Assessment

Needs assessment must be tailored to the timing, size, and impact of a specific disaster. This chapter reviews background information on vulnerability that can be assembled in advance of disaster, acute needs assessment, and longer term data collection and surveillance. Methods and limitations of data collection are examined.

PUBLIC HEALTH ROLE

- Identify disaster-related hazards and associated vulnerability in a community.

- Determine risk of public health needs likely to be created should such disasters occur.

- Prioritize health needs based on information from community needs assessment.

- Provide decision makers with objective information to guide prevention, mitigation, and response to disease.

RATIONALE FOR ASSESSING RISK

Different types of disasters are associated with distinct patterns of morbidity and mortality. To develop location-specific strategies for reducing negative health outcomes, public health officials and disaster managers must be aware of the types of hazards most likely to affect specific communities. Health planners in Florida, for example, should prepare primarily for hurricanes, while those in California should prepare for earthquakes and wildfires.

Six categories of disaster prevention measures can be implemented following the analysis of hazards, vulnerability, and risk:

- Prevention or removal of hazard (ie, closing down an aging industrial facility that cannot implement safety regulations)

- Moving those at risk away from the hazard (ie, evacuating populations prior to the impact of a hurricane, resettling communities away from flood-prone areas)

- Providing public information and education (ie, providing information concerning measures that the public can take to protect themselves during a tornado)

- Establishing early warning systems (ie, using satellite data about an approaching hurricane for public service announcements)

- Reducing the impact of the disaster (ie, enforcing strict building regulations in an earthquake prone zone)

- Increasing local capacity to respond (ie, coordinating a plan utilizing the resources of the entire health community, including health departments, hospitals, and home care agencies)

HAZARD IDENTIFICATION AND ANALYSIS

Hazard identification and analysis is used to determine which events are most likely to affect a community and to make decisions about who or what to protect as the basis of establishing measures for prevention, mitigation, and response. The National Fire Protection Association 1600 Standard[1] requires that a community's hazard identifi

---

[1]National Fire Protection Association, 1 Batterymarch Park, PO Box 9101, Quincy, MA 02269-9101 An International Codes and Standards Organization; prepared by the Technical Committee on Disaster Management.

cation include natural events, technological events, and human events (see Appendix H). Decisions about which mitigation steps to take frequently require a cost-benefit analysis and a prioritization of the assets being protected.

Data Collection

Information from several sources, including data from previous hazards, is needed to predict future events. This information can assist in the development of appropriate mitigation measures. Historical data include the nature of previous hazards, the direct causes or contributing factors of previous events (ie, failure to observe industrial regulations led to chemical release), the frequency and intensity of past disasters, the magnitude or power (as measured with established standards, such as the Richter Scale for earthquakes or the Saffir-Simpson scale for hurricanes), and the reported effects of an event at a given location (ie, number of homes destroyed by tornado, number of people displaced by flood).

Baseline data should be collected to assess current potential hazards in a community:

- Laboratories located in academic or other research institutions

- Agricultural facilities

- Chemical manufacturing and storage

- Dams, levies, and other flood control mechanisms

- Facilities for storage of infectious waste

- Firework factories

- Plants for food production or storage

- Military installations

- Munitions factories or depots

- Pesticide manufacturers or storage

- Petrochemical refineries or storage facilities

- Pharmaceutical companies

- Radiological power plants or fuel processing facilities

- Water treatment and distribution centers

- Ventilation systems for high occupancy buildings

Hazard Mapping

With these data, the location of both previous and potential hazards can be mapped. Aerial photography, satellite imagery, remote sensing, and geographic information system technology can all provide information through hazard mapping. Remote sensing can show changes to land-use maps over time. Geographic information system models enable managers to develop plans with information consolidated from numerous disciplines, including engineering, natural sciences, and public health. Various types of maps are available for different hazards, including inundation maps for floods and seismic zoning maps for earthquakes. Maps detailing the location of industrial sites and hazardous material storage facilities can also be used. Hazard maps may be macro or micro in scale. Multihazard maps are available from the scientific community, industry, the media, and governmental jurisdictions.

Scientific Resources

Use data from meteorology, seismology, volcanology, and hydrology to provide important predictive information concerning hazards. These data can be obtained from a variety of government agencies and private institutions, including the National Oceanic and Atmospheric Administration, the National Weather Service, the US Geological Survey, and the Natural Hazards Center at the University of Colorado.

In addition, decision-support systems can analyze data from several core databases, such as data on building inventories, infrastructure, demographics, and risk. These systems can stimulate "what if" scenarios to aid in planning.

Hazardous Materials Documentation

In the United States, the Superfund Amendment and Reauthorization Act requires that all hazardous materials manufactured, stored, or transported by local industry that could affect the surrounding community be identified and reported to health officials. In most communities, gasoline and liquid petroleum gas are the most common hazardous materials, but other potential hazards include chlorine, ammonia, and explosives. Material Safety Data Sheets provide a standardized method of communicating relevant information about each material, including its toxicity, flammability, and known acute and chronic health effects. Material Safety Data Sheets are provided by the manufacturers of individual chemicals and can be searched via databases available on the Internet.

Hazard Assessment

Following compilation, the data are analyzed to determine which hazards are most likely to affect a given community. Data analysis attempts to predict the nature, frequency, and intensity of future hazards; the area(s) most likely to be affected; and the onset time and duration of future events. The hazard assessment and data analysis should be conducted at a level appropriate to both the perceived risk and the availability of resources.

Probability Estimate

The probability estimate attempts to determine the probability of an event of a given magnitude occurring in a certain area over a specified time interval. This estimate cannot predict the exact timing or the effects on the surrounding community. Several statistical formulations can be used to determine the probabilities. More complicated formulations take into account not only the hazard and vulnerability estimates, but also vulnerability mitigation efforts and disaster management issues.

Vulnerability Analysis

A vulnerability analysis is used to obtain information about the susceptibility of individuals, property, and the environment to the adverse effects of a given hazard to develop appropriate prevention strategies. The analysis of this information helps determine who is most likely to be affected, what is most likely to be destroyed or damaged, and what capacities exist to cope with the effects of the disaster. A separate vulnerability analysis should be conducted for each identified hazard. There are five categories of vulnerability (Table 10).

TABLE 10. CATEGORIES OF VULNERABILITY

Category	Measures
Proximity and exposure	Identify population(s) vulnerable because they live or work near a given hazard
Physical	Assess vulnerability of buildings, infrastructure, agriculture and other aspects of the physical environment due to factors such as site, materials used, construction technique, and maintenance
	Evaluate transportation systems, communication systems, public utilities (water, sewage, power), and critical facilities (ie, hospitals) for weaknesses
	Estimate potential short- and long-term impact of hazard on crops, food, livestock, trees, and fisheries
	Identify people who require special planning because of demographics or physical condition
Social	Identify population most vulnerable to the effects of disaster (e.g, older adults, children, single-parent families, the economically disadvantaged, the disabled)
	Estimate the level of poverty, jobs that are at risk, and the availability of local institutions that may provide social support
Economic	Determine the community's potential for economic loss and recovery following a disaster
Capacity	Evaluate the availability of human resources, material resources, and the presence of mutual aid agreements with neighboring communities
	Review the existence and enforcement of government regulations that mitigate the effects of certain disasters (ie, building codes)

A community's capacity to withstand disaster conditions is determined by collecting data on the several variables. Information on the size, density, location, and socioeconomic status of the at-risk community can be obtained from local governmental officials. Public utility companies, health departments, hospital associations, and school authorities can provide data on the location and structural integrity of lifeline structures (ie, electricity, gas, water, sewer) as well as buildings with high occupancy. Information on the location and structural integrity of private dwellings is also useful. A structural engineer may be required to review these data. Additional community capacity elements to be assessed include the presence of early warning systems, the number of available emergency responders and medical personnel, the level of technical expertise among emergency responders, the availability of supplies, and the status of emergency transportation and communication systems.

Risk Assessment

Risk assessment is used during the prevention and preparedness phases as a diagnostic and planning tool to determine how many excess cases of outcome A will occur in a population of size B, due to a hazard event C of severity D. Key lessons learned from the risk assessment can be used in the development of local and regional disaster plans. Major objectives of risk assessment include:

- Determining a community's risk of adverse health effects due to a specified disaster (ie, traumatic deaths and injuries following an earthquake)

- Identifying the major hazards facing the community and their sources (ie, earthquakes, floods, industrial accidents)

- Identifying those sections of the community most likely to be affected by a particular hazard (ie, individuals living in or near flood plains)

- Determining existing measures and resources that reduce the impact of a given hazard (ie, building codes and regulations for earthquake mitigation)

- Determining areas that require strengthening to prevent or mitigate the effects of the hazard (ie, constructing levees to protect the community from flood waters)

Modelling in Risk Assessment

Risk assessment uses the results of the hazard identification and vulnerability analysis to determine the probability of a specified outcome from a given hazard that affects a community with known vulnerabilities and coping mechanisms (risk = hazard × vulnerability). The probability may be presented as a numerical range (ie, 30% to 40% probability) or in relative terms (ie, low, moderate, or high risk). A good example of how such models are used is the environmental and climate prediction services provided by the National Weather Service. The results of this modelling are broadcast by the media to warn communities of the risks of thunderstorms, blizzards, tornadoes, and hurricanes.

Models can also be used to guide appropriate responses to disasters. For example, plume dispersion modelling has shown that the most appropriate response to a major chemical release is evacuation of the surrounding community. Other strategies, such as "sheltering in place" (ie, remaining indoors with windows and doors closed), provide less protection to the population. Similar dispersion models are also used to determine the risks of other technological hazards, including releases from nuclear installations.

Rapid Health Assessment

Rapid health assessments are used in the early stages of disaster response, often simultaneously with emergency response, to characterize the health impact of the disaster on the affected community. The primary task of the assessment team is to collect, analyze, and disseminate timely, accurate health data. These data assist public health professionals in determining the health needs, in prioritizing response activities, initiating an appropriate emergency response, and evaluating the effectiveness of the response. Even if the rapid health assessment is only a basic estimate, it facilitates the rational allocation of available resources according to the true needs of the emergency.

Community plans for disaster response should include teams to provide medical care that are functionally separate from the rapid health assessment team(s). Appropriate medical responses can be planned in advance since specific disasters are associated with predictable patterns of morbidity and mortality. While rapid health assessments provide for the early collection of health data, emergency response activities to save life and limb and to rescue trapped or isolated individuals may be initiated before the results of the rapid health assessment are available. Subsequent detailed needs assessments are often conducted during the recovery and rehabilitation phases of the disaster cycle to provide information over time.

Objectives and Methods

The primary objectives of rapid health assessments are to assess:

- The presence of ongoing hazards (ie, a persistent toxic plume following a major chemical release)

- The nature and magnitude of the disaster (ie, number of people affected or geographic area involved)

- Major medical and public health problems of the community (including risk of further morbidity and mortality; observed patterns of injury, illness, and deaths; need for food, water, shelter, and sanitation)

- Availability of resources within the local community and the impact of the disaster on those resources

- Community need for external assistance

- Augmentation of existing public health surveillance to monitor the ongoing health impact of the disaster

Before field visits and preliminary data collection can begin, a team must be assembled. Members of this multidisciplinary team could include an epidemiologist, a clinician, an environmental engineer, and a logistician. If the area affected by the disaster is large and crosses jurisdictions, several assessment teams may be required, as might specialty teams to concentrate on transportation, communications, and infrastructure. If more than one assessment team is required, all teams should use the same standardized assessment form. Data forms can be developed in advance using existing protocols, such as the World Health Organization's Rapid Assessment Protocols.

Baseline data gathered prior to the field visit are essential. This information includes background on the population size and demographics, including the presence of vulnerable groups such as older adults, children, and disabled persons. Census data can provide an accurate estimate of the number of people affected by the disaster, though estimating the actual number of individuals present in the disaster area at the time of impact (ie, after evacuation following hurricane warnings) can be difficult.

Advanced information on the health care infrastructure is also critical. The location, bed capacity, and capabilities of local and regional health facilities must be documented. The status of local Emergency Medical Services must be assessed as well, including search and rescue capabilities, which can serve as surrogate measure of likely response in case of disaster. Similar information on the location and status of public utilities (ie, provision of water, sanitation, electricity) will likewise assist assessment efforts.

Detailed maps are absolutely essential for rapid health assessments. These maps should show high-risk areas (including vulnerable populations), major transport routes, main utility lines, locations of health facilities and water sources, and concentrations of residential, office, shopping, and industrial areas. These maps are often available from government departments, academic institutions, and utility companies.

All these data will be wasted if not supplied to decision makers with authority to shape the disaster plan. The rapid health assessment should be an integral component of emergency response planning.

Timeline

For acute onset disasters, such as transportation crashes and hazardous material incidents, conduct initial on-scene assessments within minutes to a few hours if possible. Where multiple casualties are suspected, such as following an earthquake or tornado, the initial assessment should be completed within several hours of impact. The assessment should be completed as soon as possible as the majority of deaths will occur within the first 24 to 48 hours. This early information will be critical in identifying the need for emergency medical services and urban search-and-rescue teams.

For slower-onset disasters, information can be collected in the first two to four days (ie, floods, epidemics, population displacements). An even longer time frame may be used for assessments of droughts and famines. In these settings, it is often more appropriate for health officials and disaster managers to collect baseline data and then follow trends with ongoing public health surveillance.

Categories of Data and Priorities for Collection

Data collection priorities differ for sudden impact disasters (ie, earthquake, tornado) and gradual onset disasters (ie, famine, complex humanitarian emergency). Teams often have limited time in which to collect data for a rapid health assessment. In these situations, only the most relevant health-related information should be collected. The specific elements of data will vary according to the type of disaster and the stage of the response. A concise checklist, developed prior to the field visit, will ensure that the most critical health issues are assessed. Disaster assessment protocols have been developed by the World Health Organization for various events, including sudden impact natural disasters, chemical emergencies, and sudden population displacements.

Sudden Impact Disaster

Days 1–2. Baseline information should be gathered as discussed previously. The sole objective is to collect information needed for immediate relief. The priority at this stage is the emergency medical response to save life and limb. Since obtaining accurate data can be difficult directly after impact, initial relief efforts are frequently guided by rough estimates. Key data include:

- Ongoing hazards, since persistent hazards that pose a risk to rescue personnel must be eliminated or controlled prior to initiating relief efforts.

- Injuries, since the number, categories, and severity of injuries help characterize the impact of the disaster and prioritize relief activities.

- Deaths, since the number and causes of death help characterize the impact of the disaster (however, information about deaths is not as important in guiding relief efforts as injury data).

- Environmental health and the status of community lifelines (ie, water, sewer, power), since an early estimate of the population's needs for shelter, food, water, and sanitation may prevent secondary disaster-related health problems.

- Health facilities, since the impact of the disaster on the physical integrity and functioning of the health infrastructure may indicate the need for temporary medical shelters and external medical assistance.

Days 3–6. At this stage, information will be needed to guide secondary relief. Emergency medical interventions and search and rescue activities are less important, as more than 96% of critically injured patients will already have received medical care. If disaster-related deaths are still occurring, any persistent hazards causing or contributing to these deaths must be identified. Injuries due to clean-up activities and secondary impact from the disaster (ie, fire, electrocution, hazardous material release) must be monitored carefully to optimise recovery efforts. Ensuring the availability of and access to primary health care becomes more important at this point than emergency care since disaster-affected populations still require routine medical services.

Assessment of environmental health and utilities must clarify the longer term needs related to food, water, sanitation, shelter, and energy.

Day 6+. During the recovery stage, disaster plans should be fully implemented, and resources made available for all sectors. Surveillance should concentrate on illness and injuries based on information available from all health facilities and infectious disease, since outbreaks are uncommon after sudden impact disasters unless major population displacement or disruptions of the public health system occur. The surveillance system should track diarrheal disease and acute respiratory infections if people are displaced into overcrowded shelters or if there is a disruption of environmental health services. The status of health facilities, the number of health personnel, and the availability of medical and pharmaceutical supplies should be accurately tracked. Environmental health (ie, water quantity and quality, sanitation, shelter, and solid waste disposal) and vector populations must be monitored carefully. Floods are often associated with swells in mosquito populations, increasing the risk of arboviral infections, such as St. Louis encephalitis. Surveillance for arboviruses can assist in determining the need for vector control following flooding.

Gradual Onset Disaster

Baseline assessments are conducted, and a surveillance system established. Background information must include population size and demographics, major causes of morbidity and mortality, sources of health care, and the status of pre-existing public health programs, such as immunizations. Key health indicators address both morbidity and mortality. For mortality, the crude mortality rate (deaths/10,000/day) is the most sensitive indicator of the population's health. Age- and sex-specific rates should be collected. The under-6 mortality rate is used to assess the health status of one of the most vulnerable groups in the population. For morbidity, information must be collected on rates of disease with public health importance, including diarrheal disease, respiratory infection, measles, malaria, and hepatitis. Rate of malnutrition in children under 6 years of age is the second most important indicator of the population's health. Data on environmental health should be collected and compared with the standards of 16 to 20 liters of water per person per day and one pit latrine per family. The disaster impact on the health system can be assessed by measuring loss of staff, since major population displacements and complex humanitarian emergencies are frequently associated with health professionals not being available to communities; the status of health infrastructure, as populations may no longer have ready access to health facilities, and hospitals and clinics are frequently damaged or destroyed; and the status of public health programs, as immunization programs, maternal and child health services, and vector control programs may all have been disrupted.

Sources and Methods of Data Collection

Data collection methods may be classified as primary (direct observation or surveys) or secondary (interviews with key informants or review of existing records.)

Direct observation can be completed on the ground or from the air. Direct on-the-ground observations can provide team members with first-hand view of the impact and extent of the disaster. Major health problems in the observed area may be identified but may not be generalizable to other sites. Where possible, team members should conduct informal interviews with victims and responders. Aerial observation allows team members to confirm the geographic extent of the disaster and to view the impact in inaccessible areas. In addition, by viewing the entire geographic region, the most severely affected areas may be identified, so that relief efforts can be more appropriately targeted.

Four types of surveys can be conducted. Focused surveys may be used to collect health data. These are relatively resource-intensive and should therefore be reserved for data that are necessary but are not available through other sources. Surveys based on convenience samples may be conducted relatively rapidly and provide a gross estimate of the health care needs of the affected community. However, convenience samples do not provide population-based information, so are likely to be sources of bias. Telephone surveys using randomly selected telephone numbers may be useful in determining the impact of the disaster and the health care needs of the community. Phone surveys require an intact communications system and may not provide a representative sample. People who are at home during the time of calling (ie, elderly) may be over-represented, introducing a potential source of bias. Surveys based on cluster-sampling methods are being used more frequently in disaster settings. Methods such as simple random sampling, stratified random sampling, and systematic random sampling are time- and resource-intensive, making them impractical for the purposes of a rapid health assessment. Cluster-sampling methods for natural disasters are based on the World Health Organization's Expanded Programme on Immunization method for estimating immunization coverage.

Cluster-sampling techniques provide population-based information both to guide and to evaluate relief operations. Modified cluster-sampling methods can be used to estimate the size of the population in the disaster-affected area, the number of people with specific health care needs, the number of damaged or destroyed buildings, and the availability of water, sanitation, food, and power in the community. Cluster surveys can usually be conducted rapidly, and the results made available within 24 hours. Follow-up surveys can be repeated in the same area over the following 3 to 14 days. Cluster surveys are particularly useful when the area of damage is generally uniform, such as after a hurricane. They have been less useful following earthquakes, where the distribution of damage may vary widely between locations. Among displaced and famine-affected populations, such as large refugee settlements, cluster surveys have been used to estimate the prevalence of acute malnutrition, disease rates, the major causes of mortality, and access to health care services.

For secondary data collection, interviews with key health and emergency personnel can be useful in obtaining qualitative data concerning the disaster. Gross estimates of the impact and population needs may also be available. Attempts should be made to corroborate these data with those collected through primary methods. Interviews may be conducted with hospital emergency room staff, medical personnel at temporary health facilities, community providers, public health officials, incident commanders, paramedics, police and fire department officials, American Red Cross representatives, and coroners. To augment and confirm these interviews, an effort should be made to review documented medical records from health facilities. Health data may be available from hospital emergency rooms and inpatient units, temporary health facilities, community providers, public health officials, and coroners' offices.

Limitations of Data Assessment

Health officials and disaster managers should be aware of the limitations of data that are collected during the rapid health assessment. Assessment team members must balance their preferences for sound epidemiological methodology against the time constraints and other limitations of the data collection process. Inaccuracies may result from logistical, technical, and organizational problems. Potential limitations include incomplete data, poor internal or external validity, and reliance on secondary sources of information. Unless population-based methodologies are used, data collected may not be representative of the community being assessed, and data collected from one population may not be generalizable to those in other regions. Further, information may not be available from certain disaster-affected areas due to poor access and communications. Finally, under-reporting of health events by rescue and medical personnel may occur because accurate documentation ranks as a low priority during the initial disaster response, particularly during sudden impact disasters.

Chapter 6

Disaster Communications

Communications before, during, and after disaster strikes dictate the success of prevention and relief efforts. This chapter reviews internal and external communications, communications systems, and goals for disaster-related communications.

PUBLIC HEALTH ROLE

- Communicate about health and public health matters with:

  - those providing medical care (hospitals and their emergency departments, community providers, and other public health and social service agencies)

  - first responders (fire, police, EMS) and other responders (national guard)

  - local and regional laboratories

  - general public

  - officials, mayors, governor(s)

  - partners (American Red Cross, public works)

• Set up communication network with health-related agencies, the media, and the public by providing public health reports to the media on regular basis.

INTERNAL AND EXTERNAL DISASTER COMMUNICATIONS

With modern mass media, even a relatively small disaster can become an international event within minutes. Electronic news reporting can raise concern about friends and relatives located in the impacted geographic area, especially when there are dramatic images of great destruction. When the media reports these stories, which may omit how much of the region is not damaged, the stricken community will be inundated with requests for information about the welfare of loved ones thought to be living or visiting where the disaster occurred. These requests for information interfere with the more urgent need to educate the public about injury prevention and food and water safety, to request supplies, and to share surveillance information with community officials.

During the impact and post-impact phases of a disaster, communications occur both internally and externally. Public health communicates internally to provide information to other responders and to solve problems. External communication occurs among health departments, hospitals, community providers, ambulatory care facilities, emergency management and first responders, laboratories, pharmacies, veterinarians, and community decision-makers. Communication lines must also be available between fixed and mobile locations. External communication to the media and public must provide factual information that the public finds credible.

Public health agencies must create advance protocols for releasing information about disasters. A public information officer, through whom all information is provided to the media, must be appointed. Arrangements for release of public information should be worked out in advance. Web sites can be used for communication to both the press and the public. As part of this effort, the public must be enjoined against flooding emergency response officials with requests about specific individuals in the disaster area so that relief operations can proceed quickly and efficiently.

COMMUNICATING WARNINGS AND RESPONSE NEEDS

With improved forecast data and models, warnings can be issued to allow timely evacuation before hurricanes, taking shelter against tornadoes, and taking active steps toward vector control. Messages communicated to the public should be positive and reassuring yet factual. These bulletins must translate technical information into lay language that people can act upon. The messages must be congruent for both the internal and external audiences so consistency exists between the actions of the response agencies and the actions requested of the public. Messages should be clear, concise, and credible and include information about the expected hazards, precautions to take, and requirements for evacuation or shelter-in-place, where necessary. Communication can be a weak aspect of a disaster response without safeguards to ensure both the transmission and reception of information. Senders of all messages must request and receivers supply verification that the transmission was both received and understood. Validation that the intent of the message was understood is evident by safety responses by citizens, use of shelters, and other appropriate actions.

Often residents do not want to evacuate areas threatened by impending disasters. In disasters for which adequate warning times are available, such as hurricanes, communities can prevent morbidity and mortality by making appropriate decisions, disseminating information, coordinating warnings, and writing messages that are easily understood and motivate evacuation. In disasters such as earthquakes and tornadoes, for which advanced warning is rare, the risk of injury and death increases. However, even with tornadoes, morbidity and mortality can be lessened by telephone or media warning as soon as condusive weather conditions are identified or the funnel cloud itself is spotted. Nocturnal tornadoes result in the most injuries because people do not hear the warnings.

Unfortunately, some officials withhold warnings until the last possible moment, sometimes until it is too late to take effective protective action. This has been attributed to the disaster myth that panic is a likely response and that panic following a call for evacuation might cause more deaths and injuries than the disaster itself.

Requests for aid following a disaster require the same clarity as warnings in advance. Otherwise, donations may be inappropriate (ie, wool blankets shipped to hurricane victims in the Caribbean, shipment of outdated medications) and cause additional problems on the receiving end. The Pan American Health Organization has developed a supply management system called SUMA that facilitates the sorting, classifying, and inventorying of the supplies sent to a disaster-stricken area. However, monetary donations are much less disruptive to the disaster response and can be used more flexibly. Preventing the broadcast of broad appeals for help and volunteers often requires advance education of the media, local government officials, and even disaster relief organizations.

COMMUNICATION SYSTEMS

Responding agencies should prepare to use an integrated system to communicate during the impact and post-impact phases of a disaster. Redundancy in systems is essential due to technological limitations and the vulnerability of public networks.

For office-based communication about disaster-related activities, public health officials need basic computer equipment. Computers must have a CD drive, continuous Internet email capacity, and sufficient security (ie, firewall, password protection, virus scanning) to protect data and prevent against intrusion. Back-up power supplies are essential, as is off-site data back up and storage. A system for broadcasting health alerts 24 hours a day, 7 days a week, must also be maintained.

Public health officials must have alternative systems for communication and be able to establish a link to the community's emergency alert system. Radio systems and radio frequencies must be established, with staff trained on the use of these systems. Protocols should be developed between the 911 system and health departments so public health agencies are among the parties regularly notified as part of the community's emergency response.

Following earthquakes, hurricanes, and tornadoes, landline services (traditional phone lines) are likely to be nonfunctional. Arrangements must be made to receive calls through an emergency telecommunications system if the landline circuits are overloaded or not operational. Health departments and hospitals should have several unlisted phone numbers so that they can more easily make outgoing phone calls. Telephone lines coming into communication centers should be buried, clearly marked, and protected from damage. Records of the location of telephone lines must be maintained and updated so they can be located quickly post-impact. The emergency management sector will have radio networks available, and public health can disseminate health advisories through both radio and television.

To avoid overload on radio frequencies, protocols must be in place to limit the length of conversations and to establish several radio transmitter-receivers operating on multiple frequencies. Fixed facilities (hospitals and health departments) should have standby sources of power to support lighting, ventilation, heating, air-conditioning, and communication equipment.

Cellular telephones, one solution for telecommunications during disaster response, depend on the existence of relay stations or cells. Each cell has a limited capacity for simultaneous communications and covers only a defined radius. If too many people are using their cellular telephones, these systems will crash. More importantly, cells are usually located in urban areas and along major traffic routes. Rural areas, where disasters are as likely to occur, may not be covered by such systems. Satellite systems are costly and may not work if weather interrupts the wavelength transmission. The federal government uses the Radio Amateur Civil Emergency Services (RACES) licensed amateurs who provide communication support. The Amateur Radio Services operate on the same radio wavelengths and currently provide support to the American Red Cross. Citizen band radio operators run the General Mobile Radio service, which requires repeaters and whose systems require battery back-up because it will go down if not hardened. Users of cellular, analog, and radio communications must recognize that these networks are not secure and that anyone with a receiver can hear the conversations.

TABLE 11. COMMUNICATIONS EQUIPMENT

Radio Equipment	Wire Lines	Combination
Two-way radios	Telephone	Cellular telephone
Pagers	Facsimile machine	Satellite telephone
Broadcast radio	Computer modem	
Television		
Satellite		

Reprinted with permission from Glass CJ. How hospitals use communication in disaster. In: Landesman L, ed. Emergency Preparedness in Healthcare Organizations. Oakbrook Terrace, Ill: Joint Commission on Accreditation of Healthcare Organizations, 1996.

SATELLITE COMMUNICATIONS

Although satellite communications may seem ideal when disaster disrupts all ground-based lines, if one link of a fixed satellite service goes down, the whole system goes down. In addition, mobile satellite receivers are expensive. A relatively new category of service, which uses dozens of low-orbiting satellites, is called the Global Mobile Personal Communications Systems (GMPCS). This system uses hand-held satellite phones and helps address the problems of geographical coverage. However, network overload is also a possibility with this system, depending on the number of satellites used, or the size of the antenna footprint. The Inmarsat system, commonly used in international disaster relief operations, is based on only four main footprints, each covering up to one third of the earth's surface. This allows for a large number of simultaneous links over any one satellite. As a result, a sudden increase of traffic from a disaster-affected area would have little impact on the overall volume of traffic. All GMPCS systems are based on costly infrastructures. Like all communication systems, the GMPCS should be used as a redundant system.

RADIO AMATEUR CIVIL EMERGENCY SERVICE

The Radio Amateur Civil Emergency Service was founded in 1952 as a public service to provide a reserve communications group within government agencies in times of extraordinary need. The Federal Communications Commission (FCC) regulates RACES operations; the amateur radio regulations (Part 97, Subpart E, §§97.407) were created by the FCC to describe RACES operations in detail.

Each RACES group is administrated by a local, county, or state agency responsible for disaster services, such as emergency management, police, or fire. In some parts of the United States, RACES may be part of an agency's Auxiliary Communications Service. Some RACES groups refer to themselves by other names such as Disaster Communications Service or Emergency Communications Service. The Federal Emergency Management Agency provides planning guidance, technical assistance, and funding for establishing RACES organizations at the state or local government level.

RACES provides a pool of emergency communications personnel prepared for deployment in time of need. Local, county, or state government agencies activate their RACES group. Traditional RACES operations involve the handling of emergency messages on amateur radio frequencies. These operations typically involve messages between critical locations such as hospitals, emergency services, shelters, and other locations where communication is needed. RACES communicators may become involved in public safety or other government communications, emergency operations center staffing, and emergency equipment repair. RACES groups develop and maintain their communications ability by training throughout the year with special exercises and public service events. A comprehensive RACES manual, Guidance for Radio Amateur Civil Emergency Service, is available on the FEMA Web site: http://www.fema.gov/library/civilpg.htm.

Chapter 7

Environmental Health Issues

Maintaining environmental health is essential to preventing disease following disasters. This chapter addresses public health interventions to maintain safety of water and food supplies, to ensure proper sanitation and waste disposal, and to control vector populations.

PUBLIC HEALTH ROLE

- Quantitative monitoring of environmental services, including ensuring the replacement or repair of existing sanitary barriers.

- Promoting changes in the behavior of victims by providing guidance, education, and assurance of safe water, safe food, and safe shelter to compensate for disrupted sanitary environments.

REDUCING EXPOSURE TO ENVIRONMENTAL HAZARDS

Disrupted environments have variable effects on health depending on the presence of endemic disease, the susceptibility and habits of the population, and the availability of protective measures. The types of disease most often spread, such as respiratory infections and diarrhea, are those that have a short transmission cycle and incubation period and are widespread.

Public health can use three major approaches to reduce exposure to environmental hazards: measures of control, establishment of multiple barriers, and providing distance between the hazard and populations at risk.

Measures of Control. Certain hazards move through the environment and cause harm to humans. Public health professionals can control disease by preventing the hazard from being released or occurring, by preventing the transport of the hazard, or by preventing people from being exposed to the hazard. For example, malaria control involves a three-pronged approach of draining stagnant water to prevent mosquito breeding, spraying for mosquitoes to prevent the transport of pathogens, and diminishing exposure by encouraging the use of treated bed-netting and insect repellent.

Establishing Multiple Barriers. Since no single environmental measure is failsafe, redundant barriers must be set up between hazards and populations. Multiple sanitary barriers provide redundant protection where, for example, public health protects surface water used for drinking. If on a given day, any of the redundant measures is not functioning, the others will reduce the hazard. Most water-borne outbreaks in the United States occur when multiple barriers fail simultaneously. Protection from environmental hazards depends on awareness of the risk, diligence in surveillance, and investment in the multiple barriers needed to keep the population risk low.

Providing Distance Between Hazards and Populations. In general, the distance needed to protect a population from exposure to a hazardous substance varies according to the volume and nature of a hazardous substance. The greater the distance existing between a hazard and a population, the greater the amount of time before an inadvertent release of the hazardous material reaches the populated area. With a longer time delay, the release is more likely to be detected in time for the population to take protective measures. Since most pollutants degrade or disperse over distance, providing space between hazardous materials and populations may by itself reduce human exposure.

ENVIRONMENTAL SURVEILLANCE

Three conditions should be monitored to estimate the number of individuals whose environment is affected by a disaster: access to excreta disposal facilities, water consumption, and the percentage of people consuming safe water.

Access to Excreta Disposal Facilities. Public health officials must assess the number of people per latrine to determine the relative availability of latrines and the amount of sharing required. To estimate people per latrine, conduct a walk through survey or interview people. For those who indicate that they have a family latrine, ask how many people are in their family and if they share the latrine with anyone else. If families are using communal latrines, calculate sanitation coverage as the number of latrines divided by the number of people using them. Where people continue to live in dwellings in which not all toilets are functional, monitor the fraction of households with a functioning toilet or latrine as a proxy for sanitation coverage.

Water Consumption. Water consumption depends both on water availability and the population's ability to obtain the water. Bucket shortages, security concerns, and long lines can all prevent plentiful sources from being fully utilized. Public health officials must survey the population and estimate water consumption by asking for a 24-hour recall of water use or by monitoring how much water is collected at the various sources and dividing this by the number of people being served. Water consumption is defined in terms of gallons or liters per person per day.

Percentage of People Consuming Safe Water. In settings where ground-water supplies at wells or springs are determined to be safe, monitor the fraction of people obtaining water from the safe sources versus unsafe sources. Public health workers should monitor the percentage of people who are getting "safe" water when it is being collected, remembering that collecting "safe" water from a source does not assure that the water is safe at the time of ingestion. With piped systems, workers must collect samples at household taps throughout the system, with a collection scheme such that each sample represents a similar number of people (ie, 1 sample per 10,000 people). The fraction of water samples that are safe to drink corresponds to the fraction of people whose water arrives safely at the point where the water is collected.

SANITATION DURING DISASTER SITUATIONS

Sewage systems are a network of pipes that carry wastes away from a population. Sewers often become flooded or clogged during hurricanes, earthquakes, and floods. Hurricanes or other storms may cause untreated sewage to be washed into waterways. Clogged sewer lines may also cause waste to spill into the environment at locations where it is likely to expose large numbers of people to biological or chemical hazards. Typically, problems within sewage networks are mitigated by pumping or re-routing the sewage, which may not be possible following a disaster. Public health officials should document the location of by-pass valves, confirm that they are functional and that auxiliary pumping capacity exists, and have an operational plan for storm events as part of a disaster preparedness program.

Where sanitation systems are destroyed, one of the first activities should be the reestablishment of a system of latrines since containing human excreta is the most protective environmental measure that can be taken following disaster. Proper spaces for defecation fields must be set aside, and latrines should be built before the population arrives at a relocation site. When defecation fields are used, they must be planned in advance and located away from water sources and downhill from living quarters. The World Health Organization recommends the provision of one pit latrine per family. Where that is not possible, both the United Nations High Commission for Refugees and United Nations International Children's Education Fund have set a maximum target of 20 people per latrine. To the extent possible, households should not share latrines or toilets. Efforts should be made to build separate latrines for men and women or separate latrines for children. Privacy screens should be constructed. Establishing one latrine per household, rather than sharing latrines, will increase the likelihood that the facilities will be kept clean. With mortality and morbidity rates among displaced populations often higher in the first days and weeks following an event, it is essential to persuade everyone to use the latrines that have been set up.

To increase use of latrines by young children, two approaches may be useful. First, educate child-care providers about proper handling of children's feces and the importance of washing their hands after cleaning the child or handling the child's feces. Second, establish excreta disposal facilities that are child-friendly (ie, well-lit, have an opening smaller than that used in adult latrines).

To ensure personal hygiene, paper, water, and soap must be readily available in or near the latrine, especially where diarrheal diseases and dysentery are likely to occur. Public health information officers should promote hand washing, particularly after defecating and before preparing food to protect against fecal-oral illnesses. The information campaign should promote measures known to prevent specific health threats. Educational messages should be short, relate to the route by which disease may be transmitted, and focus on behaviors that are not presently practiced by a significant portion of the population. Public health workers should likewise establish a simple monitoring component to assure that increased hand washing (or other preventive behavior) is actually occurring.

ENSURING WATER SAFETY

Providing people with more water is *more* protective against fecal-oral pathogens than providing people with *cleaner* water. Public health officials should work closely with the agencies that are monitoring the availability of water. Estimate water consumption at least weekly during the post-impact phase. Measure water consumption by what people receive, not what the water operators produce. Water consumption can be measured through sampling, such as household interviews, or by the actual collection of water at watering points.

Attempts should be made to provide each family with their own water bucket to reduce the risk of illness. The average water consumption should be 15 liters per day or more, with no one consuming less than 5 liters or 1 gallon per person per day. The World Health Organization recommends 16 to 20 liters per day. A three to five day supply of water (five gallons per person) should be stored for food preparation, bathing, brushing teeth, and dish washing. Where residents are preparing supplies in advance of a disaster, such as earthquake-prone California, they should store water in sturdy plastic bottles with tight fitting lids. Stored water should be located away from the storage of toxic substances and should be changed every six months.

WATER FOR DRINKING AND COOKING

Safe drinking water includes bottled, boiled, or treated water. Residents should drink only bottled, boiled, or treated water until the supply is tested and found safe. They must be instructed not to use contaminated water to wash dishes, brush teeth, wash and prepare food, or make ice. All bottled water from an unknown source must be boiled or treated before use. To kill harmful bacteria and parasites, residents should bring water to a rolling boil for one minute. Water may also be treated with chlorine or iodine tablets or by mixing six drops (1/8 teaspoon) of unscented household chlorine bleach (5.25% sodium hypochlorite) per gallon of water. Mix the solution thoroughly, and let stand for about 30 minutes. This treatment, however, will not kill parasitic organisms.

The United Nations High Commission for Refugees considers water with less than 10 fecal coliforms per 100 ml to be reasonably safe, while water with more than 100 fecal coliforms is considered unsafe. Contaminated water sources should not be closed until equally convenient facilities become available.

It may be necessary to transport safe drinking water to the disaster site by truck. Trucks that normally carry gasoline, chemicals, or sewage should not be used to transport water. Trucks should be inspected and cleaned and disinfected before being used for water transportation because they may be contaminated with microbes or chemicals. Containers, such as bottles or cans, should be rinsed with a bleach solution before reusing them. Do not rely on untested devices for decontaminating water.

WATER SUPPLY

There are three sources of water: groundwater, surface water, and rainwater. Groundwater, while generally of higher quality microbiologically, is relatively difficult to access because it is located within the earth's crust. Surface waters, found in lakes, ponds, streams and rivers, have predictable reliability and volume and are relatively easy to gather but are generally microbiologically unsafe and require treatment. Rainwater is seldom used because collection is unreliable.

COLLECTING AND TREATING SURFACE WATER

Once collected, water quality deteriorates over time. The handling and storing of water is the main determinant in water safety. Where water is collected in buckets, it should be chlorinated either in the home or by health workers at the point of collection. Residents should be instructed to add an initial dose of 2.5 mg/l chlorine to the bucket so that after 30 minutes, at least 0.5 mg/l free chlorine remains in the water. People should be encouraged to wait for 30 minutes after chlorination before consuming water to allow for adequate disinfection to occur. The dipping of water from household storage buckets causes considerable contamination. To maintain clean stored water, residents should add a chlorine residual.

With a piped system, typically chlorine levels are adjusted to assure that 0.2 to 0.5 mg/l free chlorine is in the water at the tap level where it is collected. During times of outbreaks or in systems in there are broken distribution pipes, workers should aim to have 0.5 to 1.0 mg/l free chlorine.

To prevent cross-contamination, health officials should increase the pressure in the water pipes and increase the level of residual chlorine. Pressure can be augmented by increasing the rate of pumping into the system, by cutting down on water wastage, or by closing off sections of the distribution system. Because cross-contamination usually occurs in unknown locations in a distribution system, the chlorine residual must be kept high throughout the network. Monitoring of chlorine should be done throughout the system, and the dose put into the system should be set so that there is free chlorine in at least 95% of locations.

ACCESSING AND TREATING GROUNDWATER

To collect spring water without contamination, workers should build a collection basin that has an outflow pipe constructed at or just below the point where the water comes to the surface. To prevent contamination in wells, they can build a skirt around the opening of the well or a plate sealing off the surface at the top of the well.

Water should be disinfected when household water contamination is high, when there is a high risk of a waterborne outbreak, or when the groundwater is of poor quality. Chlorine can be used in buckets when the water is collected or stored at people's homes. To chlorinate wells, use a chlorine pot or the method of shock chlorination as described below.

A chlorination pot includes a small container, such as a one-liter soda bottle, with a few holes punched in it. This container is filled with a chlorine powder and gravel mixture and placed inside a larger vessel (such as a four-liter milk jug or a clay pot) that also has holes punched in it. The chlorine disperses from the double layered pot slowly. The number and size of holes in the vessels controls the disinfectant dose and must be tailored to match a specific well volume and withdrawal rate. Invariably, the first water drawn in the morning will have an offensively high level of chlorine, and if a well has hours of very high use, the dose may become too low. Thus, pot chlorination schemes are not widely used and should not be commenced during the acute phase of a crisis when a lack of time and attention will prevent proper monitoring and adjustment of the chlorine levels.

Shock chlorination is conducted by adding 5-10 mg/l to the water in a well and allowing it to sit unused for a period of hours. The first water drawn from the well after the disinfection period is discarded, and normal use is subsequently resumed. When a well is drawing from safe groundwater but has been contaminated by people or an unusual event (such as a major rainstorm), shock chlorination can eliminate a transient threat to water quality. Shock chlorination does not provide chlorinated water to the people in their homes because after the first few hours of use after treatment, little or no residual chlorine will remain in the drawn water.

DISINFECTING WELLS

Although recommendations and regulations vary from state to state, the same general principles apply to disinfecting wells. To disinfect bored or dug wells, use Table 12 to calculate how much bleach (liquid or granules) to use. To determine the exact amount required, multiply the amount of disinfectant needed (according to the diameter of the well) by the depth of the well. For example, a well 5.0 feet in diameter requires 4.5 cups of bleach per foot of water. If the well is 30 feet deep, multiply 4.5 by 30 to determine the total cups of bleach required (135 cups). Add this total amount of disinfectant (in this case, 135 cups ÷ 16 cups per gallon = 8 gallons and 7 cups of bleach) to about 10 gallons of water. Splash the mixture around the wall or lining of the well. Be certain the disinfectant solution contacts all parts of the well. Seal the well top. Open all faucets, and pump water until a strong odor of bleach is noticeable at each faucet. Then stop the pump and allow the solution to remain in the well overnight. The next day, operate the pump by turning on all faucets, continuing until the chlorine odor disappears. Adjust the flow of water faucets or fixtures that discharge to septic systems to a low flow to avoid overloading the disposal system.

TABLE 12. BLEACH REQUIRED TO DISINFECT A BORED OR DUG WELL

Well Diameter (feet)	Liquid bleach (5.25%) per Foot of Water	Chlorine granules (70%) per Foot of Water
3	1.5 cups	1.0 ounce
4	3.0 cups	2.0 ounces
5	4.5 cups	3.0 ounces
6	6.0 cups	4.0 ounces
7	9.0 cups	6.0 ounces
8	12.0 cups	8.0 ounces
10	18.0 cups	12.0 ounces

To disinfect drilled wells, determine the amount of water in the well by multiplying the gallons per foot (see Table 13) by the depth of the well in feet. For example, a well with a 6-inch diameter contains 1.5 gallons of water per foot. If the well is 120 feet deep, multiply 1.5 by 120 to calculate the amount of water as 180 gallons.

TABLE 13. WATER VOLUME OF DRILLED WELLS

Well Diameter (inches)	Gallons per Foot of Water
3	0.37
4	0.65
5	1.00
6	1.50
8	2.60
10	4.10
12	6.00

SOURCE: ILLINOIS DEPARTMENT OF HEALTH. RECOMMENDATIONS MAY VARY FROM STATE TO STATE.

After calculating the total amount of water in the well (see Table 13), determine the amount of liquid or granular chlorine to add: use three cups of liquid laundry bleach (5.25% chlorine) or two ounces (four heaping tablespoons) of hypochloride granules (70% chlorine) per 100 gallons of well water. In the example above, the 180-gallon well would require 5.4 cups of liquid bleach or 3.6 ounces of granular chlorine.

Mix the total amount of liquid or granules with about 10 gallons of water. Pour the solution into the top of the well before the seal is installed. Connect a hose from a faucet on the discharge side of the pressure tank to the well casing top. Start the pump. Spray the water back into the well and wash the sides of the casing for at least 15 minutes. Open every faucet in the system and let the water run until the smell of chlorine can be detected. Then close all the faucets and seal the top of the well. Let stand for several hours, preferably overnight. Afterward, operate the pump by turning on all faucets continuing until all odor of chlorine disappears. Adjust the flow of water from faucets or fixtures that discharge into septic tank systems to a low flow to avoid overloading the disposal system.

EMERGENCY BASIC SERVICES

In catastrophic events, all basic services may need to be reestablished. Where the infrastructure to provide safe water and food is not intact, interim measures must be established to provide services until systems are fully operational. In catastrophic circumstances, public health officials may issue orders to boil water, warn about foods that may have spoiled during electrical outages, or announce where potable water will be provided.

Boil Water Orders

Through the Safe Drinking Water Act, Congress requires the Environmental Protection Agency (EPA) to regulate contaminants that may be health risks and that may be present in public drinking water supplies. The EPA sets legal limits on the levels of certain contaminants in drinking water and establishes the water-testing schedules and methods that water systems must follow. The rules also list acceptable techniques for treating contaminated water. The Safe Drinking Water Act gives individual states the opportunity to set and enforce their own drinking water standards so long as the standards are at least as strong as EPA's national standards. Most states and territories directly oversee the water systems within their borders.

The Total Coliform Rule sets legal limits for total coliform levels in drinking water and specifies the type and frequency of testing to determine if legal limits are exceeded. Coliforms are a broad class of bacteria that live in the digestive tracts of humans and many animals. The presence of coliform bacteria in tap water suggests that the treatment system is not working properly or that a problem exists in the pipes. Exposure to coliform can cause gastroenteritis, which is characterized by diarrhea, cramps, nausea, and vomiting.

Coliforms cannot be found in more than five percent of the samples tested each month. If more than five percent of the samples contain coliforms, water system operators must report this violation to the state and the public. If a sample tests positive for coliforms, the system must collect a set of repeat samples within 24 hours. When a routine or repeat sample tests positive for total coliforms, it must also be analyzed for fecal coliforms and *Escherichia coli (E. coli)*, which are coliforms directly associated with fresh feces. A positive result to this last test signifies an acute Maximum Contaminant Level (MCL) violation, which necessitates rapid state and public notification due to its direct health risk.

Following a disaster that may compromise a community's water supply, those responsible for monitoring water safety may use the regular water-sampling plan or make modifications, depending on the severity and geographic location of concern. When a decision has been made that water sampled from one or more sites exceeds the maximum contaminant level and poses a threat to the public's health, a decision may be made to issue a boiled water order or advisory.

The EPA issued a revised set of Drinking Water Standards and Health Advisories in 2000. With few exceptions, the health advisory val-

TABLE 14. DRINKING WATER CONTAMINANTS

Microorganism	Maximum Contaminant Level Goal (mg/L)	Maximum Contaminant Level or Treatment Technique	Potential Health Effects from Ingestion of Water	Sources of Contaminant in Drinking Water
Giardia lamblia	0	99.9% killed or inactivated	Giardiasis, a gastroenteric disease	Human and animal fecal waste
Heterotrophic plate count	n/a	≤500 bacterial colonies/ml	HPC has no health effects, but can indicate how effective treatment is at controlling microorganisms	n/a
Legionella	0	Use treatment technique for Giardia	Legionnaire's disease (pneumonia)	Found naturally in water; multiplies in heating systems
Total Coliforms (including fecal coliform and *E. Coli*)	0	≤5.0% samples total coliform-positive in a month	Used as an indicator that other potentially harmful bacteria may be present*	Human and animal fecal waste
Turbidity	n/a	Systems that filter must ensure that the turbidity ≤1 NTU (0.5 NTU for con-ventional or direct filtration) in at least 95% of the daily samples in any month	Turbidity has no health effects but can interfere with disinfection and provide a medium for microbial growth. It may indicate the presence of microbes.	Soil runoff

*Drinking Water Standards and Health Advisories, EPA, 2000

ues have been rounded to one significant figure. Table 14 summarizes the section on microorganisms. The maximum contaminant level goal refers to the maximum level of a contaminant in drinking water at which no known or anticipated adverse effects occur and that allows for an adequate margin of safety. These are nonenforceable public health goals. The maximum contaminant level, which is an enforceable standard, identifies the maximum permissible level of a contaminant in water that is delivered to any user of a public water system. Treatment technique is an enforceable procedure or level of technical performance that public water systems must follow to ensure control of a contaminant.

The Surface Water Treatment Rule requires systems using surface water or ground water under the direct influence of surface water to disinfect their water and to filter their water or meet criteria for avoiding filtration so that the following contaminant are controlled at the following levels:

- *Giardia lamblia*: 99.9% killed/inactivated.

- Viruses: 99.99% killed/inactivated.

- *Legionella*: No limit, but EPA believes that if Giardia and viruses are inactivated, Legionella will also be controlled.

- Turbidity: At no time can turbidity (cloudiness of water) go above 5 nephelolometric turbidity units (NTU); systems that filter must ensure that the turbidity go no higher than 1 NTU (0.5 NTU for conventional or direct filtration) in at least 95% of the daily samples in any month.

- Heterotrophic Plate Count: No more than 500 bacterial colonies per milliliter.

- Total Coliforms (including fecal coliform and *E. Coli*): No more than 5.0% samples total coliform-positive in a month. For water systems that collect fewer than 40 routine samples per month, no more that one sample can be total coliform-positive. Every sample that has total coliforms must be analyzed for fecal coliforms. There cannot be any fecal coliforms.

Public Notice Templates

The EPA has developed templates that can be used by water suppliers to ensure that the notice that they provide is complete. These templates can be downloaded from the EPA website: http://www.epa.gov/safewater/pws/pn/templates.htm.

Food Safety

Improper food storage is associated with *B. cereus, C. perfingens, Salmonella, S. aureus,* and group A *Streptococcus.* Lack of hand washing and personal hygiene are associated with shigellosis, hepatitis A, gastroenteritis, and giardiasis. Three food-handling techniques are a major source of food-borne illness following disaster: improper storage, inadequate cooking, and poor personal hygiene. In addition to careful hand washing, cooking utensils must be washed in boiled or treated water before being used.

Stored Food. When preparing for disasters, residents should store at least a three-day supply of food. Canned foods and dry mixes will remain fresh for about two years when stored in a cool, dry, dark place away from ranges or refrigerator exhausts at a temperature of 40 to 60°F. Residents should date all food items and use or replace food before it loses freshness. Food items should be heavily wrapped or stored in airtight containers above the ground to both prolong shelf life and to protect it from insects and rodents. Cans that bulge at the ends or that are leaking should be discarded.

Refrigerated Food. Refrigerators, without power, will keep foods cool for about four hours if left unopened. Block or dry ice can be added to refrigerators if the electricity is off longer than four hours. Perishable food in the refrigerator or freezer should be used before stored food. Unrefrigerated cooked foods should be discarded after two hours at room temperature regardless of appearance. Only foods that have a normal color, texture, and odor should be eaten.

Frozen Food. Twenty-five pounds of dry ice will keep a ten-cubic-foot freezer below freezing for three to four days. Dry ice freezes everything it touches and must be handled with dry, heavy gloves to avoid injury. Thawed food can usually be eaten or refrozen if it is still refrigerator cold or if it still contains ice crystals. Any food that has been at room temperature for two hours or more or that has an unusual odor, color, or texture should be discarded.

Flooded Food Supplies. Discard all food not stored in a waterproof container. Undamaged, commercially canned foods can be saved by removing the can labels, thoroughly washing the cans, and then disinfecting them with a solution consisting of one cup of bleach in five gallons of water. Cans should be relabeled, including expiration date, with a non-erasable marker. Food containers with screw caps, snap-lids, crimped caps (soda pop bottles), twist caps, flip tops, and home canned foods cannot be disinfected. Only pre-prepared canned baby formula that requires no added water should be used for infants.

Feeding Large Numbers of Displaced People

Food requirements can be estimated by assessing the effect of the disaster on food supplies and the number of people who are without food. Seasonal variations may affect the availability of food. Estimates of food requirements should be calculated for one week and one month: 16 metric tons of food are needed for 1,000 people for one month, and 2 cubic meters of space are needed to store 1 metric ton of food.

Control Strategies for Epidemic Diarrheal Diseases

Environmental measures and education campaigns should be specific to the fecal-oral disease public health officials seek to protect against.

Cholera. Public health bulletins must instruct residents to consume only chlorinated or boiled fluids and to eat only hot, cooked foods or peeled fruits and vegetables. Emphasize hand washing in food preparation and before eating. During a cholera outbreak, ensure that the water being consuming is chlorinated. Where chlorination is not possible, order the boiling of water or the addition of a lemon per liter. Acidic sauces added to foods, such as tomato sauce, can provide some protection against food-borne cholera.

Typhoid fever. As with cholera, residents must be told to consume only chlorinated or boiled fluids and to eat only hot, cooked foods or peeled fruits and vegetables. Public health officials must ensure that the water supply is chlorinated and emphasize hand washing in food preparation and before eating. Workers must also ensure that infected residents do not prepare food for others for three months after the onset of their symptoms.

Shigella. Public health campaigns must educate residents about a comprehensive personal hygiene program. Public health workers must provide soap and lots of water and promote hand washing, the chlorination of water, and the proper handling and heating of food. Educational efforts should be focused in households where cases have occurred because secondary cases within households are common.

Hepatitis A. Water is the main route of transmission during major outbreaks. The most common form of fecal-oral hepatitis, hepatitis A, is transmitted by food and other routes. Control measures should therefore concentrate on the chlorination of water. Since pregnant women are particularly vulnerable, special efforts should be made to educate them and help them carry out personal and food hygiene.

HEATING AND SHELTER

Provision of sufficient shelter following disaster prevents, depending on weather conditions, hypothermia, frostbite, malaise, heatstroke, and dehydration.

In cold climates, higher caloric intake is required to maintain the same activity level. For each degree below 20° C, about 1% more calories is required. If a house is 10° C, residents will require 10% more food intake to sustain their activity level. Public health interventions following cold-weather disasters include making high energy foods available, providing blankets and sleeping bags, distributing plastic sheeting to cover windows and unused doorways, encouraging the sharing of a heated place by several people or households, and instructing residents of multistory buildings to heat the same room, allowing heat lost from one floor to augment heat in the room above. Educational messages should warn people about the signs of carbon monoxide poisoning and provide instructions to check for gas leaks.

In warmer climates, sheeting should be provided to keep people dry during rainstorms and to provide shade in the daylight.

INTEGRATED PEST MANAGEMENT

The most effective way to control vector-borne disease is to establish sanitary disposal of waste as soon as possible. Where vector-borne disease is known to be endemic, control programs should be accelerated in the post-impact phase of a disaster. The principles of integrated pest management are to eliminate breeding sites, to eliminate food, and to control harborage (where pests can live). A community vector-control program includes several components:

• Collect and dispose of garbage as soon as possible.

• Educate the public about rat and mosquito control.

- Eliminate mosquito breeding sites by overturning receptacles, covering swimming pools, and draining or covering other stagnant water sources.

- Reduce rat population and spread by closing up cracks in walls and bring cats to chase the rats.

- Store food in enclosed, protected areas.

In flooded areas, rats will search for dry places to hide. Rats and other vectors can feed off dead animals and other organic waste. Therefore, animal carcasses should be sprinkled with kerosene to protect them from predatory animals.

Chapter **8**

Mental Health Strategies

Most victims and workers in disasters respond normally to an abnormal situation. This chapter reviews the psychosocial affects of natural and technological disasters on all who are impacted and the interventions needed by special populations (ie, children, older adults, emergency workers). Post-traumatic stress disorder is examined at length as well.

PUBLIC HEALTH ROLE

- Help restore the psychological and social functioning of individuals and the community.

- Reduce the occurrence and severity of adverse mental health outcomes due to exposure to natural and technological disasters through prevention, assessment, and response.

- Help speed recovery and prevent long-term problems by providing information about normal reactions to disaster-related stress and how to handle these reactions.

PSYCHOSOCIAL IMPACTS OF DISASTER

The long-term psychosocial effects of disasters are mitigated by understanding what is likely to occur and preplanning the management strategy. Living through the experience of a disaster can have profound psychosocial effects and can alter social structure. When planning a response to or delivering services in the aftermath of a disaster, public health professionals must consider the wide range of responses among victims and responders.

Disasters are very stressful, disruptive experiences that can be life-changing. However, human behavior in emergency situations generally adapts to meet immediate needs, with people behaving within their usual patterns pre- and post-disaster. The challenge of dealing with a disaster can also result in positive responses by both individuals and communities. Residents typically work together and support one another as they rebuild their lives and their communities. Residents of disaster-stricken areas tend to exhibit prosocial behaviors, are proactive in remediating the effects of the event, and are willing to help one another in their recovery. People generally provide assistance to one another and support those managing the response to the emergency. Volunteer activity increases at the time of the impact and continues throughout the post-impact period. Many disaster tasks are carried out spontaneously by civilian bystanders (ie, family, friends, co-workers, neighbors) rather than trained emergency or relief personnel.

In terms of morbidity, the social and psychosocial impacts of a disaster can greatly exceed physical injuries. The social and psychosocial effects of disasters can last months, years, or an entire lifetime. People who are involved in disasters, as either victim or responder, may experience a wide variety of stress symptoms. These symptoms can have the broadest range of emotional, physical, cognitive, and interpersonal effects. In some disaster situations, victims recover quickly without long-lasting effects. In others, victims and responders suffer major mental health problems both immediately and for years after the event. They may have lost loved ones, need to adjust to new role changes, need to clean and repair property, or need to move from their home and neighborhood.

Both victims and responders experience a disaster as a crisis. Unusual events exacerbate the trauma, as there may be deaths of family or friends, injuries, job difficulties, illness, loss of personal belongings, and disruption of the regular routine. Initially, people feel numbness rather panic. Those who experience a disaster want to talk about it with everyone who will listen. Victims exhibit anger toward "the system," such as a perceived slow response by responding agencies. In time, everyone attempts to return to normal, but delays in normalcy delay emotional recovery.

Normal Reaction To Abnormal Situations

In general, the transient reactions that people experience after a disaster represent a normal response to a highly abnormal situation. Victims of a disaster should be viewed as normal persons, capable of functioning effectively, who have been subjected to severe stress and may be showing signs of emotional strain. Mild to moderate stress reactions during the emergency and in the early post-impact phases of a disaster are highly prevalent among survivors, families, community members, and rescue workers. While some individuals may exhibit symptoms of extreme stress, these reactions generally do not lead to chronic problems. However, public health professionals should not ignore common stress reactions. Counselors can help speed recovery and prevent long-term problems by providing information about normal reactions and educating victims about ways to handle these reactions.

A portion of the population will suffer more serious, persistent symptoms. While most individuals exposed to traumatic events and disasters recover and do not suffer prolonged psychiatric illness, some exhibit behavioral change or develop physical or psychiatric illness. Psychosocial problems can result from exposure to both natural and technological disasters and can include depression, alcohol abuse, anxiety, somatization, domestic violence, difficulties in daily functioning, and post-traumatic stress disorder (PTSD). While less serious, insomnia and anxiety may also be experienced by disaster victims and workers.

Symptoms of Distress

Adults and children manifest symptoms of distress differently. Disasters can have emotional, cognitive, physical, and interpersonal effects. For adults, the initial emotional response is usually shock and disbelief. This lasts from a few minutes to a few hours. Behavior is dazed or stunned. For the next several days, victims are willing to follow directions and are grateful for assistance. They may fell guilty for surviving.

In the next several weeks, victims will likely seek out others who were affected and participate in group activities of recovery. This activity is often followed by despair and depression. Victims can experience anger, emotional numbing, or a dissociation, perceiving their experience as "dreamlike." Cognitive effects can include impaired memory, concentration, and decision-making ability. Some victims worry about their futures and blame themselves.

Long term, there is a risk of decreased self-esteem and self-sufficiency. Some victims experience intrusive thoughts and memories. Physical effects can include sleep disturbances leading to insomnia and fatigue. Some victims and responders experience hyperarousal or a startle response. There can be somatic complaints such as headaches, gastrointestinal problems, reduced appetite, and decreased libido. Finally, disasters can have profound and widespread interpersonal effects such as alienation, social withdrawal, increased conflict within relationships, and both vocational and school impairment.

Those most at risk for psychosocial impacts are children, older adults, people with serious mental illness, families of people who die in a disaster, and special needs groups. Different age groups are vulnerable to stress in different ways. Most people do not see themselves as needing mental health services following disaster and will not seek out such services.

Children

Although a disaster affects everyone in the community, children are a particularly vulnerable group and require special attention and programs. Helping children will likely involve working closely with teachers and schools. The goal for those intervening with children is to help them integrate the experience and to reestablish a sense of security and mastery. Children who are most at risk are those who have lost family members or friends, who had a previous experience with a disaster, or who have preexisting family or individual crises. Children may not be able to describe their fears, which are a normal reaction stimulated by real events. Fear can outlast the event and can persist even if no physical injury occurred.

Preschool children needing extra help may appear withdrawn or depressed, or they may not respond to directed attention or to attempts to "draw them out." They may exhibit thumb-sucking, bedwetting, fears of darkness or animals, clinging to parents, night terrors, incontinence or constipation, speech difficulties, or changes in appetite. Preschoolers are vulnerable to disruptions in their environment, are affected by the reactions of their family, and are disoriented by changes to their regular schedule. Interventions to help preschoolers include reenactment of the events in play (ie, with fire trucks, dump trucks, ambulances) and games that involve touching (ie, ring around the rosie, London bridge, duck-duck-goose). Verbal reassurance, physical comforting, frequent attention, expressions regarding loss of pets or toys, and sleeping in the same room as their parents may be helpful as well.

Children aged 5 to 11 years may exhibit irritability, whining, clinging, aggressive behavior, competition for parent's attention, night terrors or nightmares, fears of darkness, withdrawal from peers, and avoidance, disinterest, or poor concentration in school. Interventions for this age group include patience and tolerance, play sessions with adults and peers, discussions with adults and peers, relaxed expectations, structured free time with activities, and rehearsal of safety measures for the future.

Children aged 11 to 14 years can experience sleep disturbances, changes in appetite, rebellion at home, physical complaints, and problems with or less interest in school activities. At this age, children may benefit from encouraging the resumption of normal routines, organizing groups with peers, engaging in group discussions about the disaster, relaxing expectations temporarily, taking on structured responsibilities, and receiving additional attention as needed.

Children aged 14 to 18 years may exhibit psychosomatic symptoms, disturbances of sleep and appetite, hypochondriasis, changes in energy level, apathy, decline in interest in opposite sex, irresponsible or delinquent behavior, fewer struggles for emancipation from parents, and poor concentration. Interventions include encouraging participation in community reclamation, resumption of social activities, discussion of experience with peers, reducing expectations temporarily, and discussion of experience with family. Adolescent activities should end on a positive note, such as talk of heroic acts, helping the community, and preparing for the next time. Small groups could develop a plan to help the community rehabilitate.

Older Adults

Older adults are in the highest risk group following a disaster. Generally, older adults have fewer support networks, limited mobility, or pre-existing illness. In addition, disasters can trigger memories of other traumas experienced earlier in life. Older persons worry about their deteriorating health and needing to be institutionalized and as a result may conceal the full extent of their physical problems. This population experiences a higher proportion of personal injury or loss because they often live in places more vulnerable to damage, such as trailer parks. Since they experience a greater loss of mobility, their independence and self-sufficiency are damaged because they are less able to rebuild their homes, businesses, and other losses due to disaster.

Responders

Those whose job is to respond to disasters "are repeatedly exposed to mutilated bodies, mass destruction, and life-threatening situations while doing physically demanding work that itself creates fatigue, sleep loss and often risk to one's life."[1] Their role as a help provider is also very stressful. Some responders experience similar feelings to those experienced by the victims. They can be irritable, finding fault with things that never bothered them before. They can be suspicious and resent authority. They can be concerned for their own safety and the safety of their children. Responders can be stressed by their working environment, particularly in the presence of understaffing of their units, being overworked, and conflicts with other professionals. Responders may face anxiety about their competence, are more affected by the impact of the sights and smells, and can also struggle to balance family responsibilities and work demands in the face of an emergency.

Some responders may develop a condition known as critical incident stress. This syndrome must be recognized and treated because critical incident stress lowers group morale, increases absenteeism, interferes with mutual support, and adversely affects home life. The symptoms include deterioration in sense of well-being, exhaustion, depression, hostility, lost tolerance for victims, dread of new encounters, guilt, helplessness, or isolation. "Burn out" is often recognized by looking for detachment or overinvolvement.

POST-TRAUMATIC STRESS DISORDER

Post-traumatic stress disorder (PTSD) is a prolonged stress response associated with impairment and dysfunction. PTSD usually appears within three months of the trauma but may surface months or years later. The duration of the disorder varies. Sometimes the symptoms of PTSD disappear over time, and sometimes PTSD persists for many years. While PTSD has been the subject of considerable research in

---

[1]Ursano RJ et al, "Trauma and Disaster" in Individual and Community Responses to Trauma and Disaster: The Structure of Human Chaos, eds RJ Urbano et al, Cambridge, England: Cambridge University Press, 1994, 3-27.

recent years, other serious problems that can develop after a disaster include acute stress disorder, major depression, generalized anxiety disorder, and substance abuse. Acute stress disorder is characterized by post-traumatic stress symptoms lasting at least two days but not longer than one month following the trauma.

Criteria for PTSD

A diagnosis of PTSD, as listed in the Diagnostic and Statistical Manual of Mental Disorders (DSM-IV)[2], requires that several criteria be met. PTSD symptoms can be acute, chronic, or delayed in their onset.

The first criterion relates to the nature of the traumatic event and the response it evokes:

> The person has been exposed to a traumatic event in which both of the following were present: (1) the person experienced, witnessed, or [has] been confronted with an event or events that involved actual or threatened death or serious injury, or a threat to the physical integrity of self or others ... [and] (2) the person's response involved intense fear, helplessness or horror ... (p. 209)

The second criterion relates to the *reexperiencing* of the traumatic event:

> The traumatic event is persistently reexperienced in one (or more) of the following ways: (1) recurrent and intrusive distressing recollections of the event ... (2) recurrent distressing dreams of the event ... (3) acting or feeling as if the traumatic event were recurring ... (4) intense psychological distress at exposure to internal or external cues that symbolize or resemble an aspect of the traumatic event; (5) physiological reactivity on exposure to internal or external cures that symbolize or resemble an aspect of the traumatic event. (p. 209-210)

The third criterion relates to *avoidance*, that is, the person avoiding things that remind him or her of the traumatic event:

> Persistent avoidance of stimuli associated with the trauma and numbing of general responsiveness (not present before the trauma), as indicated by three (or more) of the follow-

[2]Diagnostic Criteria from DSM-IV. Washington, DC: American Psychiatric Association, 1994: 209-211

ing: (1) efforts to avoid thoughts, feelings or conversations associated with the trauma; (2) efforts to avoid activities, places or people that arouse recollections of the trauma; (3) inability to recall an important aspect of the trauma; (4) markedly diminished interest or participation in significant activities; (5) feeling of detachment or estrangement from others; (6) restricted range of affect (e.g. unable to have love feelings); (7) sense of a foreshortened future ... (p. 211)

The fourth criterion relates to the person experiencing *increased arousal* after the traumatic event:

Persistent symptoms of increased arousal (not present before the trauma), as indicated by two (or more) of the following: (1) difficulty falling asleep; (2) irritability or outbursts of anger; (3) difficulty concentrating; (4) hypervigilance; (5) exaggerated startle response. (p. 211)

The fifth criterion relates to the duration of the symptoms just described. In particular, for a diagnosis of PTSD to be made, the duration of the symptoms in the second, third, and fourth criteria must exceed one month.

Finally, the disturbance must cause "clinically significant distress or impairment in social, occupational or other important areas of functioning."

PTSD Risk Factors/Predictors

Several factors can help predict which individuals might be at risk for PTSD. The nature or severity of the trauma the person has experienced plays a major role. Higher risk scenarios potentially leading to long-term adjustment problems include exposure to life-threatening situations, having a loved one die, loss of home and belongings, exposure to toxic contamination, and exposure to terror, horror, or grotesque sights, such as multiple casualties. Additional risk factors relate to life events before the disaster. A history of prior exposure to trauma, concurrent stressful life events, and lack of social support all predispose to PTSD.

Family members of trauma victims and family members of disaster workers may also develop PTSD and related symptoms. Spouses and significant others should be included in debriefing, education programs, and treatment programs as indicated.

Ethnocultural Issues in PTSD

Rates of PTSD or other disaster-related impairment can differ among groups of different race or ethnicity due to culturally varying perceptions of what constitutes a traumatic experience as well as individual and social responses to trauma. PTSD has been detected in traumatized cohorts from very different ethnocultural backgrounds, and refugees from non-Western cultures who meet PTSD diagnostic criteria have shown a similar clinical course and response to treatment as have Euro-American individuals. Assessments of the stress reaction of non-Western individuals should be carried out in a culturally sensitive manner, accounting for factors that may be unknown. Major depression, generalized anxiety disorder, and substance abuse are well documented after exposure to trauma and disasters.

NATURAL DISASTERS AND TECHNOLOGICAL DISASTERS

The similarities and differences between human-made and natural disasters are the degree to which the events are felt to be preventable and controllable. The two types of disasters have in common the immediate threat and the potential for ongoing disruption. However, they differ with regard to whether someone can be "blamed" for the event and whether it could have been prevented. People understand that man has little control over nature and that some geographic locations are more prone to some natural disasters than others. In contrast, they believe people can control technology and thus feel a greater sense of a loss of control with technological events, since these events could have been prevented.

Residents who are victimized by technological disasters may have their stress exacerbated by knowing that their tragedy was caused by other human beings. Technological disasters of the same magnitude as natural disasters generally cause more severe mental health problems because it is harder in the former to achieve psychological resolution and to move on.

For several reasons, technological disasters present complex challenges for public health professionals. First, unlike the community cohesiveness that occurs after natural disasters, communities are often in conflict after an environmental disaster. Where the disaster involves contaminants, which are usually invisible, great uncertainty often exists as to exposure. Contaminants may not have dispersed evenly, resulting in very different perceptions of the events by people living in the same community. Victims of technological disasters often feel a great deal of uncertainty about the risks of exposure and the long-term risks. Because of this ambiguity and uncertainty, neighbors can become bitterly divided, and their support networks may be irreversibly damaged. Worse, residents of affected communities can be stigmatized by society due to the unknown risks of their exposure.

Technological disasters often cause chronic uncertainty and distress. Unlike natural disasters, which generally have a low point after which things can be expected to improve, in disasters involving chemicals and radiation, those affected often do not know when all of the recovery activities will resolve. Uncertainty continues about the chronic health effects of exposure to invisible contaminants. Furthermore, long-term consequences, such as cancer, may take years to develop. Events that have a beginning and an end, such as tornadoes or hurricanes, allow for a process of recovery. Technological disasters do not have this defined timeline, and as a result, the psychological threat can be continual and chronic.

Morbidity and Mortality

Mental health–related morbidity and mortality following a natural disaster include poor concentration, phobia, substance abuse, absenteeism, deteriorating relationships, anxiety, depression, recurrent recollections, suicidal thoughts, and critical incident stress. Among junior and high school age children, mental health symptoms include being disoriented (ie, to name, town or date), despondent, agitated, restless, severely depressed and withdrawn, unable to make simple decisions, and unable to carry out daily activities. These children may also pace, appear pressured, hallucinate, become preoccupied with one idea or thought, engage in self-mutilation, abuse drugs or alcohol, experience significant memory gaps, and become delusional or suicidal. Following a technological disaster, psychophysiological symptoms are prevalent, along with chronic stress and demoralization.

PUBLIC HEALTH INTERVENTION

Psychosocial services strongly emphasize the principle of prevention using a multifaceted, multilevel approach aimed at helping individuals, groups, and the community as a whole. Most of the early work will be the provision of concrete services to normal people under stress, such as information about available services, how to get insurance benefits or loans, assistance with applications at government agencies, health care, child care, transportation, and other routine needs. Public health workers should initiate counseling as a preventive measure and encourage open communication. Some of the most important ways of helping may be in simply listening, providing a ready ear, and indicating interest or concern.

If evacuation is required, responders should keep families together and try to keep support systems intact. Workers can also help in the rebuilding of support networks as quickly as possible. During the short- and long-term recovery phases, public health and human service professionals must go to community sites where survivors are involved in the activities of their daily lives. Such places include neighborhoods, schools, shelters, disaster application centers, meal sites, hospitals, churches, community centers, and other central locations. Among the services typically provided after disaster are telephone helplines, information and referral services, literature on the emotional effects of disaster, facilitation of self-help, support groups, crisis counseling, public education through the media, information sessions for community groups, grief support services, and advocacy services.

Throughout the disaster relief effort, several general management strategies should be followed:

- Show clear decision-making in actions so victims feel that the designated leaders are active in the response.

- Issue warnings with instructions of specific actions to take.

- Plan ahead for necessary resources, with call-up procedures in place.

- Tailor activities and services provided in the aftermath of disaster to the community being served and involve them in the development and delivery of services.

- Target psychosocial services toward "normal" people responding normally to an abnormal situation.

- Identify persons at risk for severe psychological or social impairment due to their experience of the disaster.

Chapter 9

Essentials of Disaster Planning

While disasters are often unexpected, disaster planning can anticipate common problems raised and tasks required following large-scale emergencies. This chapter considers the principles of disaster planning, the common tasks of disaster response, and the components of a disaster preparedness plan.

PUBLIC HEALTH ROLE

- Use traditional planning principles in preparing for the delivery of public health and health care services during the impact and post-impact phases.

- Participate as full partners with the emergency management community in disaster response and recovery.

- Participate in the development of and serve as an integral part of a community's disaster preparedness plans.

PRINCIPLES OF DISASTER PLANNING

Along with their differences, disasters have similarities in that certain problems and tasks occur repetitively and predictably. On the other hand, disasters differ not only quantitatively but also qualitatively from common daily emergencies. Thus, effective disaster response involves much more than an extension of routine emergency response (ie, the mobilization of more personnel, facilities, equipment, supplies). Understanding the planning process and the lexicon of emergency management increases the effectiveness of public health professionals.

Effective disaster plans are based on empirical knowledge of how people normally behave in disasters. Plans are easier to change than human behavior, so disaster plans should be based on what people are likely to do rather than on the expectation that the public will behave "according to the plan." Plans must be flexible and easy to change due to the number of laws, organizations, populations, technology, hazards, resources, and personnel involved in disaster response.

Disaster planning should focus on a *local* response with federal and state support. In any major natural disaster, the main rescue effort will most likely be executed by local authorities during the first 48-hour period to ensure a timely response for the severely injured (ie, those trapped in a collapsed building). Thus, disaster plans must be acceptable to the elected officials, to the departments that will implement them, and to those whom the plan is intended to benefit. Plans should be widely disseminated among all those involved and should be exercised regularly as discussed later in this chapter.

Similarly, disaster plans should provide for some authority at the lowest levels of the organization since workers in the trenches must make many decisions during the impact and immediate post-impact phases. Disasters often present decision-making demands that exceed the bureaucratic capacities and information-processing abilities of the day-to-day management structure. Disaster plans that require all decisions to be made from the top-down do not optimize the resources of the organization.

INCREASED NEED FOR PLANNING

With the rising occurrence and greater damage associated with natural disasters, public health agencies should give priority to planning for disasters. No region of the United States is free from all disaster risk. In fact, the effects of disasters escalate each year due to increases in population and development in vulnerable areas (ie, seismic fault lines, coastal areas, flood plains, wilderness areas). At the same time, immigration, imported goods, rapid international transportation, emerging and resident pathogens, and terrorism (chemical, nuclear, biological) increase the potential for technological disasters and epidemic spread of disease. Finally, the economic health of the United States affects the number of displaced persons following disaster (ie, homeless, working poor) and recovery from disaster.

CONSTRAINTS ON ABILITY TO RESPOND

Trends in health care reimbursement and delivery interfere with efforts by health care facilities to prepare for disasters. First, decreasing reimbursement reduces the likelihood that facilities will allocate funds for disaster preparedness. Even if the budgetary allocations are adequate, fewer resources are available for the delivery of unusual services. Fewer supplies may be available for disaster response because hospitals and other health facilities have eliminated the local warehousing of supplies and instead reorder as needed. The trend to outsource services (ie, laundry, kitchen, security) reduces the availability of important resources that would be needed post-impact. With shorter inpatient lengths of stay and greater use of ambulatory care, fewer hospital beds will be available or sufficiently staffed in a disaster. The availability of beds post-impact will be further complicated by the trend to hospitalize sicker patients who require more intensive care, so few patients will be ready for discharge to create room for victims seriously injured in the disaster. Finally, while the focus on delivering care in nonhospital settings has increased, a parallel effort to ensure disaster readiness in nonhospital health care settings has not been made.

PLANNING FOR VARIOUS DISASTERS

Two strategies for disaster planning include the agent-specific and the all-hazards approaches. In agent-specific planning, communities only plan for threats most likely to occur in their region (ie, earthquakes, hurricanes, floods, tornadoes). For example, planning for earthquakes, floods, and wild fires will be more useful in California than planning for hurricanes and tornadoes. Further, officials and taxpayers are more likely to be motivated by what are perceived locally as the most viable threats.

With the all-hazards approach to disaster planning, the level of preparedness is maximized for the effort and expenditures involved. Since many disasters pose similar problems and similar tasks, an all-hazards approach involves planning for the common problems and tasks that arise in the majority of disasters.

Common Tasks of Disaster Response

Twelve tasks or problems are likely to occur in most disasters, as summarized below.

- *Interorganizational coordination* is critical and has been discussed in Chapters 2 and 3.

- *Sharing information* among organizations is complicated by the amount of equipment needed and the number of people involved. In the impact and post-impact phases, two-way radios are often the only reliable form of communications across distances. Even if ground and cellular telephone systems are not damaged, they are generally congested or overloaded. Communication via radio frequencies is difficult as no common frequency has been designated for mutual aid. The Federal Communications Commission has assigned public safety frequencies to several different bands, making it difficult for one agency to communicate with another on a common frequency. While newer radios can be programmed to operate on a different frequency or frequencies, they cannot be reprogrammed to a different band. A few radios can now operate on more than one band, but this is the exception.

- *Resource management*—the distribution of supplemental personnel, equipment, and supplies among multiple organizations— requires a process to identify which resources have arrived or are in transit and to determine where those resources are most needed. Once a security perimeter has been established at the disaster site, a check-in or staging area is usually established outside this boundary. Each staging area has a manager who has radio contact with the disaster command post or emergency operations center. Law enforcement or security personnel are usually notified to refer all responders or volunteers to the closest check-in area. There, personnel will be logged in, briefed on the situation, given an assignment, and provided with a radio, communications frequency, or hardware to link them to the broader response effort.

- When advance *warnings* are possible, *evacuation* from areas of danger can be the most effective life-saving strategy in a disaster. The warning process is complex and requires precise communication among numerous agencies. A threat must be detected and analyzed to assess the specific areas at risk as well as the nature of that risk. Warnings should be delivered in such a manner that the population at risk will take the threat seriously and take appropriate action based on the warning. Detection and assessment are usually the responsibility of one agency (ie, the US Weather Bureau, flood districts, dam officials). The decision to order an evacuation is the responsibility of other organizations (ie, the sheriff's office), and the dissemination of the warning is the responsibility of a third group (ie, commercial television or radio stations).

- The public tends to underestimate risks and downplay *warnings* if messages are ambiguous or inconsistent. Factors that enhance the effectiveness of warnings include the credibility of the warning source, the number of repetitions (especially if emanating from multiple sources), the consistency of message content across different sources, the context of the warning (ie, a visible gas cloud or odor accompanying warnings about a hazardous substance leak), the inclusion of information that allows recipients to determine if they are personally in danger (ie, details on location or track), the inclusion of specific information on self-protective actions, and invitations from friends or relatives to take shelter.

- *Search and rescue* is an important aspect of post-disaster response. In many disasters, casualties are initially treated in the field, and this process influences their entry into the health care system. To the extent that search and rescue is uncoordinated, the flow of patients through the emergency medical services system and the health care system is also uncoordinated. Several characteristics of disaster search and rescue create problems amenable to improvement through organizational planning. Most disaster search and rescue, particularly in the immediate post-impact period, is not initiated by trained emergency personnel but by the spontaneous efforts of untrained bystanders who happen to be in the area. Care of patients also becomes complicated when the disaster occurs across jurisdictional boundaries or involves emergency responders from many agencies (ie, private ambulance

providers, municipal first responders, and county, state, and
federal agencies).

• *Using the mass media* to deliver warnings to the public and to
  educate the public about the avoidance of health problems in
  the aftermath of a disaster—such as food and water safety,
  injury prevention through chain saw safety, avoidance of nail
  punctures, and monitoring carbon monoxide exposure from
  charcoal and unvented heaters—can be an effective public
  health tool.

• *Triage*, derived from the French verb trier or to sort, is a
  method of assigning priorities for treatment and transport for
  injured citizens. Untrained personnel and bystanders who may
  do the initial search and rescue often bypass established field
  triage and first aid stations because they do not know where
  these posts are located or because they want to get the victims
  to the closest hospital.

• In most domestic disasters, several medical resources can handle the *casualty distribution*. Often, the closest hospitals receive
  the majority of patients, while other hospitals await casualties
  that never arrive. Transport decisions made by untrained volunteers are difficult to control. Established protocols between
  emergency medical services and area hospitals will ensure the
  more even distribution of casualties.

• *Patient tracking* is complicated by the fact that most persons
  evacuating their homes do not seek lodging in public shelters
  where their presence will be registered by the American Red
  Cross. Tracking the location of victims is further obfuscated
  because no single agency serves as a central repository of
  information about the location of victims from area hospitals,
  morgues, shelters, jails, or other potential locations. Tracking
  of the injured is also confounded because most patients get to
  hospitals by nonambulance means, leaving emergency medical
  services with an incomplete record of injuries. When hospitals
  themselves are damaged, the evacuation of hospitalized
  patients further complicates tracking where victims might be
  located.

- *Caring for patients when the health care infrastructure has been damaged* requires careful advance planning. Following natural disasters, hospitals should plan to care for high numbers of minor injuries than for major trauma. Substantial numbers of patients seeking hospital care do so because of chronic medical conditions rather than trauma due, in part, to damage to or loss of access to usual sources of primary medical care. Persons often evacuate their homes without prescription medications or underestimate how long they will be prevented from returning home. In addition, many injuries are sustained not during the disaster impact but during rescue or clean-up activities. Hospitals, urgent care centers, home health care agencies, pharmacies, and dialysis centers must make appropriate plans to ensure that their facilities will not be damaged or disabled in a disaster and that they have backup arrangements for the care of their patients post-impact. This includes providing backup supplies of power and water; building structures resistant to wind, fire, flood, and seismic hazards; maintaining essential equipment and supplies that will be damaged by earthquakes or other disasters; supplying surge protection and data backup for computers with patient accounts, charts, or pharmacy information; making plans for alternative office, business, or clinical sites for displaced local health care resources (ie, physicians, pharmacists, radiology); and developing plans to relocate the site of "home" health care to sites where the patients have temporarily relocated.

- The *management of volunteers and donations* is a common problem in disasters. Disaster planning often focuses on the mobilization of resources, when not infrequently more resources arrive than are actually needed, requested, or expected. Procedures should be established to manage large numbers of resources. First, expect large numbers of donations and unsolicited volunteers (spontaneous civilian bystanders, family members, neighbors, co-workers, other survivors). Second, channel public requests for aid to a locality outside the disaster area where resources can be collected, organized, and distributed without disrupting ongoing emergency operations.

- Plan for organized improvisation in response to the *disruption of shelter, utilities, communication systems, and transportation.*

Regardless of the level of preplanning, disasters will require some unanticipated tasks. Public health officials must develop the capacity, mutually agreed upon procedures, and training to participate in the community's coordinated, multiorganizational response to unexpected problems.

Components of a Plan

A regional plan will identify the potential jurisdictions that could be affected by a disaster and the corresponding agencies with assigned disaster response and recovery responsibilities. Such a plan will bring together the chief executives and operational leaders of these agencies, initiate a joint coordination and situation assessment process, identify likely types of disasters, establish communication channels for sharing information, and create a standard protocol to assess the scope of damage, injuries, deaths, and secondary threats.

Baseline Assessment

To develop a regional plan, public health agencies must first work with the emergency management sector to assess the status of the health and health risks of the community, the status of health care facilities, the protection of vital records, the potential requirements for public shelters, available resources for alternative emergency and primary care, and the availability of and procedures for obtaining state and federal assistance.

Efforts to assess the health condition of the community must examine:
• Prevalent disease and persons with special needs who will need assistance related to evacuation and continuity of care.
• Ability of the affected population to obtain prescription medications.
• Building safety and ability to protect victims from injury, the elements, and hazardous material release.
• Ability to maintain air quality, food safety, sanitation, waste disposal, vector control, and water systems.

Hospitals, urgent care centers, physician offices, outpatient medical clinics, psychiatric clinics, dialysis centers, pharmacies, custodial facilities for aged or disabled, and home health care services must have the capacity to meet patient needs and to ensure continuity of power, communications, water, sewer, and waste disposal in disaster situations. Data processing and exchange of patient information will be particularly important in the post-impact and recovery phases.

Disaster plans must take into account the availability of alternate treatment facilities when any or all of these locations are closed. Public health departments should work with hospitals and community providers to develop a plan for providing both routine and continuity of care for victims experiencing acute exacerbations of chronic medical problems such as asthma, emphysema, diabetes, and hypertension. If their normal source of care is not available and no alternative plan is communicated to the public, patients could be expected to seek care from overburdened hospital emergency departments. Following Hurricane Andrew, for example, more than 1000 physician offices were destroyed or significantly damaged, greatly adding to hospital patient loads.

In addition, plans should be developed for patients in both hospitals and residential care facilities (ie, long-term care, assisted living, psychiatric treatment, rehabilitation) who may need to be evacuated and placed elsewhere. Plans should also be made to maintain poison control hotlines and to continue home health care services (ie, dialysis, intravenous antibiotic, visiting nurses services, medical supply) at sites to which patients have been relocated.

Public health departments must collect background data on requirements for the medical needs, lodging, water, sanitation, and feeding arrangements for both victims and rescue and relief personnel. Plans for resource management—including directing incoming responders and volunteers to designated check-in or staging areas and determining what resources are present, available, or committed to the incident—should be established in advance. Assignments regarding which tasks will be coordinated or implemented by which agency or individual worker must be designated. This is particularly true for responsibilities that cross functional, geographic, or jurisdictional boundaries and for tasks for which no single person or agency has clear-cut statutory or contractual responsibility. Priorities for resource distribution, cost sharing, acquisition, training, and coordination must be set jointly and disseminated widely.

Finally, public health officials should ensure that the disaster preparedness plan identifies state and federal assistance programs (ie, Stafford Act as explained in Chapter 3) for reimbursement and establishes procedures to verify that full reimbursement for disaster-related health care has been recovered.

Drills and Training

Ideally, local public health and health care facilities are integrated into a community-wide emergency response plan that is exercised at least once every 12 months. However, the existence of a written plan does not ensure that it will be used or that the plan will be effective if needed. When all of the agencies that will be called upon to respond to a disaster, including public health, have participated in the plan's development, they are more likely to ensure that the full needs of the community can be met and that individual organizations are not overburdened due to poor planning.

A disaster plan can be exercised in one of three ways. The first involves desktop simulation exercises using paper or computer-based scenarios to improve coordination, to share information, and to practice decision-making. The second method relies on field exercises, which, however, are expensive because they test the disaster plan in simulated field conditions. The third method, drills, is effective because responders get to know each other and each other's roles, gain experience working with the community's plan, and understand what must be done—thus enhancing their ability to rely on each other's activities. Drills are based on valid assumptions about what happens in disasters. Because disasters often cross political, geographical, functional, and jurisdictional boundaries, drills and training are most effective when carried out on a multiorganizational, multidisciplinary, multijurisdictional basis. Coordination is also facilitated when participants are familiar with the skills, level of knowledge, and dependability of other responders on whom they may one day need to rely.

Identifying Available Resources

Disaster response may call for the use of resources (ie, personnel, equipment, supplies, information) that do not commonly reside in one location or under the jurisdiction of one agency. Reducing morbidity and mortality in the early hours after disaster has struck may depend on locating resources that are not commonly used in routine emergency responses or are in short supply. A comprehensive plan should establish procedures for locating specialty physicians, search dogs, specialized devices for locating trapped victims in the rubble of collapsed buildings, tools for cutting through and lifting heavy reinforced concrete blocks, dialysis centers or equipment to treat crush injury, laboratories to rapidly analyze hazardous chemicals or biological agents, radiation detection instruments, confined-space rescue teams, and hazardous materials response teams with appropriate protective gear.

Chapter 10

Public Health Response to Emerging Infections and Bioterrorism

A s invisible disaster threats, epidemics of infectious disease and bioterrorism agents pose special concerns and response requirements for public health departments. This chapter reviews covert and overt threats, categories of bioterrorism agents and the response required, and bioterrorism response plans at the community, regional, and federal level.

PUBLIC HEALTH ROLE

- Develop and use multidisciplinary protocols for collaboration among state and local public health agencies, community hospitals, academic health centers, community health care providers, laboratories, professional societies, medical examiners, emergency response units, safety and medical equipment manufacturers, the media, government officials, and federal agencies such as the US Office of Emergency Preparedness and Centers for Disease Control and Prevention.

- Establish specific criteria for emerging infections, activate surveillance systems that can quickly identify emerging or re-emerging diseases, and closely monitor unexplained morbidity and mortality due to infectious disease (because many bioterrorism agents present as flu-like illness, improve surveillance for flu-like illness).

• Increase lab capacity, educate microbiologists about reporting, and establish communication linkages with a laboratory response network for the rapid evaluation and identification of bioterrorism agents.

• Develop and activate diagnostic clinical and treatment protocols that are communicated to the medical community to improve rapid reporting of suspect cases, unusual clusters of disease, and unusual manifestations of disease.

• Plan for and respond, where necessary, to reduce the morbidity and mortality from a bioterrorism event by stockpiling antibiotics, preparing multilingual patient information, developing contingency plans for quarantine, and developing community plans for the delivery of medical care to large numbers of patients and care to the "worried well."

• Develop, test, and implement the Health Alert Network.

• With the local medical examiner, develop contingency plans for mass mortuary services, including plans for the utilization of Federal Disaster Medical Assistance (DMAT) and Mortuary Teams (DMORT).

• Train all health organizations that may be required to participate in delivering care following a bioterrorism attack.

• Resolve legal issues related to public health authority in emergencies.

RESPONSE TO UNKNOWN DISEASE

Unlike the response to an overt chemical event where fire, police, or hazardous material units are the first responders, the public health department is charged with identifying infectious disease in a community. The public health response to unknown disease outbreaks has four components: detection of usual events, investigation and containment of potential threats, laboratory capacity, and coordination and communication. This response to bioterrorism requires an interdependent working relationship among local, state, and federal agencies and among community clinicians, emergency responders, and local public health personnel.

A biologic event would most likely present as a cluster of cases of an unusual disease in the population, with the initial detection likely to take place at the local level. Members of the local medical community may be the first to recognize unusual disease incidence, with state and local health departments most likely to initiate a community-wide response. A potential bioterrorism event might be a group of patients with a similar clinical syndrome with unusual characteristics, such as age distribution, unusually high morbidity or mortality without obvious explanation for the illness, unusual concurrence of geographic exposure, unusual disease not previously found in the region, a case of inhalation anthrax or smallpox, or unexplained increase in a common syndrome above seasonally expected levels (ie, cluster flu epidemic in summer with negative virology, food poisoning without a single source). If a release of a contagious disease occurred, such as smallpox, several patients will appear in emergency rooms with rash illness that should be reported to authorities as "suspect smallpox." In addition to surveillance and activating the participation of other agencies, public health officials may initiate actions to protect the community, including quarantine and immunization.

OVERT AND COVERT RELEASES

Overt releases are those where an assessment of the threat is made before the response is initiated, perhaps because the threat is announced. Public health officials should assume that potential hoaxes are in fact real when accompanied by increased morbidity or mortality even if the microorganisms have not been confirmed. Communities may choose a limited response to hoaxes based on a sophisticated analysis of the situation and a relatively easy resolution of the incident.

Covert releases are those without prior warning in which a biologic agent presents as illness in the community and where traditional surveillance methods are needed to detect the agent. With covert releases, patients fall ill or die from unknown causes or unusual origins. An unusual cluster of cases or an unusual geographic distribution may also be noted. Covert dissemination of a biological agent in a public place will probably not have an immediate impact due to the incubation period of the disease, resulting in a delay between exposure and onset. Consequently, the first casualties of a covert attack probably will be identified by primary health care providers.

The covert release of a contagious agent has the potential for multinational spread prior to detection. Release in a transportation hub or in a highly mobile population could disseminate a highly contagious agent such as smallpox across boarders before the epidemic is recognized. As person-to-person contact continues, successive waves of transmission could carry infection to other localities around the globe. In a very short time, public health authorities would be asked to determine that an attack has occurred, identify the organism, and prevent more casualties through prevention strategies (ie, mass vaccination or prophylactic treatment). The ability to detect covert releases depends on enhancing public health infrastructure and increasing the skills of front line medical practitioners so they recognize and report suspicious syndromes.

CRITICAL BIOLOGICAL AGENTS

The Centers for Disease Control and Prevention (CDC) identify three major categories of agents.

Category A

Category A is a list of the nine highest priority agents. While the frequency of these diseases is relatively low, their impact is high because of the speed with which they spread. The agents on the Category A list pose a risk to national security because they can be easily disseminated or transmitted person-to-person; cause high mortality, with potential for major public health impact; could cause public panic and social disruption; and require special action for public health preparedness.

Variola major. Smallpox, for which dissemination requires person-to-person transmission, is highly contagious in unimmunized populations and has a mortality rate as high as 35%. Smallpox has a cycle time of 10 to 14 days and an attack rate of up to 90%. Bioterrorism using smallpox is considered less likely than the use of other agents because the World Health Organization's eradication program eliminated the natural illness from the planet. While evidence suggests that live smallpox is held by other parties, only two known samples of live virus remain. One is under the control of the United States at the Centers for Disease Control and Prevention, and the other is held by Russia.

Bacillus anthracis. Anthrax is considered to be a highly efficacious biological warfare agent because it forms spores (providing stability in aerosol form), is relatively easy to disseminate using off-the-shelf technology, and is frequently fatal if inhaled. While preparing an aerosol-stable form of the agent is challenging, these difficulties were overcome in the former Soviet Union, and it is possible that well-informed terrorists could replicate those procedures.

Yersinia pestis. Plague is a respiratory-acquired illness that is spread from person-to-person. Plague occurs as an enzootic disease of rodents in the United States, making it relatively easy to attain an isolate for use as a terrorist agent.

Clostridium botulinum. Botulism is an environmental organism that can be easily cultured from soil. Victims of the toxin often require intensive supportive medical care. The treatment for botulism, in the form of antitoxin, is limited in both supply and availability.

Francisella tularensis. Tularemia can be disseminated in water. In aerosol form, the organism produces a severely debilitating pneumonia but with a lower mortality rate than anthrax.

Two filoviruses, Ebola hemorrhagic fever and Marburg hemorrhagic fever, and two arenaviruses, Lassa fever and Argentine hemorrhagic fever (Junin), complete the Category A agents.

Category B

Category B agents are considered the second highest priority because they are moderately easy to disseminate, cause moderate morbidity and low mortality, and require specific enhancements of CDC's diagnostic capacity as well as enhanced disease surveillance. Category B agents include:

- *Coxiella burnetii* (Q fever)

- *Brucella species* (brucellosis)

- *Burkholderia mallei* (glanders)

- alphaviruses (Venezuelan encephalomyelitis, eastern and western equine encephalomyelitis), and ricin toxin from Ricinus communis (castor beans)

- *epsilon toxin* of Clostridium perfringens

- *Staphylococcus enterotoxin B*

A subset of List B agents includes pathogens that are food- or water-borne. These pathogens include but ae not limited to:

- *Salmonella species*

- *Shigella dysenteriae*

- *Escherichia coli O157:H7*

- *Vibrio cholerae*

- *Cryptosporidium parvum*

Category C

Category C, the third highest priority agents, include emerging pathogens that could be engineered for mass dissemination in the future due to availability, ease of production and dispersion, and potential for high morbidity, mortality, and major public health impact. Preparedness for List C agents requires ongoing research to improve disease detection, diagnosis, treatment, and prevention. Category C agents include:

- Nipah virus

- Hantaviruses

- Tickborne hemorrhagic fever viruses

- Tickborne encephalitis viruses

- Yellow fever

- Multidrug-resistant tuberculosis

TABLE 15. BIOTERRORISM AGENT SUMMARY
ADAPTED FROM HTTP://WWW.BT.CDC.GOV/DOCUMENTS/PPT/RESPONSE/TABLE1AGENTSUMMARY.PDF

	Inhalation Anthrax	Brucellosis	Botulism	Tularemia	Pneumonic Plague	Smallpox	Viral Hemorrhagic Fever
Infective Dose	8,000-50,000 spores	10-100 organisms	0.001 g/kg (type A)	10-50 organisms	<100 organisms	10-100 particles	1-10 particles
Incubation	1-6 d	5-60 d	6 h to 10 d	1-21 d	2-3 d	7-17 d	4-21 d
Duration	3-5 d	Weeks to months	24-72 h	~ 2 wk	1-6 d	~4 wk	7-16 d
Mortality Untreated	~100%	~5%*	1st case: 25% Subsequent cases: 4% Overall: 5-10%	33%	40%-70%	Variola minor: <1% Variola major: 20%-50%	53%-88%
Mortality Treated	~99%	<1%	1st case: 25% Subsequent cases: 4% Overall: 5-10%	<4%	5%	Variola minor: <1% Variola major: 20%-50%	53%-88%
Person to Person Transmission†	No	No	No	No	Yes (high)	Yes (high)	Yes (moderate)
Isolation Precautions‡	Standard	Standard	Standard	Standard	Droplet§	Airborne§	Airborne and Contact§
Persistence	40 y in soil	10 wk in water/soil	Weeks in food/water	Months in moist soil	≥1 y in soil	Very stable	Unstable

*Endocarditis accounts for the majority of brucellosis-related deaths.
†For inhalation anthrax, brucellosis, botulism, or tularemia, no evidence of person to person transmission exists; for pneumonic plague, for 72 h following initiation of appropriate antimicrobial therapy or until sputum culture is negative; for smallpox, approximately 3 weeks, which usually corresponds with the initial appearance of skin lesions through their final disappearance, though most infectious during the first week of rash via inhalation of virus released from oropharyngeal-lesion secretions of the index case; for viral hemorrhagic fever, varies with virus but at minimum, all for the duration of illness and for Ebola/Marburg, transmission via semen may occur up to 7 weeks after clinical recovery.
‡Garner JS, Hospital Infection Control Practices Advisory Commitee. Guideline for isolation precautions in hospitals. Infect Control Hosp Epidemiol 1996;17:53-80, and Am J Infect Control 1996;24:24-52. (http://www.cdc.gov/ncidod/hip/isolat/isolat.htm)
§In addition to standard precautions that apply to all patients.

BIOTERRORISM RESPONSE PLAN

Chapter 9 describes general principles that apply to disaster planning for natural hazards or technological events. Tasks related to bioterrorism that require similar preparation include interorganizational coordination, sharing information, resource management, using the media to communicate to the public, triage, casualty distribution, and patient tracking. Because of the potential for the rapid spread of disease, however, planning for emerging infections or bioterrorism events relies heavily on skills that are uniquely those of public health and health care systems.

While incidents involving weapons of mass destruction may involve mass casualties and damage to building and other property, these incidents are dissimilar to typical disasters. Officials may not recognize that an incident has occurred until there are several casualties. By this time, multiple releases may have occurred. Responders and health care personnel can unknowingly become contaminated and are at higher risk to become casualties themselves. Victims may unknowingly carry the agent to critical facilities and across large geographic areas. The scope of the incident may expand geometrically and may affect multiple jurisdictions. The fear of the unknown may generate a strong response from the public, resulting in larger numbers of "worried well" than of actual victims. Finally, specialized response units may quickly be overwhelmed.

The Federal Emergency Management Agency (FEMA) established an Office of National Preparedness to coordinate federal programs and to assist local governments in responding to terrorist attacks involving so-called weapons of mass destruction and consequence management. The federal plan to provide guidance to federal, state, and local agencies regarding a national response to a potential or actual terrorist threat—US Government Interagency Domestic Terrorism Concept of Operations Plan—is commonly referred to as CONPLAN. Relevant sections of the plan provide for FEMA to implement the federal response plan, including the terrorism annex, and to manage and coordinate the federal response in support of state and local officials. The Environmental Protection Agency will provide technical personnel and supporting equipment. Under CONPLAN, the US Department of Health and Human Services, with its own Counter-Terrorism Concept of Operations Plan, has lead responsibility for the medical response to national emergencies in support of local authorities.

As in all disaster plans, federal activities are initiated to support local activities, not supplant them. Local officials are expected to establish control at the scene of the incident, initiate appropriate protective and response measures, establish distribution systems, organize mass immunization or prophylactic centers, maintain records, refer to treatment centers, and inform the public. The US Department of Health and Human Services will coordinate the provision of federal health and medical assistance when local and state health care delivery systems require augmentation.

At the local or regional level, public health planning for a bioterrorism event can be modeled after planning models for pandemic influenza. A planning committee should be established with key representatives from the health, emergency management, and public safety sectors. This committee is responsible for establishing an overall command and control structure (see Chapter 3 on incident command); for overseeing the prevention, planning, response, and recovery activities; and for ensuring that a jurisdiction's plan is developed, reviewed, and revised when needed. Because bioterrorism response will require cooperation from a broad variety of community groups, it is important to identify who the stakeholders are and to solicit their support. Participation from the community should involve personnel knowledgeable about communicable disease and immunization, laboratories, specialists in information systems, the media, citizen band radio groups, social service agencies, the American Red Cross, law enforcement, fire and emergency medical services, the medical community, the medical examiner and coroner, funeral directors, local utilities, and local government officials, among others. The planning committee will ask that stakeholders develop the components of the plan for which they have expertise.

Communities or regions should plan for three levels of response to a bioterrorism event. Examples of this three-tiered approach include separate plans for incidents with up to 100 victims, for incidents with 100 to 10,000 victims, and for incidents with more than 10,000 victims. An important part of each plan will be the logistics of obtaining and distributing vaccines and antibiotics. Plans should identify the location of local or federal depositories, designate distribution sites, and establish priorities for distribution. Stockpiles will most likely be flown into commercial airports. A protocol must be established for off loading antibiotics and supplies, and a site located for packaging the materials into smaller units. In addition, a system must be established for ensuring that the antibiotics are used before their expired shelf life.

While hospitals are required to have a disaster plan to be accredited by the Joint Commission on Accreditation of Healthcare Organizations, a sequence of stand-alone facility plans do not prepare a community to respond to bioterrorism. The hospitals in a community must coordinate their efforts, including the transport of patients, the ordering and stockpiling of supplies and pharmaceuticals, communications during the event, the handling of bodies, and other major tasks. The planning committee should ensure that a community-wide plan incorporates all hospitals and provides for multihospital drills.

While estimates vary widely of those who might seek care because they think they are sick, a comprehensive plan should arrange for triage of a large number of unaffected patients who are the "worried well." In major metropolitan regions, the estimated ratio of "worried well" to affected patients has been as high as 30 to 1. Large numbers of potential patients would require the rapid establishment of alternative care facilities. Because patients have been found to seek health care from locations where they regularly receive care, alternative care facilities should be set up as close to hospitals as possible.

COMMUNITY PLAN FOR BIOTERRORISM RESPONSE

In addition to a description of a unified command and control and management structure and responsibilities (including protocols for coordinating activities of the health sector with those of the emergency management sector), a community plan for bioterrorism includes the following:

- Protocols for large-scale surveillance and epidemiological investigations for detecting bioterrorism or natural biologic disaster, including coordination with local poison control centers.

- Notification and response protocols for suspected and confirmed emergencies, including arranging for rapid diagnostic testing, providing disease-specific information to the health care community on medical management of cases and those exposed, implementing active surveillance and epidemiological investigations, initiating mass medical care and prophylaxis, distributing protocols to providers, and setting up communication hotlines for providers, the media, and the public.

- Protocols to ensure rapid laboratory confirmation of samples.

- Stockpiling and monitoring of expiration dates of pharmaceutical inventories for a range of potential agents (see Table 16).

- Plans for mass medical care, including patient overflow, turning shelters into hospitals, establishing patient isolation in many locations, mass prophylaxis (ie, vaccinations or medication distribution), drug distribution to large numbers of the population, transportation of patients, triaging the "worried well", and mortuary care.

- Resolution of legal issues related to authority to establish quarantine, blockade, zone perimeters, requisitions, curfews, governance, restricted access, and emergency credentialing of providers who are not credentialed through the federal response.

- Coordination among all participating stakeholders, including local veterinary facilities capable of handling affected animals.

- Protocols for both external communication to the public and internal communication among those coordinating the public response, including managing the media and keeping the general public accurately informed.

- Assessment of facility needs for drugs, vaccines, and beds as well as needed equipment, including type, availability, and location.

- Plan to establish arrangements for mutual aid among hospitals, communities, states, and regions.

- Assessment of staffing, including outreach criteria, guidelines for worker safety, and training needs.

- Measures to assure biosafety, arrangements for mass burials, and mortuary management.

- Protocols for management of mental health issues, including the "worried well," critical incident stress debriefing, grief counseling, and support.

- Baseline data with scheduled updates on:

  –hospital admissions

  –acute bed occupancy

  –intensive care unit bed occupancy

  –emergency room visits for infection

  –ambulatory department utilization

  –influenza-like illness

  –flu cases in patient billing and emergency department visit data

  –unexplained deaths

  –unusual syndromes in ambulatory patients

  –911 calls

  –calls to poison control centers

  –antibiotic and other pharmaceutical supplies

  –total number of respirators

  –workforce and school absenteeism

DETECTING AND RESPONDING TO BIOTERRORIST EVENTS

Since accurate diagnosis of diseases caused by the most likely bioterrorist agents may be delayed due to the initial flu-like presentation and the several days needed for a positive laboratory identification, public

TABLE 16: SUPPLIES AND ANTIDOTES FOR POTENTIAL BIOTERRORISM AGENTS

Agent Supplies	Needed
Bacterial Agents	Ciprofloxacin, doxycycline, penicillin, chloramphenicol, and azithromycin
Botulinum toxin	Mechanical respiratory ventilators and associated supplies
Burn/Vesicants	Sterile bandages, intravenous fluids, and broad spectrum antibiotics
Cyanide	Cyanide antidote kits containing amyl nitrite, sodium nitrite, and sodium thiosulfate
Lewisite	British anti-Lewisite
Nerve Agents	Atropine, pralidoxime, chloride, and diazepam
Radiologic Exposure	Potassium iodide
All	Resuscitation equipment and supplies, vasopressors

health officials cannot depend on passive surveillance systems. Labor-intensive active surveillance requires outreach and can be costly but will be essential in identifying when "the flu" is not "the flu."

A full mobilization of public health efforts includes sending suspected samples to reference laboratories for rapid confirmation of bioterrorist agents, the galvanizing of active surveillance and epidemiological teams to review charts of suspected patients, the initiation of treatment and prophylaxis to reduce morbidity and mortality, and the launching of pre-established communication protocols among many medical community and emergency management agencies and between government and the public. The public health team should be organized to respond to potential biological, chemical, or radiological events and include professionals from multiple disciplines, such as chemists, emergency management, emergency medical technicians and paramedics, environmental health scientists, epidemiologists, hazardous material response teams, health physicists, industrial hygienists, infectious disease specialists, medical examiners, occupational health physicians, public health laboratory designees, toxicologists, and veterinarians. A detailed template for health care facility planning for bioterrorism is available online (http://www.apic.org). Other relevant websites are listed in Appendix C.

An effective surveillance system will be able to rapidly track changes in disease trends, be based on clinical syndromes, and be generated by data that are collected continually, reviewed daily, and remain geographically representative. An "alert" in these systems prompts an epidemiological investigation to determine if there is an outbreak and to identify the potential microbial etiology and the source of transmission. Sources of data for bioterrorism and emerging disease include:

- Hospital reports (admissions to intensive care units of previously healthy persons with unexplained febrile illnesses)

- Infectious disease and laboratory reports

- Diagnostic categories with trends and unusual patterns from emergency departments

- Outbreaks in institutional settings (ie, nursing homes)

- Workforce and school absenteeism

- Prescription and over-the-counter medication sales

- Animal outbreaks and deaths

- Police and emergency medical services reports

- Geographic analyses of 911 calls categorized by disease syndrome (ie, codes for difficulty breathing, respiratory distress, and other markers for influenza-like disease)

While medical examiner reports are useful a two to three day delay often occurs between the time of death and the filing of the death certificate. In addition, it is difficult to identify clusters using death certificates. Optimally, electronic death reporting can be instituted so that this information is more timely. In addition, epidemiologists will want to look at environmental factors, such as food, the presence of vectors (ie, ticks, fleas, flies, rodents, cats, mosquitoes, bats), and trends in animal populations and food crops.

Case Definition of Potential Bioterrorist Event

A possible bioterrorist event includes one of the following:

- A single, definitively diagnosed or strongly suspected case of an illness due to a recognized bioterrorist agent occurring in a patient without a plausible explanation for his/her illness.

- A cluster of patients presenting with a similar clinical syndrome with either unusual characteristics (age distribution) or unusually high morbidity or mortality, without an obvious etiology or explanation.

- An unexplained increase in the incidence of a common syndrome above seasonally expected levels.

Active Surveillance and Epidemiological Investigations

If there is a confirmed bioterrorist event, health departments will be responsible for tracking the cases and performing epidemiological investigations to determine the source and sites of exposure. This information will be essential in determining who else might have been exposed and requires prophylaxis. Epidemiological investigations will help identify the determinants, the distribution, and the frequency of disease in both human and animal populations. Epidemiology will detect possible vector-control requirements and the likelihood of secondary spread. These investigations will be coordinated with neighboring health departments as well as interstate and international agencies.

To activate a rapid surveillance, materials must be prepared in advance. Essential tools include instruments of preplanned generic questions to determine case and risk exposure, a sampling strategy, a centralized database with fields defined, and a mechanism to call-up and deploy 24-hour/7-day-a-week teams to conduct the surveillance. The instrument might ask questions about location of residence and work, usual commuter routes, and a detailed diary of the patient's activities during the incubation period of the suspected agent.

Mass Prophylaxis/Immunization

A plan for mass immunization of the population should include:

- Description of the decision-making process that would be used to initiate a mass immunization campaign

- Method of identifying the affected population

- Distribution plan for the vaccine or antibiotics that would ensure coverage of an affected population

- Plans for moving a pharmaceutical stockpile to distribution points

- Designated personnel who will manage the arrival, distribution, and local dissemination of vaccines and antibiotics

- Plans for the storage, transportation, and handling of pharmaceuticals

- Procedures for immunization of differing age groups

- Procedures for record keeping

- Plans for the availability of protective clothing by personnel

- Plans for ensuring community participation

Mass Medical and Mortuary Care

In addition to baseline surveys that provide information about a community's capacity to care for patients exposed to bioterrorist agents, guidelines are needed for the care of exposed patients. Community care guidelines include physician education, broadcast alerts, and a medical hotline. Hospitals plans for responding to a large infectious disease outbreak include provisions for triaging large numbers of patients in the emergency department, increasing bed capacity, calling in additional staff, and establishing isolation units on short notice. Hospital plans establish the medical protocols that will be followed, the stockpiling and distribution of medications or vaccines, and whether to set up community-based mass prophylaxis clinics. Multilingual information sheets and consent forms should be prepared. In addition, instructional sheets on the methodology for administering vaccines (ie, smallpox) should be ready for use.

Legal Issues

Should a community need to consider the quarantine of infected persons or their close contacts, the local authority to establish a quarantine must be clarified. Public health authorities should identify who has the authority, what criteria must be met, what legal mechanism must be followed, and who is responsible for enforcement. Contingency plans should define the legal mechanism to initiate a quarantine and should establish protocols for implementation and enforcement.

LABORATORY RESPONSE NETWORK

The laboratory response network has been established to assist in a response to bioterrorism. Public health laboratories support surveillance and epidemiological investigations by identifying disease, providing direct and reference services, and conducting environmental, rapid, and specialized testing. The network consists of four levels of laboratories, which are connected with redundancy and with an emphasis on rapid turnaround and accuracy.

Five of the major threats (ie, botulism, plague, anthrax, tularemia, poxvirus illnesses) occur naturally in the United States, and specimens for these diseases are routinely evaluated by public health laboratories. In addition, the standard techniques for detecting bacterial agents (ie, gram stain, culture on selective media, visual colony morphology, growth after heat shock and confirmatory methods using phage and direct immunofluorescence) are well recognized for establishing definitive diagnosis. Methods such as isolation in cell culture, inoculation of animals, direct fluorescence methods, and electron microscopy are considered definitive methods in virology.

The personnel who work in public health laboratories are highly skilled and familiar with following complex identification algorithms. The procedures used can be readily adapted to environmental samples that might be collected after an overt threat or in the attribution of the source of a sample. Further, the laboratories are all certified under the clinical laboratory improvement act as employing appropriate quality assurance and quality control procedures. Although definitive identification requires a day or two, preliminary results can be available in minutes or hours. In particular, the minimum response time for a definitive negative result with a rapidly growing organism such as anthrax may be 16 hours. More slowly growing organisms or complex procedures may take 48 hours or more. Further, many methods require a fixed facility with traditional lab techniques not readily adaptable to a field situation.

The laboratory response network has four levels of performance defined as A, B, C, and D.

Level A laboratories are clinical labs that screen presumptive cases early and rule-out or refer. They may assess risks for aerosol agents. They use BioSafety Level 2 (BSL) techniques.

Level B laboratories are county or state laboratories that perform first-level confirmation, such as direct fluorescence or phage testing. Level B labs perform susceptibility testing. They isolate and identify, rule-in and refer, and use BSL-3 techniques. Highly dangerous pathogens must be sent to BSL-3 and BSL-4 laboratories.

Level C laboratories are major state public health laboratories that provide the second level of confirmation with more complicated methods, such as molecular diagnostics. Level C labs provide rapid identification, rule-in and refer, and work at BSL-3.

Level D laboratories are the network of federal and private partners in the US Public Health Service, Department of Defense, national laboratories, and industry that can perform research on and development of new techniques that are disseminated to the other levels of the network. Level D labs probe for the universe of agents with a high level of characterization and function at BSL-4. Laboratory services to detect biological, chemical, and radiological agents should be available to investigate emergency releases within four hours of being notified. Guidelines on the handling of laboratory specimens should address collection, transportation, safe disposal, labeling, chain of custody, and referrals to state or federal laboratories as well as whether laboratory reports require the attention of the local public health department.

If a covert event occurs that is not recognized immediately, the incidence of disease in the community would trigger public health to submit samples to the laboratory and report to the surveillance network. With an announced threat or an overt event, the situation would be reported to the Federal Bureau of Investigation, which would in turn determine which level of laboratory is required and transport samples to the nearest appropriate laboratory resource in the network.

HEALTH ALERT NETWORK

The Health Alert Network is a nationwide, integrated information and communications system whose goal is to strengthen state and local preparedness by serving as a platform for the distribution of health alerts, dissemination of prevention guidelines and other information, distance learning, national disease surveillance, and electronic laboratory reporting. Locally, the health alert network has daily practicality, including online dialogues where clinicians can confer with each other about syndromes presenting in their offices, emergency departments, and hospitals.

Chapter 11

Public Health Considerations in Recovery and Reconstruction

Disaster preparedness plans must also consider the long-term process of recovery and reconstruction. This chapter examines the three post-impact phases of disaster and the priorities in planning for each. Particular attention is paid to transitional services, such as special needs shelters.

PUBLIC HEALTH ROLE

Organize community-wide programs for delivery of health care and public health services, including special needs shelters.

- Provide community education to enhance public awareness (ie, injury control), to aid community adjustment, to form the basis for future disaster mitigation, and to educate the community about likely health risks and how to deal with them.

- Assess health needs in the community.

PRINCIPLES OF DISASTER RECOVERY AND RECONSTRUCTION

Factors that influence recovery planning and policy include the accuracy of needs assessments, intense pressure by citizens to rebuild as soon as possible, the amount of time and resources allocated to problem solving and to recovery, and the many and often conflicting preferences of affected groups. Community participation is essential for planning the rehabilitation phase because local people better understand their own needs and the problems that create these needs. Residents should be the direct beneficiaries of rehabilitation projects since they will be responsible for monitoring development projects that continue after relief workers have left.

In planning each activity, aid agencies and the community must consider the positive and negative impacts, both short term and long term. For example, aid should be provided in such a way that people can stay at home (ie, not building relocation camps) and continue with what more closely approaches normal life and promotes resumption of other normal activities when possible. Integrated recovery programs may include work schemes to repair community facilities that pay residents cash to replace lost possessions. This injection of money will stimulate local markets and help speed recovery. To aid recovery further, loans or grants can be made available to small business.

PHASES OF RECOVERY AND RECONSTRUCTION

Three phases describe what happens post-impact in the affected community: emergency, transition or recovery, and reconstruction. The timing of each phase varies with the nature of the disaster, its location, and the capacity of the community to recover.

In the *emergency phase*, activity focuses on saving lives through search and rescue, first aid, emergency medical assistance, and overall disaster assessment. Efforts immediately begin to repair critical facilities, to restore communications and transportation networks, and, in some cases, to evacuate residents from areas still vulnerable to further disaster.

During the *transition or recovery phase*, people return to work, repair damaged buildings and infrastructure, and initiate other actions that allow the community to return to normal as soon as possible. Victims begin their emotional recovery and may experience depression and post-traumatic stress disorder (see Chapter 8). External assistance is provided in the form of cash and credit. Construction projects and other types of job creation are the most appropriate types of aid.

Traditionally, four stages of recovery have been categorized. These stages are not necessarily sequential, and different parts of a community can be at different stages, depending on the extent of devastation and resources available. These include emergency response, including debris removal, provision of temporary housing; restoration of public services, including electricity, water, and telephone; replacement and reconstruction of capital stock; and initiation of improvements and developmental reconstruction that stimulate economic growth and local development.

The *reconstruction phase* is characterized by physical reordering of communications, utilities, roads, and general physical environment. Residents repair or rebuild their housing, and agricultural activities resume. The timeframe for reconstruction may span years, especially for the restoration of housing and other buildings.

Factors affecting recovery time include the risk of secondary disasters, motivation, communications, technical assistance, conflicts in technical advice, cash flow, reuse of salvaged materials, cost and supply of materials, general economy, public rejection of recovery plans, irrelevant aid, bureaucracy in government and other responding agencies, and efforts by interest groups to channel aid to rebuild their areas first.

POST-DISASTER ASSESSMENTS

Post-impact needs assessments provide information necessary to begin recovery. The first step is to assess community capacities and vulnerabilities, including physical environment (ie, intact infrastructure, resources), social conditions (ie, existing organizations, support networks), and population attitude toward and motivation to recover. Communication must be established between the people affected by the disaster and responding jurisdictions and organizations. Needs are determined by visiting representative areas, by talking to selected groups in affected communities, and by conducting rapid health assessment surveys (see Chapter 5). Emergency needs are more easily apparent than long-term needs, and long-term needs vary over time. When possible, needs should be quantified, (ie, percentage of families without running water, number of patients served by pharmacies that were destroyed), even if the number is determined by extrapolation. Public health workers should highlight gaps in the community's emergency response, where identified. Once the baseline capacities and vulnerabilities have been assessed, this information must be gathered again over time.

POST-DISASTER PRIORITIES

Local people must set the priorities and direct the use of resources. In the recovery phase, priorities include the assurance of adequate shelter, medical services, infrastructure, utilities, business, economic activity, and social networks.

Post-impact, shelter may be provided as emergency or temporary housing and permanent structures. Securing permanent shelter is a top priority. When establishing an emergency shelter, the American Red Cross allocates 40 to 60 square feet per person. Emergency or temporary shelters require a facility that can withstand a disaster and that has communication capabilities, power, and running water. The ideal shelter would have separate areas for registering residents, conducting physical examinations, offering mental health treatment, sleeping, eating, and recreation. American Red Cross shelters do not permit pets but do allow service animals (ie, seeing eye or hearing dogs).

SPECIAL NEEDS SHELTERS

Disaster victims who cannot be evacuated to a regular American Red Cross shelter include those with certain health or medical conditions, such as an infectious disease requiring isolation, serious injury or disease requiring regular medication or monitoring, or a chronic illness requiring assistance with activities of daily living. Those who need special medical equipment, such as Foley catheters or intravenous therapy, can not be housed in a routine shelter either.

For these patients, communities must establish plans for alternative care facilities referred to as special needs shelters (SNS). These facilities can be associated with a hospital such that persons requiring medical management but not hospital-level care can be safely housed. These SNS are generally intended to operate for a limited period of time (ie, one to four days).

SNS Facilities

Special needs shelters are usually refuges of last resort intended to maintain the current health, safety, and well-being of the individuals who are medically dependent yet are not acutely ill or injured. SNS must be set up to meet a range of physical and psychological human needs under adverse conditions. Most SNS operate out of school buildings, churches, or other community buildings. Facilities that must accommodate expanded medical needs should provide 100 square feet per person. These shelters are usually not equipped as a medical care facility. Some have bedding, while others require residents using the shelter to bring their own. Staffing often relies on volunteers. Planning for SNS should include discussions with local hospitals and home care agencies regarding possible assistance if higher-level skilled staff are needed.

The SNS may not have the supplies needed by those who must take shelter there. Home care agencies should prepare a cardex (indicating all of their treatment information) that can accompany the patient during relocation. In addition, patients must prepare a portable kit (preferably housed in a waterproof plastic box) that includes sufficient medical supplies and medication for one week.

As part of their plan for SNS facilities, communities should include a unit that coordinates emergency replacement of medical supplies, prescriptions, glasses, teeth, hearing aids, prosthetic devices, mobility aids, and other medical necessities often lost in disaster situations. Plans should detail how bed-ridden patients will be moved if additional evacuation is necessary (ie, flat-bed trucks). Planning can be facilitated by identifying in advance those who will need the services of a SNS and by matching that population with the appropriate shelters, supplies, and resources.

Triage

Public health should establish a system to triage the patients who require SNS. Advance identification of the medical needs of community's residents will facilitate this triage. The following example, derived from the Training Guide prepared by the Florida Department of Health as part of the Public Health Nursing Disaster Resource Guide (August 2000), suggests criteria that can be used to determine appropriate shelter assignment.

Category 1: Special Needs Shelter

Patients should be ambulatory, though they can have a medical problem and be accompanied by a care giver. These patients can be divided according to whether they need assistance in activities of daily living or whether they need monitoring by a nurse or require the use of medical equipment and assistance with medication. Patients directed to a SNS may have the following medical needs: Foley catheter, diabetes care, maintenance of medication, blood pressure monitoring, nasogastric tube feeding, ostomy care, or oxygen or nebulizer therapy. Patients with severe arthritis, stable stroke, heart disease, cancer, and Alzheimer's disease can also be accepted at SNS, as can those with disabilities (ie, blind, hearing impaired, amputee, wheelchair-bound). Bedridden and total care patients must bring a responsible caregiver and not require a hospital bed.

Category 2: Inpatient Hospital Care

For category 2 patients, public health officials are advised to make arrangements with providers and hospitals as part of global community planning. In the event of natural disasters such as hurricanes, earthquakes, and tornados, hospitals themselves may be damaged or may receive large numbers of severely injured patients, necessitating the discharge of stable medical patients and the inability to handle medical patients whose conditions have become acute.

Category 2 patients include those who require infusion therapy, complex sterile dressing changes, hyperalimentation, oxygen (including ventilator care), dialysis, intensive care, or life-support equipment. Medically complex, unstable, and terminally ill patients with "do not resuscitate orders" must also be hospitalized.

Supportive Care in SNS

Communities should establish protocols for staff assistance and procedures for triage, supportive care, and universal precautions (ie, no smoking, proper handling of body fluids and medical waste, continuous monitoring of patients by caregivers). Nurses and other staff at SNS can offer supportive care while patients and their caregivers manage routine needs. Caregivers focus on helping with activities of daily living, administering medications, and providing oxygen and other medical support. SNS nurses offer supervision and assistance, if needed, when patients or caregivers assume responsibility for their own procedures.

The community plan must anticipate SNS staffing requirements, including the types of personnel (ie, medical director, nurses, emergency medical technicians, social workers, support staff), credentialing process, scheduling, and onsite recruitment, registration, and supervision of volunteers. Plans for SNS must ensure cultural and linguistic competence among staff members. Protocols must be established for admitting and registering patients and caregivers and for acquiring and storing supplies. Staff members must be capable of handling a range of medical and nursing requirements, including labor in pregnant women, violent situations, and deaths. Procedures for closing down the SNS and relocating patients as needed must be established as part of the overall plan.

REESTABLISHING LOCAL BUSINESS AND ECONOMIC ACTIVITY

When reestablishing lost infrastructure, communities should take the opportunity to make improvements and to reduce future vulnerability to disaster. Local efforts can influence the pace, location, type, density, design, and cost of redevelopment. In addition to providing guidance on disaster-resistant building techniques, community leaders can aid reconstruction by ensuring optimal urban planning, letting families rebuild housing according to their tastes and incomes, and financing the delivery of electricity, water, and sewer lines.

A major disaster usually causes a decline in income and employment, thus reducing the resources of the population at their time of greatest need. This reduction in income cuts the tax base when increased government resources are needed. Jobs and economic activity give people a sense of return to normalcy (reestablishing schools also serves this function). Jobs, economic growth, and housing repair influence long-term recovery more than disaster relief efforts.

SOCIAL ENVIRONMENT

To aid in social recovery, local leaders must be familiar with basic family structure, economic patterns, governmental structure, religious affiliations, customs and practices, and power relationships within their community before disaster strikes. Effective intervention after a disaster requires an understanding of coping mechanisms. Each community has a variety of internal social structures that help individuals and families through difficult periods. Coping mechanisms exist at the level of the individual, family, community, and regional levels.

Strengthening horizontal community ties provides a means of redevelopment and of preparing for future disasters. In some cases, the disaster may provide an opportunity for the community to work together in ways it never has before, resulting in a stronger community and a stronger sense of community than existed before the crisis.

Emphasis on reestablishing community means that, where options exist, leaders should choose the option that strengthens or maintains the community. For example, disaster recovery plans should avoid building camps or large shelters wherever possible and instead provide aid in such a way that people can stay at home or in their neighborhood, which will allow residents to rely on preexisting social connections and to promote resumption of other normal activities.

INCORPORATING DISASTER PREPAREDNESS INTO RECOVERY

Vulnerability assessments require a review of land use based on post-disaster needs. Vulnerability assessments can also be used to predict the effects (both positive and negative) of redevelopment by projecting the impact of anticipated changes. The assessment of vulnerabilities should be used to avoid or reduce negative outcomes from future disasters. Encouraging communities to rebuild and commit to their communities long term requires attracting investment and demonstrating that the community has worked to reduce the negative impact if disaster repeats. For example, if housing is needed following a flood, a vulnerability assessment can tell officials where to build new houses to reduce the risk of damage from future flooding. Reconstruction should use improved designs and standards that reduce the vulnerability of structures. Reconstruction may also involve the erection of structures to reduce future mortality, such as cyclone shelters, and to detect possible events, such as early warning systems.

Chapter 12

Evaluation Methods for Assessing Medical and Public Health Response to Disasters

Evaluating disaster response is essential for preparedness planning. This chapter addresses the principles involved in comprehensive and objective disaster plan assessment and provides details on how to develop effective evaluation tools.

PUBLIC HEALTH ROLE

- Conduct systematic reviews of health and public health aspects of disaster response to improve efforts to reduce morbidity and mortality.

- Use professionally recognized measures of process and outcome to monitor health and public health programs and to direct resources in all phases of disaster response and recovery.

EVALUATION METHODS

Evaluation has several purposes, the most fundamental of which is to determine the extent to which an organization, program, or unit achieves its clearly stated and measurable objectives in responding to a disaster. Evaluations are used to adjust disaster plans, to focus practice drills and preparedness, to improve planning for rapid assessment and management of daily response operations, to provide input for the refinement of measures of effectiveness, and to collect data for hypothesis-driven research. Evaluations provide objective information for managers to formulate and revise policy through a retrospective and descriptive design for capturing information. While disaster response evaluation cannot always use traditional experimental design for data collection or analysis, administrators can improve their management of health systems affected by disasters from retrospective studies that draw information systematically from a variety of sources. For example, collecting information from broad categories of personnel and lay informants could be used in lieu of probability sampling.

Disaster evaluation research seeks to obtain information that can be used in preparation for future disasters by:

- Developing profiles of victims and types of injuries to inform the revision of existing or preparation of enhanced disaster plans.

- Assessing whether program adjustments can reduce disability and save lives.

- Determining if better methods to organize and manage a response exist, including the use of resources in a relief effort.

- Identifying measures that can be implemented to reduce damage to communities.

- Assessing the long-term physical and emotional effects of a disaster on individuals and communities.

Evaluations should examine the structure of the health system's response to the disaster, the allocation of health and public health resources, the sequence of events, the impact of the program at each stage, issues that arose during the health system's response to the disaster, the limitations of the response, and policy lessons.

DATA COLLECTION

During the impact and post-impact phases of a disaster, a record of important medical, environmental, and social events is usually created in journalistic features, photographs, videos, official records, recollections of participants, and other trained reporters. To study these events, information must be obtained from a variety of informants, documents, and records. Thorough preplanning of the evaluation is essential to ensure that the evaluation will yield valid findings. Multidisciplinary teams must design studies, collect data, and interpret the findings. A typical team consists of a physician, Emergency Medical Services specialist, social or behavioral scientist, epidemiologist, and disaster management specialist. This research team should hold daily debriefings to discuss issues and problems related to the implementation of the evaluation protocol.

While record keeping during a disaster is difficult and gaps often occur, some written record on a case-by-case basis is usually available. Public health officials can look for data in the hospital patient record, hospital E-codes, emergency department records, field station logs, and autopsy reports. Impressions of patient treatment can be made by reviewing available patient records, supplemented by interview data. Other sources of evaluation data include journalistic accounts and interviews with injured survivors, public health and health care professionals, search and rescue personnel, relief workers, lay bystanders, and disaster managers.

For interviews, a series of questions designed to probe the effectiveness of the disaster relief operation can be incorporated into the administered questionnaire. The questions should be structured, calling for a fixed response, although a small number of open-ended questions can provide useful information. Use medical record abstract forms to collect hospital and autopsy data. The data should be validated by cross-checking multiple sources.

DESIGNING EVALUATION STUDIES

Evaluations begin by reviewing the disaster response plan and its measurable objectives. Without measurable objectives, a disaster response plan cannot be evaluated. A structured evaluation must begin before the disaster with preparedness activities and participants and plans for rapid surveillance. Equipment needs, strategies for medical and public health intervention, and the chain of command among participating response organizations must all be assessed. Internal and external communication methods and participants must be examined. All personnel who participate in disaster response must be evaluated for the timing and execution of duties in relation to their planned assignments and actual implementation in the field.

In the process of conducting an evaluation, assessments are directed for five domains of activity: structure, process, outcomes, response adequacy, and costs. The following sections describe each domain and provide sample questions that might be asked to evaluate the response to a disaster involving a large number of casualties.

Structure

Evaluation of structure examines how the medical and public health response was organized, what resources were needed, and what resources were available. Questions used to evaluate structure for the response to mass casualty incidents include:

- Were ambulances, hospital emergency departments, and critical care units sufficiently equipped and supplied to meet the demands of the disaster?

- Were sufficient numbers of properly trained staff available, especially volunteers, first responders, ambulance personnel, emergency department nurses, critical care physicians, and communications staff?

- Did staff receive prior training in methods specific to the provision of public health and medical care during a disaster?

- Did the communications system have sufficient capacity, flexibility, and back-up capabilities during the disaster for both internal and external communications?

- How were patients transported to the hospital? To what extent was the ambulance system overloaded? What equipment shortages were experienced?

- How well did the following functions operate during the impact and post-impact phases: resource management (ie, dispatch, coordination with Emergency Medical Services and public services), medical supervision, and communication among hospitals, mobile units, and other services?

Process

Process assesses how the system (both medical and public health components) functioned during the impact and post-impact, how well individuals were prepared, and what problems occurred. The process questions should be sorted into those that probe the operation of the disaster response system and those that assess the process of treating patients. Process questions to ask in a mass casualty incident include:

- Were medical staff available during the search and rescue of patients? How soon after the response as initiated did they arrive?

- Did medical staff trained in detection and extrication have the skills and knowledge required to perform their functions during the disaster?

- Were medical staff trained in detection and extrication able to apply their medical knowledge under disaster conditions? What factors, if any, prevented optimum performance?

- How effectively was the triage function performed? What, if any, factors interfered?

- Was there adequate control over the management and deployment of resources during the post-impact response? Was responsibility for decision making clear? Were appropriate decisions made concerning the process of patient triage, transfer, and treatment?

- What first aid was provided to victims, by whom, and when? Was this appropriate and effective?

- How were patients transferred from the scene of the disaster to treatment sites?

- Did effective coordination and communication among agencies occur?

- How did the hospital respond to the volume of patients?

- How did volunteers function? Was their participation support-ive, or did it interfere with the treatment of patients? What controls, if any, were exercised?

- Did any compromises in standard medical care occur? Were these compromises necessary and acceptable?

- Was the public prepared to act appropriately when the disas-ter occurred? Should the plan to provide public education and information be modified to facilitate a future public health or medical response?

Outcomes

Outcomes assessments identify what was and was not achieved as a result of the medical and public health response. This assessment focuses on the impact of care provided to patients during the disaster. Outcome assessment can be achieved using either implicit or explicit criteria through a review of patient records. If implicit standards and criteria are used, a panel of critical care and emergency care specialists can review a sample of patient records and make judgments about the appropriateness of treatment related to patient outcomes. If explicit standards and criteria are employed, the reviewer uses written guide-lines to determine the adequacy of treatment. Forms for summarizing patient treatment and outcome data should be developed well in advance of their use and evaluated for completeness after use to assess a disaster response. Data to be collected should include at a minimum:

- Personal characteristics of patient (ie, age, sex, residence)

- Medical condition/status prior to injury

- Principal diagnosis, secondary diagnosis, type of injury

- Body location of injury (ie, extremities, back, chest, head, neck, abdomen)

- Prehospital care provided and by whom

- Method of transportation to hospital

- Hospital treatment provided

- Patient status on discharge

- Cause of death, if applicable

Response Adequacy

Assessing the adequacy of the disaster response examines the extent to which the response systems were able to meet the needs of the community during the disaster. The analysis of the adequacy of the response is valuable for planning for future disasters. The main concern is, overall, how much death and disability occurred that could have been prevented? To assess this dimension of the response for a mass casualty incident, obtain information about the following:

- To what extent was the prehospital system able to function as designed?

- What types of victims were cared for and what types were the hospital and prehospital systems unable to treat? For what reasons?

- How many victims were transported to more than one hospital due to limitations in hospital beds, intensive care beds, supplies, or staff?

- How effectively did hospitals cooperate to distribute patients to share the burden of treatment and to refer patients in need to specialty care?

Costs

Disaster response costs can be measured in several ways: the total cost of the relief effort, the cost per every life saved, the cost for various subsystems that operated during the response phase, and the costs of preparedness. Questions to ask include:

- What were each of the previously defined costs?

- Did the cost of the program correlate with the benefits to the community?

EPILOGUE

In 1983, participants of an international earthquake conference at the University of Southern California heard a leading terrorism expert declare that it was only a matter of time before the U.S. experienced the same violent terrorism that was felt abroad. A decade later, the first World Trade Center (WTC) attack occurred. Then Americans witnessed Oklahoma City. Because of geography, history of occurrence, and prediction, it is possible for localities to prepare for the most likely natural hazards. Events in September, 2001 taught us that preparation for technological disaster must now be universal. In addition to the morbidity and mortality, financial experts predict that the short term impact will be a 1% decrease in the Gross National Product of the U.S.

Tuesday, September 11, 2001 was the first time that terrorists used Weapons of Mass Destruction (WMD) on U.S. soil. At 8:48 am, a domestic Boeing 767 commercial airplane struck the North Tower of the World Trade Center in New York City. Fifteen minutes later, a second plane struck the South Tower, which collapsed at 9:59 am. The North Tower collapsed 29 minutes later. A third plane hit the Pentagon in Washington D.C., leaving hundreds dead and injured.

While thousands of occupants successfully evacuated the WTC, as of this writing, over 6,000 were missing and presumed dead. Over 6,400 people sought medical treatment for injuries in New York City and New Jersey hospitals immediately after the collapse, of which, 1,000 were seen at one of the city's eleven public hospitals. Eleven thousand body bags were requested and provided. Most would be used for parts of bodies, as the force of the blast tore people apart. Initially, two temporary morgues were set up. Subsequently, eighteen refrigerated trucks were dispatched to Bellevue Hospital, to be used to store the bodies. Identification of victims would involve procedures used by the Federal Aviation Administration following airplane crashes. In the days following the attack, a secondary wave of people sought care in emergency departments for eye irritation and breathing problems.

The federal NDMS was activated and DMAT and DMORT teams were mobilized to New York. At two treatment stations, HHS sent about 100 doctors, nurses and other health care professionals to provide round-the-clock medical care to rescue and recovery workers in New York City. In addition, CDC has dispatched occupational health specialists to New York to assess rescue worker safety needs and the Administration for Children and Families has provided grant money to New York City to provide emergency child care for relief workers and victims.

After the earlier WTC bombing in 1993, New York City built a state-of-the art command center at 7 World Trade Center, across the street from the 100 floor towers. This command center was considered impenetrable. Immediately after the first plane struck on September 11, emergency service personnel responded to the burning tower and liaisons from the breadth of government agencies reported to the command center. In the lobby of 7 WTC, some were thrown to their feet when the second plane hit the taller tower. Agency leaders had scrambled down over 20 flights of stairs to evacuate before 7 WTC collapsed, after being fatally damaged by the implosion of its neighboring towers. The city immediately set up a command center at an undisclosed location. Bellevue Hospital became a command center for health.

THE RESPONSE

Most city agencies, including the New York City Department of Health (NYCDOH) and Health and Hospitals Corporation (HHC), are located in close proximity to the WTC. Personnel at the 125 Worth Street central offices of the health department and public hospitals evacuated immediately after the planes struck. In the days that followed, the offices were initially inoperable and DOH temporarily relocated its headquarters to the department's Public Health Laboratories at 455 First Avenue. HHC moved some staff to it's offices at 41st, and some were temporarily dispatched to specific hospitals. Inspectors evaluated the soundness of the building at 125 Worth before allowing staff to return. Senior managers were resourceful, such as arranging for 75 Nextel phones so that staff could communicate, as all phones, email, beepers, and external servers were inoperable, even a week after the blasts. Temporary phone lists were created and emailed to senior staff at HHC. Some were traveling at the time of the blast and had difficulty returning to the city when flights were repeatedly canceled as security at all airports tightened.

In August, almost 900 NYCDOH field nurses received disaster training at the American Red Cross headquarters as part of the joint activities of the Center for Public Health Preparedness at the Mailman School of Public Health at Columbia University and the NYCDOH. The hundreds of public health nurses learned about the organization of an emergency response, the organization of the New York City response, and shelter management. This training was useful as after the WTC attack, tens of thousands of NYC residents were unable to return to their homes and numerous shelters were opened. Immediately after the attack, the CDC sent an additional 35 members of the Epidemic Intelligence Service (EIS) to assist the New York City Health Department and EIS officers already in place in the ongoing monitoring of public health matters. The EIS officers were assigned to hospitals to assist New York health officials and physicians monitor diseases; conduct a medical and health needs assessment; identify existing health problems such as allergic reactions; and determine if there are new medical needs and if already deployed resources could be better used elsewhere.

Victim location services were established at the armory. Behavioral health personnel, including providers from HHC and the New York City Department of Mental Health, the Red Cross, and various members of the clergy helped surviving family and friends complete and file very lengthy, detailed forms. Requests were made for significant others to bring in hair, toothbrushes, and dental records so that victims could be identified by DNA analysis. Within a week after the incident, New York City established a family center for relatives of people missing in the terror attack. The center offered hot meals, child care, telephones and Internet access, a television lounge and cafeteria, interpreters and curtained interview cubicles. In addition to local red cross and mental health agency efforts, federal hotlines were also initiated for those seeking counseling.

IMPLEMENTATION OF DISASTER PLANS

The disaster response involved the activation of actions found in the typical emergency response plan. These included establishment of incident chain of command, immediate triage and transport of victims, rescue and recovery using assets deployed through mutual aid agreements and a Presidential Declaration through the Stafford Act, resource acquisition of both personnel and hardware, and communication both internally among the responding agencies and externally to the public. The attack at the WTC was unique from other disaster responses because of the military and national security issues and the loss of senior emergency management command (ie. Fire Department of New York/EMS and New York Police Department managers). The response was complicated because the event was a combination of disasters: fire, water, smoke, potential bio-hazards, environmental, and transport. The instability of the buildings in this complex environment and the significant number of potential victims stretched the response capabilities of all involved and the potential psychological impact for the entire country.

PUBLIC HEALTH INFORMATION PROVIDED

Numerous agencies provided information to public health and emergency management personnel. The NYCDOH worked closely with other City, State and Federal agencies, including the Centers for Disease Control and Prevention, in a coordinated response to the World Trade Center disaster. Joel Ackelsberg, MD, MPH, Medical Director of the Emergency Readiness and Response Unit, Communicable Disease Program, and Marcelle Layton, MD, Assistant Commissioner, Communicable Disease Program provided broadcast alerts to emergency medicine directors, infection control practitioners and infectious disease physicians, and other persons on the NYCDOH Broadcast Alert System. These alerts were intended for:

• Hospital administration

• Medical and Nursing Staff

• Emergency Departments

• Hospital Safety Directors, and

• Hospital Pharmacy and Laboratories

The following is excerpted from Alert #3:

CONCERNS ABOUT PUBLIC HEALTH ISSUES RELATED TO THE DISASTER SITE

A) There is no threat to the health of the general public from decomposing human remains at the disaster site: There are no risks of infectious disease epidemics among the general public related to the disaster site. Bad odors that are likely to arise from decomposing bodies, although unpleasant, are not harmful. The NYCDOH is working closely with other local, state and federal agencies to ensure that workers on-site adhere to strict standard precautions to avoid contact with blood or body fluids.

During rescue operations, some rescue workers may come in contact with potentially contaminated body fluids. If such exposures occur percutaneously, to non-intact skin, or to mucous membranes, facilities should refer to their institutional protocols for managing potential exposures to blood-borne pathogens, or consult the infectious disease experts who routinely manage these situations in their hospitals.

B) Acute Stress Disorders: Given the traumatic experience of last week's plane crashes into the World Trade Center, all New Yorkers, especially those personally affected by the disaster, those providing care to the victims or their families, and those working on the relief effort are likely to experience emotional distress. American Red Cross and Department of Mental Health Hotlines can provide direct access to services (New York City numbers provided).

ENVIRONMENTAL RISKS POSED BY ASBESTOS AND DUST

Asbestos was used in the construction of the World Trade Center. Tests performed by various city, state and federal agencies indicate that asbestos may be present in low levels in the vicinity of the World Trade Center. For workers at the site, the health risk posed by short-term exposures is very low. The risk to persons who have not been present in the affected area following the disaster is also thought to be extremely low.

There are no tests that can be done, including chest radiographs, to tell if exposure has occurred, nor to predict if pulmonary disease will occur in the future.

At a minimum, anyone who needs to enter the affected area should wear a disposable cup-type (i.e., not fan-folded or duckbill) N100 or P100 respirator and goggles. Workers in contact with debris or surface dust in the affected area should contact their employers or the NYCDOH (numbers provided) for specific recommendations regarding needed protective equipment.

Increased particulate matter and dust released during the days since the attack may cause eye and/or respiratory irritation, particularly for persons with underlying pulmonary disease, including asthma or Chronic Obstructive Pulmonary Disease. Individuals who have a history of heart and lung conditions and who are in areas where smoke or dust is visible are advised to remain indoors with the windows shut. It is advised that air conditioners be operated on the "recirculate" mode, so that outside air is not pumped inside, or if this is not possible, that they should be turned off. Persons who experience difficulty breathing or chest pain are advised to seek medical care immediately.

Environmental testing is continuing to better characterize levels of asbestos, dust particulates and other potentially hazardous materials within the affected site and in other off-site locations. In addition, the NYCDOH is monitoring issues related to food and water safety, rodent control, radiation levels and worker safety in the area around the World Trade Center site.

SURVEILLANCE FOR INFECTIOUS DISEASE OUTBREAKS THAT MAY REPRESENT BIOTERRORISM

Since the terrorist attack on Tuesday, September 11, 2001, the NYC DOH has continued to monitor for the possibility of a bioterrorist event in NYC. We have found NO evidence that biological agents have been released in NYC; laboratory tests on environmental samples taken from the affected area after the attack were all negative. Moreover, biologic agents would likely not have survived an explosion the magnitude of the World Trade Center attack. Accordingly, we are not recommending any prophylaxis for NYC residents.

However, we recognize the need to remain alert to the occurrence of unusual disease clusters or manifestations, given the increased concerns raised in general about terrorism. Surveillance systems are currently in place and include:

A) Active Emergency Department (ED) Syndromic Surveillance

In 15 hospital EDs, NYCDOH has established surveillance for illness syndromes that would likely occur if a biological pathogen were released covertly in NYC. Epidemic Intelligence Service (EIS) officers from the Centers for Disease Control and Prevention are on-site 24 hours per day, working closely with ED staff at these facilities to collect clinical data on all individuals presenting for evaluation. Data are analyzed daily at the NYCDOH for trends and patterns that could signal an increase in illness consistent with a possible bioterrorist event. In the event that this surveillance system identifies a worrisome pattern of illness in the community, the NYC DOH will initiate a rapid epidemiologic field investigation to determine the etiology of the illness.

In addition, this syndromic surveillance system will also monitor for health effects associated with the aftermath of the World Trade Center attack, such as increases in respiratory illness, gastrointestinal illness, trauma and psychological distress.

B) Enhanced Healthcare Provider Reporting of Unusual Illnesses

The NYC DOH depends on local clinicians and laboratories to identify and report unusual clusters of communicable diseases in a timely fashion. Vigilance for unusual clusters or manifestations of disease is critical to the early detection of a covert bioterrorist event and rapid implementation of public health interventions.

REPORTING FATAL CASES AND INFORMATION ON MORTUARY ISSUES, INCLUDING DEATH CERTIFICATE REGISTRATION FOR DEATHS RELATED TO THIS INCIDENT

ALL deaths directly or secondarily related to this terrorist incident should be reported to the Office of the Chief Medical Examiner. The NYCDOH Burial Desk for registration of death certificates has been temporarily moved to (address and phone provided).

CLINICAL RECOGNITION AND MANAGEMENT OF SUSPECTED BIOTERRORISM EVENTS

Healthcare providers in New York City should be alert to the illness patterns and diagnostic clues that might signal an unusual infectious disease outbreak due to the intentional release of a biological agent. Look for the following clinical and epidemiological clues that are suggestive of a possible bioterrorist event:

• Suspected or confirmed communicable diseases that are not endemic in NYC (e.g., anthrax, plague, tularemia, smallpox, or viral hemorrhagic fever)

• Simultaneous disease outbreaks in human and animal populations

• Any unusual age distributions or temporal and/or geographic clustering of illness (e.g., persons who attended the same public event or religious gathering) for a rare or common disease

• Any sudden increase of illness in previously healthy individuals

- Any sudden increase in the following non-specific syndromes:

  - Respiratory illness with fever

  - Gastrointestinal illness

  - Encephalitis or meningitis

  - Neuromuscular illness (e.g., botulism)

  - Fever with rash

  - Bleeding disorders

RESPONSE TO SUSPECTED BT EVENT

Any unusual cluster or manifestions of illness should be reported immediately to the New York City Department of Health. After learning of any suspicious disease cluster, the NYC DOH will initiate an immediate investigation to determine the cause of illness as well as the mode of transmission.

RETURNING HOME

The NYCDOH offered the following recommendations for individuals re-occupying commercial buildings and residents re-entering their homes through a press release on September 17, 2001:

- Make sure conditions are safe.

- Enter your home dressed in a long-sleeve shirt and pants, and with closed shoes.

- Check for the smell of gas. If the apartment smells of gas, leave immediately and report it to your building manager and to Con Edison.

- Check for broken glass and fixtures. Wrap any broken glass in paper and mark it "broken glass." If large pieces of glass are broken, ask your building superintendent for help.

- Run hot and cold water from each of the taps for at least two minutes, or until water runs completely clean, whichever is longer.

- Flush toilets until bowls are refilled. For air pressure systems, you may need to flush several times. If there are any problems with the toilet or plumbing system, call a plumber — do not try to fix the problem yourself.

- If in doubt, throw food out. Raw or cooked meat, poultry and seafood, milk and milk-containing products, eggs, mayonnaise and creamy dressings, and cooked foods should be thrown out if power was out for two or more hours. Frozen foods that have thawed should be thrown away. Throw away any food that may have been contaminated with dust, except for food in cans, jars, or containers with tight-fitting lids. Wash dust-covered cans and jars with water and wipe clean.

- To remove dust use a wet rag or wet mop. Do not sweep with a dry broom because it can make dust airborne again. Where dust is thick, directly wet the dust with water, and remove it in layers with wet rags and mops. Dirty rags can be rinsed under running water. Used rags and mops should be put in plastic bags while they are still wet and bags should be sealed and discarded. Do not dry rags before bagging, disposal or washing. Cloth rags should be washed separately from other laundry. Wash heavily-soiled or dusty clothing or linens twice. Remove lint from washing machines and filters in the dryers with each laundry load.

- Because the dust particles are so small, standard vacuuming is not an efficient way to remove the dust and may put dust back into the air where it can be inhaled. HEPA (high efficiency particulate) efficiency filtration vacuums capable of trapping very fine particles can be used. If a HEPA vacuum is not available, either HEPA bags or dust allergen bags should be used with your regular vacuum. Carpets and upholstery can be shampooed and then vacuumed.

- If your apartment is very dusty, you should wash or HEPA vacuum your curtains. If curtains need to be taken down, take them down slowly to prevent dust releasing in the air.

- Avoid sweeping or other outdoor maintenance.

- Keep windows closed.

- Set the air conditioner to re-circulate air (closed vents), and clean or change the filter frequently.

GUIDANCE FROM THE RED CROSS

The American Red Cross developed four documents to guide providing information to families and children who are concerned about the recent terrorist attacks in New York and Washington, DC. The documents are all posted on the Red Cross public web site and are available through links at: http://www.redcross.org/services/disaster/keepsafe/ attack.html. The purpose of each document and its intended audience is described below:

1) **How Do I Deal With My Feelings?** Audience: Adults. Provides information regarding common reactions and how you can help yourself and others. (English and web-based only)

2) **Helping Children Cope With Trauma.** Audience: Parents and caregivers of children of ages 2-18. Provides information regarding children's reactions and feelings to transportation disasters. Suggestions are provided for dealing with the fears and anxieties of children in the target audience. ARC 1303.

3) **When Bad Things Happen.** Audience: Middle school aged children. Provides information about the emotional and physical reactions people may have to disaster and gives tips to help put the event in perspective in their lives. It also provides suggestions that might help manage these reactions. ARC 1356.

4) **Why Do I Feel Like This?** Audience: High school aged students. Provides information about the emotional and physical reactions people may be having in times of disaster. Helps them understand what reactions are "normal" and recommends how to deal with these reactions. ARC 1355.

Documents 2-4 are being translated and will be made available on the Red Cross public web site in: Arabic, Cambodian, Farsi, French, Hmong, Korean, Laotian, Portuguese, Russian, Tagalog, and Vietnamese in the near future. They are available for direct download from the internet in two forms: As PDF files and as HTML (web-based) documents. PDF files are "printer friendly" and may be reproduced on any photocopier. The documents are not copyrighted, and may be freely reproduced. However, the Red Cross asks that the materials not be changed or altered, except to add local Red Cross chapter contact information.

CDC OFFICIAL HEALTH ADVISORY

On September 14, 2001, CDC sent an official health advisory through the Health Alert Network in response to requests for information about management of exposures to blood or other body fluids that may pose a hazard (ie hepatitis B virus, hepatitis C virus, or HIV). Routes of exposure to blood or other body fluids that merit evaluation include percutaneous injuries with contaminated sharps, splashes to mucosal surfaces, and visible contamination of injured skin. Post-exposure management systems should address:

1. Instructions to exposed personnel about reporting exposures and the need for evaluation at sites where immediate post-exposure treatment services are provided;
2. Assessment and documentation of the nature and severity of the exposures;
3. Provision of post-exposure prophylaxis to prevent hepatitis B or HIV when indicated;
4. Referral for appropriate follow-up care.

The National Clinicians' Post-Exposure Prophylaxis Hotline (888-488-4911 toll free or 415-469-4417 back-up) is available for 24 -7advice about assessing and treating occupational exposures to blood and other body fluids that might pose a threat of hepatitis or HIV. There is no charge for this service. Additional detailed information about post-exposure care after occupational exposures to blood and body fluids can be found at <http://www.cdc.gov/ncidod/hip/guide/phspep.htm. In addition, the University of California, Los Angeles and CDC have developed an interactive website to help guide clinicians in making decisions about post-exposure care:

http://www.needlestick.mednet.ucla.edu

WE ARE ALL VICTIMS

It is doubtful that anyone in the U.S. is immune to the effects of the terrorist attack that occurred at the WTC on September 11, 2001. The effects reach around the globe as an international group worked and conducted business in the towers. New York City had honed its preparations through response to the West Nile virus, general disaster planning and preparedness with the New York City Office of Emergency Management and the Center for Public Health Preparedness at the Mailman School. While public health couldn't prevent the primary attack, the public health system of New York demonstrated that preparedness pays off. Despite losing it's own infrastructure, these professionals efficiently responded to citizen needs in secondary and tertiary prevention. Unfortunately, this lesson has been learned by everyone in the country.

TERMS COMMONLY USED IN DISASTER PREPAREDNESS AND RESPONSE

Advanced Life Support – A medical procedure performed by paramedics that includes the advanced diagnosis and protocol–driven treatment of a patient in the field.

Aftershocks – A sequence of smaller earthquakes that follow larger magnitude earthquakes. Aftershocks may be felt for many months after an earthquake and can exacerbate damage. Also a type of ground failure.

Alarm Procedure – A means of alerting concerned parties to a disaster. Various optical and acoustical means of alarm are possible including flags, lights, sirens, radio, and telephone.

Analysis–Epidemiologic Measures – Includes indicators such as descriptive statistics, specific disease and/or death rates, secular trends, and tests for sensitivity and validity.

Assessments – The evaluation and interpretation of short and long term measurements to provide a basis for decisionmaking and to enhance public health officials' ability to monitor disaster situations.

Assets –A term used for all resources required, including human, to adequately respond to a disaster.

Avalanche – The sudden slide of a huge mass of snow and ice, usually carrying with it earth, rocks, trees, and other debris.

Basic Life Support – Includes non–invasive measures used to treat unstable patients such as extraction of airway obstructions, cardio–pulmonary resuscitation, care of wounds and hemorrhages, and immobilization of fractures.

Becquerel (Bq) – A unit of nuclear activity. For example, 1 Bq represents the amount of radioactive substance that disintegrates in one second. This unit replaces the curie.

Bioterrorism – The unlawful release of biologic agents or toxins with the intent to intimidate or coerce a government or civilian population to further political or social objectives. Humans, animals, and plants are often targets.

Branch – See page 177.

Case – A unit of observation.

Case Definition – Standardized criteria for deciding whether a person has a particular disease or health–related condition. Often used in investigations and for comparing potential cases. Case definitions help decide which disaster–specific conditions should be monitored with emergency information surveillance systems.

Casualty – Any person suffering physical and/or psychological damage that leads to death, injury, or material loss.

Casualty Clearing Station – A collecting point for victims that is located in the immediate vicinity of a disaster site where triage and medical treatment can be provided.

Central Holding Area – A location where ambulances leave to pick patients up from the casualty clearing station, or deliver patients to neighboring hospitals according to a victim distribution plan.

Community Profile – The characteristics of the local environment that are prone to a chemical or nuclear accident. These characteristics can include population density; age distribution; number of roadways, railways, and waterways; type of buildings; and local relief agencies.

Comprehensive Emergency Management – A broad style of emergency management, encompassing prevention, preparedness, response, and recovery.

Consequence Management – An emergency management function that and includes measures to protect public health and safety, restore essential government services, and provide emergency relief to governments in the event of terrorism. Consequence management responses are managed by FEMA and use protocols established under the Federal Response Plan (FRP). Consequence management efforts can also include support missions as described in other Federal operations plans, such as predictive modeling, protective action recommendations, and mass decontamination.

Contamination – An accidental release of hazardous chemicals or nuclear materials that pollute the environment and place humans at risk of contamination.

Contingency Plan – An emergency plan developed in expectation of a disaster. Contingency plans are often based on risk assessments, the availability of human and material resources, community preparedness, and local and international response capabilities.

Coordinate – A systematic exchange of information among principal participants in order to carry out a unified response in the event of an emergency.

Covert Releases (of a biologic agent) – An unannounced release of a biologic agent that causes illness. Detection of the biologic agent is dependent on traditional surveillance methods. If undetected, a covert release of a contagion has the potential to spread widely before it is detected.

Crisis Management – Administrative measures that identify, acquire, and plan the use of resources needed to anticipate, prevent, and/or resolve a threat to public safety (ie terrorism).

Data Collection – Gathering, assembling and delivering data to a centralized collection point.

Decontamination – The removal of hazardous chemicals or nuclear substances from the skin and/or mucous membranes by showering or washing the affected area with water, or by rinsing with a sterile solution.

Disaster – Any event, typically occuring suddenly, that causes damage, ecological disruption, loss of human life, deterioration of health and health services AND which exceeds the capacity of the affected community on a scale sufficient to require outside assistance. These events can be caused by nature, equipment malfunction, human error, or biological hazards and disease (eg, earthquake, flood, fire, hurricane, cyclone, typhoon, significant storms, volcanic eruptions, spills, air crashes, drought, epidemic, food shortages, civil strife).

Disaster Continuum or Emergency Management Cycle – The life cycle of a disaster or emergency.

Disaster Epidemiology – The study of disaster–related deaths, illnesses, and injuries in humans. Also includes the study of the factors that affect death, illness, and injury following a disaster. Methodology involves identifying and comparing risk factors among disaster victims to those who were left unharmed. Epidemiologic investigations provide public health professionals with information on the probable public health consequences of disasters.

Disaster Field Office (DFO)– The office established in or near the disaster area that supports federal and state response as well as recovery operations. The Disaster Field Office houses the Federal Coordinating Officer (FCO), the Emergency Response Team (ERT), the State Coordinating Officer (SCO), and support staff.

Disaster Informatics – The theoretical and practical operation of processing information and communicating in a disaster situation.

Disaster–prone – The level of risk that is related to the hazard or the immediate cause of a disaster. Disaster–proneness is determined by analyzing the history of past events as well as new conditions that may increase the risk of a disaster taking place.

Disaster Severity Scale – A scale that classifies disasters by the following parameters: the radius of the disaster site, the number of dead, the number of wounded, the average severity of the injuries sustained, the impact time, and the rescue time. By attributing a numeric score to each of the variables from 0 to 2 with 0 being the least severe and 2 the most severe, a scale with a range of 0 to 18 can be created.

Disaster Vulnerability – A measure of the ability of a community to absorb the effects of a severe disaster and to recover. Vulnerability varies with each disaster, depending on the disaster's impact on the affected population or group.

Dispatch Communications System – A system used to assign ambulance personnel and other first responders.

Division – See page 177.

Emergency – Any natural or man–made situation that results in severe injury, harm, or loss to humans or property.

Emergency Operations Center (EOC)– The site from which civil government officials (eg, municipal, county, state, federal) direct emergency operations in a disaster.

Emergency Management Agency (EMA)– Also referred to as the Office of Emergency Preparedness (OEP). The EMA, under the authority of the governor's office, coordinates the efforts of the state's health department, housing and social service agencies, and public safety agencies (eg, state police) during an emergency or disaster. The EMA also coordinates federal resources made available to the states such as the National Guard, the Centers for Disease Control (eg, EIS officers), and the Public Health Service (eg, Agency for Toxic Substances Disease Registry, ATSDR).

The Emergency Medical Services (EMS) **System** – An Emergency Medical Services System is the coordination of the pre–hospital system (eg, public access, dispatch, EMTs/ and medics, ambulance services) and the in–hospital system (eg, emergency departments, hospitals and other definitive care facilities and personnel) to provide emergency medical care.

Emergency Medical Technicians (EMTs) and **Paramedics** (EMT–Ps) – Trained emergency medical respondents. Both paramedics and EMTs are trained to diagnose and treat most common medical emergencies in the field and to provide medical treatment while en route to the hospital. Paramedics are more highly trained than EMTs.

Emergency Operations Center (EOC) – See page 177.

Emergency Public Information– Information disseminated to the public in anticipation of an emergency that continues for the duration of the emergency. Emergency public information directs actions and gives instructions.

Emergency Response Team – A team of federal personnel and support staff that is deployed by FEMA during a major disaster or emergency. The duty of the team is to assist the FCO in carrying out his or her responsibilities under the Stafford Act.. Team members consist of representatives from each federal department or agency that has been assigned primary responsibility for an Emergency Support Function as well as key members of the FCO's staff.

Emergency Support Function (ESF)– A functional area of response activity established to coordinated the delivery of federal assistance during the response phase of an emergency. ESF's mission is to save lives, protect property, preserve public health, and maintain public safety. ESF represents the type of federal assistance most needed by states overwhelmed by the impact of a catastrophic event on local and state resources.

ESF 6 Mass Care – Mass Care includes sheltering and feeding victims of disaster, emergency first aid, family reunification, and the distribution of emergency relief supplies. The American Red Cross (ARC) is designated by the Federal Response Plan (FRP) as the primary agency responsible for ESF Mass Care.

ESF 8 Health and Medical – Lead by the United States Public Health Service's Office of Emergency Preparedness, ESF 8 Health and Medical serves as the basis for federal response to the health needs of disaster victims.

Epidemic – The occurrence of any known or suspected contagion that occurs in clear excess of normal expectancy. A threatened epidemic occurs when the circumstances are such that a disease may reasonably be anticipated to occur in excess of normal expectancy.

Evacuation – An organized removal of civilians from a dangerous or potentially dangerous area.

Evaluation – A detailed review of a disaster relief program designed to determine whether program objectives were met, to assess the program's impact on the community, and to generate "lessons learned" for the design of future projects. Evaluations are most often conducted at the completion of important milestones, or at the end of a specified period.

Evaluation Research – The application of scientific methods to assess the effectiveness of programs, services, or organizations established to improve a patient's health or prevent illness.

Exposure Surveillance – To look for exposure to risk. In a disaster setting, exposure may be based on the physical or environmental properties of the disaster event. Also known as a risk factor variable, predictor variable, independent variable, or putative causal factor.

Exposure Variable – A characteristic of interest. Also known as risk factor or predictor variable.

Far–field – The outlying vicinity of a nuclear accident. A far–field lies from 2 to 20 kilometers outside the accident site, depending on the strength of the source of radiation. The area closest to the nuclear accident is called the near–field.

Federal Coordinating Officer (FCO)– The person appointed by FEMA following a presidential declaration of a severe disaster or of an emergency to coordinate federal assistance. The FCO initiates immediately action to assure that federal assistance is provided in accordance with the disaster declaration, any applicable laws or regulations, and the FEMA–state agreement. The FCO is also the senior federal official appointed in accordance with the provisions of Public Law 93–288, as amended (the Stafford Act), to coordinate the overall consequence management response and recovery activities. The FCO represents the President as provided by Section 303 of the Stafford Act by coordinating the administration of federal relief activities in the designated disaster area. Additionally, the FCO is delegated responsibilities and performs those for the FEMA Director as outlined in Executive Order 12148 and those responsibilities delegated to the FEMA Regional Director in the Code of Federal Regulations, Title 44, Part 205.

Federal On–Scene Commander (OSC)– The official designated upon the activation of the Joint Operations Center that ensures appropriate coordination of the United States government's overall response with federal, state and local authorities. The OSC maintains this role until the United States Attorney General transfers the Lead Federal Agency (LFA) role to FEMA.

Federal Response Plan (FRP)– The plan that coordinates federal resources in disaster situations. The FRP is designed to address the consequences of any disaster or emergency situation in which there is need for federal assistance under the authorities of the Robert T. Stafford Disaster Relief and Emergency Assistance Act, 42 U.S.C. 5121 et seq. The FRP is also the federal government's plan of action when assisting affected states and local jurisdictions in the event of a severe disaster or emergency. The plan consists of 12 Emergency Support Functions (ESFs).

Famine Early Warning System – A system established by the United States Agency for International Development to monitor a number of factors that are predictive of famine including climate, availability of food, and nutrition related morbidity.

First Responder– Local police, fire, and emergency medical personnel who arrive first on the scene of an incident and take action to save lives, protect property, and meet basic human needs.

Functional Model of Public Health Response in Disasters – A model for identifying which disaster related activities are the responsibility of public health officials. This model also identifies the interface between the core components of professional public health training and emergency management functions as well as the relationship between the framework of activities typically conducted by the emergency management community and public health practice.

Fujita Scale – A scale used to measure the strength of tornadoes.

Golden Hour – A principle that states ABC unstable victims must be stabilized within one hour following injury to reduce the risk of death.

Group – See page 177.

Hazard – The probability that a disaster will occur. Hazards can be caused by a natural phenomenon (eg, earthquake, tropical cyclone), by failure of manmade energy sources (eg, nuclear reactor, industrial explosion), or by an uncontrolled human activity (eg, conflict, overgrazing).

Hazard Identification/Analysis – The process of determining what events are likely to occur in a specified region or environment (eg, earthquakes, floods, industrial accidents).

Hazard Surveillance – An assessment of the occurrence, distribution, and secular trends relating to different levels of hazards (eg, toxic chemical agents, physical agents, biomechanical stressors, and biologic agents) that are responsible for disease and injury.

Impact Phase – A phase during a disaster where emergency management activities focus on warning and preparedness.

Incident Action Plan (IAP) – A written document, developed by the incident commander or the planning section of the ICS, that details which actions will be conducted by the ICS in response to an incident. IAPs are developed for specific time period, often referred to as operational periods, and are based on the specific needs of an incident. The incident commander is responsible for the oversight and implementation the IAP.

Incident Command System (ICS) – ICS is the model for the command, control, and coordination of a response to an emergency and provides the means to coordinate the efforts of individual agencies.

Branch – An organizational level that has functional or geographic responsibility for major parts of the ICS or incident operations. The incident commander may establish geographic branches to resolve span–of–control issues, or functional branches to manage specific functions (eg, law enforcement, fire, and emergency medical). A Branch is managed by the Branch Director.

Division – The organizational level that has responsibility for operations within a defined geographic area. The division level is the organizational level between Single Resources, Task Forces, or Strike Teams and the Branch level.

Emergency Operations Center (EOC) – The location where department heads, government officials, and volunteer agencies coordinate the response to an emergency.

Group – The organizational level that has responsibility for a specified functional assignment in an emergency or disaster (eg perimeter control, evacuation, fire suppression, etc.). A Group is managed by a Group Supervisor.

Integrated Communications – A system that uses a common communications plan, standard operating procedures, clear text, common frequencies, and common terminology.

Resource Management – A management style that maximizes the use of and control over assets. This management style reduces the need for unnecessary communications, provides for strict accountability, and ensures the safety of personnel.

Section – The organizational level that is responsible for a major functional area of the incident. Incident is the term used to describe the event requiring emergency response management (ie. Multi–car collision, high rise fire, explosion). A section is located organizationally between Branches and the Incident Commander.

Size–up – To identify a problem and assess the potential consequences. Initially, a size–up is the responsibility of the first officer to arrive at the scene of an emergency. Size–ups continue throughout the response phase and continuously update the status of the incident, evaluate the hazards present, determine the size of the affected area as well as whether the area can be isolated. A size–up also determines if a staging area will be needed and where it should be located to allow for the best flow of personnel and equipment.

Span of Control – The number of individuals managed by a single supervisor. The manageable span on control for one supervisor ranges from between three to seven individuals, with five as optimum.

Staging Area – An area where resources are kept while awaiting assignment.

Strike Team – A group of resources of the same size and type (eg, five patrol units, three drug K–9 teams).

Task Force – A combination of single resources that is assembled for a particular operational need with common communications and one leader.

Top–down – A command function that is established by the first officer to arrive on the scene. This officer then becomes the incident commander.

Unity of Command – A hierarchical methodology that states that each person within an organization should report to only one superior.

Integrated Communications – See page 178.

Integrated Recovery Programs (IRPs) – Versatile recovery programs that respond to a variety of community needs. IRPs often coordinate recovery activities and stimulate economic rehabilitation by working with various sectors of the community. For example, IRPs may include work schemes to repair community facilities that enable disaster victims to access cash and replace their lost possessions.

Intensity – A Roman numerical index from I to XII that describes the physical effects of an earthquake to a specific area. These values are subjective. Intensity is a measurement of the nature and spatial extent of the distribution of damage. The most commonly used scale is the 12 point Modified Mercalli Intensity (MMI), developed in the 1930s. Intensity VI of the MMI represents the threshold for potential ground failures such as liquefaction. Intensity VII: The threshold for architectural damage. Intensity VIII: The threshold for structural damage. Intensity IX: Intense structural damage. Intensities X to XII: Various levels of destruction up to total destruction. An earthquake has many intensities (perceived effects), but only one magnitude (force). The MMI does not indicate an earthquake's magnitude.

International Assistance – Assistance provided by one or more governments or voluntary organizations to a country in need, usually for development or for an emergency. The four primary elements of assistance within the international community are intergovernmental agencies (eg, United Nations, Common Market) non–governmental organizations, the Red Cross, and bilateral agreements.

Joint Information Center (JIC)– A center located at the scene of an emergency established to coordinate federal public information. It is also the central point of contact for all news media. Public information officials from participating state and local agencies often collocate at the JIC.

Joint Operations Center (JOC)– The JOC acts as the focal point for the management and direction of onsite activities, coordination and establishment of state requirements and priorities, as well as the coordination of the federal response. JOCs are established by the Lead Federal Agency (LFA) and are under the operational control of the federal on–scene coordinator.

Landslide – A massive or rapid decent of damage–causing soil and rock. Landslides are the most common and wide–spread type of ground failure and may include falls, topples, slides, spreads, and flows of soil and/or rock on unstable slopes.

Lead Agency – The federal department or agency that is assigned the lead responsibility under United States law for the management and coordination of the federal response in a specific functional area. Lead agencies support the Lead Federal Agency (LFA) during all phases of the response.

Lead Federal Agency (LFA)– The agency designed by the President to lead and coordinate the federal response. The type of emergency determines which agency that becomes the LFA. In general, the LFA establishes operational procedures to assemble and work with the cooperating agencies to provide the LFA with support. These agencies support the LFA in carrying out the President's policy by furnishing the LFA with an initial assessment of the situation, developing action plans, monitoring and updating operational priorities, and by ensuring that each agency exercises its authority within the boundaries of the law. Specific responsibilities of an LFA vary according to each agency's statutory authority.

Liaison– An agency official who works with individual agencies or agency officials to coordinate interagency communications.

Liquefaction – Primarily occurs in young, shallow, loosely compacted, water saturated sand and gravel deposits that are subjected to ground shaking. Liquefaction results in a temporary loss of load–bearing strength.

Local Government – Any country, city, village, town, district, political subdivision of any state, Indian tribe or authorized tribal organization, or Alaska native village or organization including rural communities, unincorporated towns and villages, or any other public entity.

Loss – A range of adverse consequences that can impact communities and individuals (eg, damage, loss of economic value, loss of function, loss of natural resources, loss of ecological systems, environmental impact, health deterioration, mortality, morbidity).

Latrines – A pit designed to capture and contain excreta. Latrines are most often trenches with multiple platforms across it, or solitary pits surrounded by a structure.

Magnitude – A numerical quantity invented by Charles F. Richter that determines the size and scope of an earthquake by using a measure called a Richter. The magnitude of an earthquake is the total amount of energy released after adjusting for differences in epicentral distance and focal depth. Magnitude is determined on the basis of instrumental records; whereas, intensity is determined by subjective observations of an earthquake's damage. Moderate earthquakes have magnitudes of 5.5 to 6.9; larger earthquakes have magnitudes of 7.0 to 7.9; and strong earthquakes have magnitudes of 8.0 and greater. The energy of an earthquake increases exponentially with magnitude. For example, a magnitude 6.0 earthquake releases 31.5 times more energy than a magnitude 5.0 earthquake or approximately 1,000 times more energy than a magnitude 4.0 earthquake.

Manmade or Technological Disasters; Complex Emergencies – Technological events that are caused by humans and occur in human settlements. Examples of manmade or technological disasters are fire, chemical spills and explosions, and armed conflict.

Maximum Contaminant Level (MCL) – The maximum permissible level of a contaminant in water in a public water system. The MCL is established by the Environmental Protection Agency (EPA). MCLs are defined in the Safe Drinking Water Act as the level that may be achieved with the use of the best available technology, treatment techniques, and other means that EPA finds are available after taking cost into consideration.

Medical Coordination – The coordination between healthcare providers during the transition from the pre–hospital to the hospital phase of patient care . Simplification and standardization of materials and methods is a prerequisite.

Measuring Environmental Hazards – Assessing the occurrence, distribution, and the secular trends that affect the level of hazards (eg, toxic chemical agents, physical agents, biomechanical stressors, biologic agents) responsible for disease and injury.

Measures of Biological Effects – A gauge of health in humans that indicates the impact of a disaster. Examples include laboratory typing of organisms where infectious disease outbreaks occur, biochemical testing of exposures to toxic chemicals to assess exposure levels, and anthropometric measurements (eg, height to weight ratio) that indicate the type and degree of malnutrition in famine situations.

Measures of Physical Effects to Indicate Magnitude – An assessment of environmental conditions whose levels are negatively impacted due to a disaster.   Examples include the height of river above flood stage, the level of pollutants in air after forest fire, and the level of toxic chemicals in drinking water or sediment.

Mitigation – Measures taken to reduce the harmful effects of a disaster by attempting to limit the disaster's impact on human health and economic infrastructure.

Modified Mercalli Scale – A scale that indicates the intensity of an earthquake by assessing the degree of damage on a particular location.

Monitoring – A process of evaluating the performance of response and recovery programs by measuring a program's outcomes against stated objectives. Monitoring is used to identify bottlenecks and obstacles that cause delays or programmatic shortfalls that require assessment.

Mortality Data – Information about the number of deaths used to assess the magnitude of a disaster, evaluate the effectiveness of disaster preparedness, evaluate the adequacy of warning systems, and to aid in contingency planning by identifying high risk groups.

Natural Disasters – Natural phenomena with acute onset and profound effects (eg, earthquakes, floods, cyclones, tornadoes).

Na–tech (natural–technological) **Disasters** – Natural disasters that create technological emergencies such as urban fires that result from seismic motion or chemical spills that result from floods.

On–Scene Coordinator (OSC)– The federal official pre–designated by the EPA and United States Coast Guard to coordinate and direct response and removals of oil of hazardous materials under the National Oil or Hazardous Substances Pollution Contingency Plan.

Outcome Surveillance – To look for a health outcome or health event of interest, usually illness, injury, or death. Also known as the response variable, dependent variable, or effect variable. For example, the American Red Cross (ARC)/Centers for Disease Control and Prevention's Health Impact Surveillance System records mortality and morbidity in disaster events in which ARC has served.

Outcome Variable – A health event, usually encompassing illness, injury, or death. Also known as a response variable.

Overt Release – An announced release of a biological agent, by terrorists or others. This type of release allows for treatment before the onset of disease.

Phases of the Functional Model – The functional model is composed of six phases, each corresponding to a type of activity involved in preparing for and responding to a disaster. The phases include planning, prevention, assessment, response, surveillance, and recovery.

Planning – To work cooperatively with others in advance of a disaster in order to initiate prevention and preparedness activities.

Post–Disaster Surveillance – Observations conducted by health authorities after a disaster in order to monitor health events, detect sudden changes in disease occurrence, follow long term trends of specific diseases, identify changes in agents and host factors for the diseases of interest, and detect changes in health practices for treating disease.

Postimpact Phase – The period of time after a disaster event. Often associated with the activities of response and recovery.

Public Information Officer– The official at headquarters or in the field responsible for preparing, coordinating, and disseminating public information. The public information officer relies on the cooperation of federal, state, and local agencies.

Pre–impact Phase – The period of time before a disaster strikes. Often associated with mitigation and prevention activities.

Preparedness – All measures and policies taken before an event occurs that allow for prevention, mitigation, and readiness. Preparedness includes designing warning systems, planning for evacuation and relocation, storing food and water, building temporary shelter, devising management strategies, and holding disaster drills and exercises. Contingency planning is also included in preparedness as well as planning for post–impact response and recovery.

Prevention – Primary, secondary, and tertiary efforts that help avert an emergency. These activities are commonly referred to as "mitigation" in the emergency management model. For example, prevention activities include cloud seeding to stimulate rain in a fire. In public health terms, prevention refers to actions that prevent the onset or deterioration of disease, disability, and injury.

Primary Prevention – Preventing the occurrence of death, injury, or illness in a disaster (eg, evacuation of a community in a flood–prone area, sensitizing warning systems for tornadoes and severe storms).

Public Access System – An emergency telephone system by which the public notifies authorities of a medical emergency. Accessed by dialing 911.

Public Health Surveillance – The systematic collection, analysis, and interpretation of the health data that is used to plan, implement, and evaluate public health programs. Also used to determine the need for public health action.

Radio Bands – A collection of neighboring radio frequencies. Frequencies are allocated on different bands. Each two–way radio is designed for a specific band. For example, a radio designed to work on one band will not work on another band.

Rapid Needs Assessment – A collection of techniques (ie, epidemiologic, statistical, anthropological) designed to provide information about an affected community's needs following a disaster.

Readiness – Links preparedness to relief. An assessment of readiness reflects the current capacity and capabilities of the organizations involved in relief activities.

Recovery – Actions of responders, government, and the victims that help return an affected community to normal by stimulating community cohesiveness and government involvement. One type of recovery involves repairing infrastructure, damaged buildings, and critical facilities. The recovery period falls between the onset of the emergency and the reconstruction period.

Recovery Plan– A plan to restore areas affected by disaster. Developed on a state–by–state basis with assistance from responding federal agencies.

Red Cross – (also known as the American Red Cross, or the International Red Cross) A comprehensive designation used for all or one the components of the International Red Cross and Red Crescent Movement, a worldwide organization active in humanitarian work. This organization has 3 components: The International Committee of the Red Cross (ICRC), which acts primarily as a neutral intermediary during armed conflict. ICRC also includes the Guardian of the Geneva Conventions, an advocate for the protection of war victims. The League of the Red Cross and Red Crescent Societies (LRCS): an international federation of the National Societies, active in non–conflict disasters and natural calamities; and the National Red Cross or Red Crescent Society a worldwide relief organization specific to individual countries.

Rehabilitation or Reconstruction – A long–term development project that follows a disaster or emergency that reconstructs a community's infrastructure to pre–existing levels. Reconstruction is often associated with an opportunity to improve a community rather than to simply 'reconstruct' a pre–existing system.

Regional Operations Center (ROC)– Temporary operations facility used in the coordination of federal response and recovery activities. Located at the FEMA Regional Office (or at the Federal Regional Center) and led by the FEMA Regional Director or Deputy Regional Director until the Disaster Field Office becomes operational.

Relief – Action focused on saving lives. Relief activities often include search and rescue missions, first aid, and restoration of emergency communications and transportation systems. Relief also includes attention to the immediate care of survivors by providing food, clothing, medical treatment, and emotional care.

Report Format – The instrument on which surveillance data are reported.

Reporting Unit for Surveillance – The data source that provides information for the surveillance system. Reporting units often include hospitals, clinics, health posts, and mobile health units. Epidemiologists select reporting units after they define "what is a case" because the source of data is dependent on that definition.

Representativeness – The accuracy of the data when measuring the occurrence of a health event over time and its distribution by person and place.

Resource Management – See page [x].

Response – The phase in a disaster when relief, recovery, and rehabilitation occur. Also includes the delivery of services, the management of activities and programs designed to address the immediate and short–term effects of an emergency or disaster.

Richter Scale – A scale that indicates the magnitude of an earthquake by providing a measure of the total energy released from the source of the quake. The source of an earthquake is the segment of the fault that has slipped.

Risk Assessment –A systematic process that determines the likelihood of adverse health effects to a population after exposure to a hazard. Health consequences may depend on the type of hazard and damage to infrastructure, loss of economic value, loss of function, loss of natural resources, loss of ecological systems, and environmental impacts and deterioration of health, mortality, and morbidity. The major components of a risk assessment include a hazard identification analysis and a vulnerability analysis that answer the following questions: What are the hazards that could effect a community? What can happen as a result of those haazards? How likely is each of the possible outcomes? When the possible outcomes occur, what are the likely consequences and losses? Risk assessment is a fundamental planning tool for disaster management, especially during prevention and mitigation activities.

Risk as a Function of Hazard and Vulnerability – A relationship that is frequently illustrated with the following formula, although the association is not strictly arithmetic: Risk = Hazard * Vulnerability

Risk Indicator – Descriptor that denotes risks that may cause a disaster.

Risk Management – The process of deciding which action to take when a risk assessment indicates that a danger of loss exists. Risk management includes a range of actions (eg, prevention, mitigation, preparedness, recovery) that are designed to mitigate an increasing risk of natural and technological hazards; decrease a risk to existing levels; and plan ways to respond to natural and technological hazards as well as catastrophic events.

Saffir–Simpson Scale – A scale used to measure strength of hurricanes.

Secondary Prevention– Mitigates the health consequences of disasters. Examples include the use of carbon monoxide detectors when operating gasoline–powered generators after the loss of electric power, employing appropriate occupant behavior in multistory structures during earthquakes, and building "safe rooms" in dwellings located in tornado–prone areas. Secondary prevention may be instituted when disasters are imminent.

Section – See page 178.

Size–up – See page 178.

Span of Control – The number of resources under the control of one supervisor.

Staging Area – See page 178.

State Coordinating Officer– An official designated by the governor of an affected state upon the declaration of a major disaster or emergency to coordinate state and local disaster assistance efforts with those of the federal government and to act in cooperation with the FCO to administer disaster recovery efforts.

Stockpile – An area or storehouse where medicine and other supplies are kept in the event of an emergency.

Stress – Physical, mental, or emotional strain or tension.

Strike Team – See page 178.

Supply Management Program (SUMA) – A computer system that sorts and classifies supplies in order to prepare inventories of relief supplies that are sent to disaster–stricken countries. Developed by the Pan American Health Organization.

Surveillance –The ongoing and systematic collection, analysis, and interpretation of health data essential to the planning, implementation, and evaluation of public health practice. Surveillance systems are designed to disseminate data in a timely manner and often includes both data collection and disease monitoring.

Task Force – See page 178.

Technological Hazard – A potential threat to human welfare caused by technological factors (eg, chemical release, nuclear accident, dam failure). Earthquakes and other natural hazards can trigger technological hazards as well.

Tertiary Prevention – The minimization of the effects of disease and disability among those with pre–existing health conditions. Tertiary prevention shields persons with health conditions from negative health effects relating to a disaster. Examples of tertiary prevention include protecting persons with respiratory illnesses and those prone to respiratory conditions from the haze and smoke that originates from forest fires and sheltering elderly who are prone to heat illnesses during episodes of extreme ambient temperatures.

Timeliness – How quickly information or surveillance data can be made available.

Toxicological Disaster – A serious environmental pollutant that causes illness by a massive, accidental escape of toxic substances into the air, soil or water. Toxicological disasters affect man, animals and plants.

Toxin – A substance capable of causing a harmful effect.

Treatment Technique (TT) – An enforceable procedure or level of technological performance that public water systems must follow to ensure control of a water contaminant. When there is no reliable method that is economically and technically feasible to measure contaminants at particularly low concentrations, a treatment technique (TT) is set rather than a maximum contaminant level (MCL). An example of a treatment technique rule is the surface water treatment rule, which includes disinfection and filtration.

Triage – To select and categorize victims of a disaster for appropriate medical treatment according to the degree of severity of illness or injury as well as for the availability of medical and transport facilities.

Transportation to Definitive Medical Care – Ground ambulances are the vehicle of choice for most medical transports, but helicopters, boats, and snow cats may also be used. Medical transports allow for the continued medical support of patients while in transport from the field to a hospital.

Traumatic Stress – While not a clearly defined condition, traumatic stress has tended to include events and circumstances that are both extreme and outside of the realm of everyday experiences (eg, events that are dangerous, overwhelming, and sudden marked by their extreme or sudden force, typically causing fear, anxiety, withdrawal, and avoidance). Traumatic events also have high intensity, are unexpected, infrequent, and vary in duration from acute to chronic.

Tsunami – An oceanic tidal wave generated by underwater upheavals such as earthquakes and volcanic eruptions. Tsunami waves move out in all directions and can travel over 100 miles and cause massive destruction.

Tsunami Run Up – A type of ground failure that affects low lying areas along coastlines and results from long periods of high ocean waves that are generated by the sudden, impulsive, vertical displacement of a submarine earthquake.

Victim – Persons who have been affected by a disaster. There are three classes of victims:

Primary Victims – Those who are affected by the physical impact of the disaster.

Secondary Victims – Those who reside within an affected community or on the border of an affected area and suffer economic loss due to the disaster or actions taken by relief operations.

Tertiary Victims – Those who are indirectly affected. Tertiary victims may live in the same country, but not necessarily in the disaster area.

Top–down – See page 178.

Unity of Command – See page 178.

Victim Distribution – A victim distribution plan defines the transport and distribution of victims among neighboring hospitals according to their hospital treatment capacity. Victim distribution plans often avoid taking victims to the nearest hospital since walking victims will overcrowd hospitals closest to the disaster site.

Voluntary agency (VOLAG) – A non–profit, non–governmental, private association maintained and supported by voluntary contributions that provides assistance in emergencies and disasters.

Vulnerability – The susceptibility of a population to a specific type of event. Vulnerability is also associated with the degree of possible or potential loss from a risk that results from a hazard at a given intensity. The factors that influence vulnerability include demographics, the age and resilience of the environment, technology, social differentiation and diversity as well as regional and global economics and politics.

Vulnerability Analysis – The assessment of an exposed population's susceptibility to the adverse health effects of a particular hazard.

Warning and forecasting – Monitoring events to determine the time, location, and severity of a disaster.

Weapons of Mass Destruction (WMD) – A WMD is any device, material, or substance used in a manner, in a quantity or type, or under circumstances evidencing an intent to cause death or serious injury to persons or significant damage of property.

Acronyms Commonly Used in Disaster Preparedness, Response, and Recovery

ARC	American Red Cross
CAT	Crisis Action Team
CCP	Casualty Collection Point
CDC	Centers for Disease Control and Prevention, United States Public Health Service
CDRG	Catastrophic Disaster Response Group
CEPPO	Chemical Emergency Preparedness and Prevention Office
CERCLA	Comprehensive Environmental Response, Compensation, and Liability Act
CFR	Code of Federal Regulations
CINC	Commander-in-Chief
CMT	Crisis Management Team
CRC	Crisis Response Cell
CRM	Crisis Resource Manager
CWA	Clean Water Act
DAE	Disaster Assistance Employee
DFO	Disaster Field Office
DFSG	Disaster Financial Services Group
DMAT	Disaster Medical Assistance Team
DMORT	Disaster Mortuary Response Team, National Disaster Medical System
DWI	Disaster Welfare Inquiry

EC	Emergency Coordinator
ECS	Emergency Communications Staff
EEI	Essential Elements of Information
EICC	Emergency Information and Coordination Center
EMS	Emergency Medical Services
EMT	Emergency Medical Technician
EOC	Emergency Operations Center
EPA	Environmental Protection Agency
ERC	Emergency Response Coordinator
ERCG	Emergency Response Coordination Group, Public Health Service,Centers for Disease Control and Agency for Toxic Substances and Disease Registry
ERT	Emergency Response Team
ERT-A	Advance Element of the Emergency Response Team
ESF	Emergency Support Function
EST	Emergency Support Team
FAA	Federal Aviation Administration
FBI	Federal Bureau of Investigation
FCC	Federal Communications Commission
FCO	Federal Coordinating Officer
FECC	Federal Emergency Communications Coordinator
FEMA	Federal Emergency Management Agency
FERC	FEMA Emergency Response Capability
FESC	Federal Emergency Support Coordinator
FHWA	Federal Highway Administration
FNS	Food and Nutrition Services
FRCM	FEMA Regional Communications Manager
FRERP	Federal Radiological Emergency Response Plan
GSA	General Services Administration
HAZMAT	Hazardous material
HET-ESF	Headquarters Emergency Transportation – Emergency Support Function
HF	High Frequency
HHS	Department of Health and Human Services
HQUSACE	Headquarters, United States Army Corps of Engineers
HUD	Department of Housing and Urban Development
HWC	Health and Welfare Canada
IAEA	International Atomic Energy Agency
ICC	Interstate Commerce Commission
ICPAE	Interagency Committee on Public Affairs in Emergencies
ICRC	International Committee of the Red Cross

ICS	Incident Command System
IMS	Incident Management System
JCAHO	Joint Committee on Accreditation of Health Care Organizations
MARS	United States Army Military Affiliate Radio System
MASF	Mobile Aeromedical Staging Facility
MC	Mobilization Center
MMWR	Morbidity and Mortality Weekly Report, published by the Centers for Disease Control and Prevention
MOA	Memorandum of Agreement
MOU	Memorandum of Understanding
MRE	Meals Ready to Eat
NASA	National Aeronautics and Space Administration
NCC	National Coordinating Center
NCP	National Oil and Hazardous Substances Pollution Contingency Plan
NCS	National Communications System
NCS/DCA-OC	National Communications System/Defense Communication Agency – Operations Center
NDMOC	National Disaster Medical Operations Center
NDMS	National Disaster Medical System
NDMSOSC	National Disaster Medical System Operations Support Center
NECC	National Emergency Coordination Center (FEMA)
NEIS	National Earthquake Information Service
NFDA	National Funeral Directors Association
NGO	Non-Governmental Organization
NICC	National Interagency Coordination Center
NIFCC	National Interagency Fire Coordination Center, United States Forest Service
NIMH	National Institutes of Mental Health
NOAA	National Oceanic and Atmospheric Administration
NP	National Preparedness
NRC	Nuclear Regulatory Commission
NRT	National Response Team
NSEP	National Security Emergency Preparedness
NSF	National Strike Force
NTIA	National Telecommunications and Information Administration
NTSP	National Telecommunications Support Plan
NVOAD	National Voluntary Organizations Active in Disaster

NWS	National Weather Service
OCHAMPUS	Office of Civilian Health and Medical Program of the Uniformed Services, Department of Defense
OEP	Office of Emergency Preparedness, United States Public Health Service
OET	Office of Emergency Transportation
OFDA	Office of United States Foreign Disaster Assistance
OSC	On-Scene Coordinator
OSHA	Occupational Safety and Health Administration
PAHO	Pan-American Health Organization
PHS	United States Public Health Service, Department of Health and Human Services
PIO	Public Information Officer
PVO	Private Voluntary Organization
RACES	Radio Amateur Civil Emergency Services
RCP	Regional Oil and Hazardous Substances Pollution Contingency Plan
RD	Regional Director
REACT	Radio Emergency Associated Communication Team
REC	Regional Emergency Coordinator
RECC	Regional Emergency Communications Coordinator
RECP	Regional Emergency Communications Plan
REP	Regional Evacuation Point
RET	Regional Emergency Transportation
RETCO	Regional Emergency Transportation Coordinator
RHA	Regional Health Administrator (Department of Health and Human Services)
RISC	Regional Inter-Agency Steering Committee
SAMHSA	Substance Abuse and Mental Health Services Administration
S	Staging Area
SAR	Search and Rescue
SARA	Superfund Amendments and Reauthorization Act
SCO	State Coordinating Officer
SLPS	State and Local Programs and Support Directorate (FEMA)
SOP	Standard Operating Procedure
UNDRO	United Nations Disaster Relief Organization
UNHCR	United Nations High Commission for Refugees
UNICEF	United Nations International Children's Education Fund
US	United States

USACE	United States Army Corps of Engineers
USAID	United States Agency for International Development
USCG	United States Coast Guard
USDA	United States Department of Agriculture
USGS	United States Geological Survey
USPHS	United States Public Health Service
US&R	Urban Search and Rescue
VA	Department of Veterans Affairs
VHA	Veterans Health Administration, Department of Veterans Affairs
VOAD	Voluntary Organizations Active in Disaster
WHO	World Health Organization

Appendix **C**

Useful Internet Sites

Note: All web addresses are correct as of September 1, 2001.

INFORMATION ON HAZARDS:

http://www.redcross.org/disaster/safety/index.html
http://www.redcross.org/disaster/safety/cde.html
http://disaster.ifas.ufl.edu
http://www.iso.com
http://www.iso.com/docs/news.htm
http://www.paho.org.disasters

THE AGENCY FOR TOXIC SUBSTANCES AND DISEASE REGISTRY, PUBLIC HEALTH SERVICE, UNITED STATES DEPARTMENT OF HEALTH AND HUMAN SERVICE

http://www.atsdr.cdc.gov

THE AMERICAN COUNSELING ASSOCIATION

http://www.counseling.org

THE AMERICAN PUBLIC HEALTH ASSOCIATION

http://www.apha.org

THE AMERICAN PSYCHIATRIC ASSOCIATION

http://www.psych.org

THE AMERICAN PSYCHOLOGICAL ASSOCIATION'S DISASTER RESPONSE NETWORK

http://www.apa.org/practice

THE AMERICAN RED CROSS

http://www.redcross.org

ANIMAL MANAGEMENT IN DISASTERS

http://www.animaldisasters.com

THE AMERICAN PSYCHOLOGICAL ASSOCIATION'S HELPING PAGE

http://helping.apa.org

THE ARMED FORCES INSTITUTE OF PATHOLOGY

http://www.afip.org

THE ARMED FORCES RADIOBIOLOGY RESEARCH INSTITUTE

http://www.afrri.usuhs.mil

CANADIAN CENTER FOR EMERGENCY PREPAREDNESS

http://www.ccep.ca

THE CENTER FOR CIVILIAN BIODEFENSE STUDIES, JOHNS HOPKINS UNIVERSITY

http://www.hopkins-biodefense.org

THE CENTERS FOR DISEASE CONTROL AND PREVENTION

http://www.cdc.gov
http://www.cdc.gov/ncidod/diseases/bioterr.htm
http://www.cdc.gov/ncidod/diseases/foodborn/botu.htm
http://www.cdc.gov/ncidod/srp/drugservice/immunodrugs.htm
see following: http://www.cdc.gov/ncidod/hip/redirects.htm

THE CENTERS FOR DISEASE CONTROL AND PREVENTION, BIOTERRORISM PREPAREDNESS & RESPONSE

http://www.bt.cdc.gov

THE CENTERS FOR DISEASE CONTROL AND PREVENTION, HEALTH ALERT NETWORK

http://www.phppo.cdc.gov/han

THE CENTER FOR EARTHQUAKE RESEARCH AND INFORMATION AT THE UNIVERSITY OF MEMPHIS

http://www.ceri.memphis.edu

THE CENTER FOR FOOD SAFETY AND APPLIED NUTRITION, UNITED STATES FOOD AND DRUG ADMINISTRATION

http://vm.cfsan.fda.gov/list.html

THE CENTER FOR MENTAL HEALTH SERVICES

http://www.samhsa.gov/cmhs/cmhs.htm

THE CENTER FOR RESEARCH ON THE EPIDEMIOLOGY OF DISASTERS

http://www.md.ucl.ac.be/cred/front_uk.htm

THE DEFENSE THREAT REDUCTION AGENCY - CHEM-BIO DEFENSE

http://www.dtra.mil

THE DEPARTMENT OF HEALTH AND HUMAN SERVICES (DHHS), OFFICE OF EMERGENCY PREPAREDNESS (OEP)

http://ndms.dhhs.gov

THE DEPARTMENT OF HEALTH AND HUMAN SERVICES (DHHS), OEP, NATIONAL DISASTER MEDICAL SYSTEM

http://ndms.dhhs.gov/NDMS/ndms.html

THE DEPARTMENT OF DEFENSE, DEPARTMENT OF THE ARMY, DIRECTOR OF MILITARY SUPPORT

http://www.dtic.mil

THE DEPARTMENT OF DEFENSE, NUCLEAR, BIOLOGICAL, CHEMICAL MEDICAL REFERENCE SITE

http://www.nbc-med.org/others

THE DEPARTMENT OF DEFENSE, OFFICE OF COUNTERPROLIFERATION AND CHEMICAL/BIOLOGICAL DEFENSE

http://www.acq.osd.mil/cp

THE DEPARTMENT OF JUSTICE, OFFICE OF STATE AND LOCAL DOMESTIC PREPAREDNESS SUPPORT

http://www.ojp.usdoj.gov/osldps

DISASTER COMMUNICATIONS HANDBOOK

http://www.itu.int/ITU-D-StGrps/SGP_1998-2002/SG2/
documents/DocList.htm

DISASTER MEDICINE AND MENTAL HEALTH

http://www.mentalhealth.org/cmhs/EmergencyServices

THE DISASTER MENTAL HEALTH INSTITUTE (DMHI), UNIVERSITY OF SOUTH DAKOTA

http://www.usd.edu/dmhi

THE DISASTER CENTER

http://www.disastercenter.com

THE DISASTER RESEARCH CENTER, UNIVERSITY OF DELAWARE

http://www.udel.edu/DRC

EARTHQUAKES

http://www.geohaz.org/radius

EARTHQUAKE ENGINEERING RESEARCH LIBRARY CALIFORNIA INSTITUTE OF TECHNOLOGY

(National Information Service for Earthquake Engineering)

http://www.eerl.caltech.edu/#nisee

EFFECTIVE DISASTER WARNINGS

http://www.noaa.gov
http://www.fema.gov/nwz00/effectivedoc.htm

THE EMERGENCY INFORMATION INFRASTRUCTURE PARTNERSHIP

http://www.emforum.org

THE EMERGENCY NET, EMERGENCY RESPONSE AND RESEARCH INSTITUTE

http://www.emergency.com

THE ENVIRONMENTAL PROTECTION AGENCY, CHEMICAL EMERGENCY PREPAREDNESS AND PREVENTION OFFICE

http://www.epa.gov/swercepp
http://www.epa.gov/ceppo

THE ENVIRONMENTAL PROTECTION AGENCY, SAFE WATER

http://www.epa.gov/safewater/pws/pn

FEDERAL OFFICES INVOLVED IN WEAPONS OF MASS DESTRUCTION

http://www.cns.miis.edu

FEDERAL EMERGENCY MANAGEMENT AGENCY

http://www.fema.gov

THE FEDERAL EMERGENCY MANAGEMENT AGENCY'S HIGHER EDUCATION PROJECT

http://www.fema.gov/EMI/edu

FIRST RESPONDERS.COM

http://wmdfirstresponders.com

FLOOD INSURANCE MANUAL, THE FEDERAL EMERGENCY MANAGEMENT AGENCY

http://www.fema.gov/nfip/manual.htm

THE GLOBAL EMERGING INFECTIONS SURVEILLANCE AND RESPONSE SYSTEM, DEPARTMENT OF DEFENSE

http://141.236.12.246

GREEN CROSS

http://psy.uq.edu.au/PTSD/trauma/ogcross.html

HEALTH INFORMATION NETWORK FOR ADVANCED PLANNING (HINAP)

http://www.who.int/hinap

HENRY L. STIMSON CENTER, CHEMICAL AND BIOLOGICAL WEAPONS NON-PROLIFERATION PROJECT

http://www.stimson.org

HOSPITAL EMERGENCY INCIDENT COMMAND SYSTEM (HEICS III)

http://www.emsa.ca.gov/dms2/history.htm

INTERNATIONAL ASSOCIATION OF EMERGENCY MANAGERS

http://www.iaem.com

INTERNATIONAL CRITICAL INCIDENT STRESS FOUNDATION (ICISF)

http://www.icisf.org

INTERNATIONAL FEDERATION OF THE RED CROSS

http://www.ifrc.org

INTERNATIONAL RESCUE COMMITTEE

http://www.intrescom.org

INTERNATIONAL SOCIETY FOR TRAUMATIC STRESS STUDIES (ISTSS)

http://www.istss.org

JOINT PROGRAM OFFICE-BIODEFENSE, DEPARTMENT OF DEFENSE, OFFICE OF BIODEFENSE EQUIPMENT DEVELOPMENT

http://www.jpobd.net

JOINT SERVICE CHEMICAL BIOLOGICAL INFORMATION SYSTEM, DEPARTMENT OF DEFENSE, TRACKING SYSTEM FOR EQUIPMENT DEVELOPMENT

http://206.37.238.107/jscbis/jscbis.cfm

THE LAWRENCE LIVERMORE NATIONAL LABORATORY

http://www.llnl.gov

THE NATIONAL ACADEMIES OF SCIENCE, INSTITUTE OF MEDICINE

http://www4.nas.edu/IOM/IOMHome.nsf

THE NATIONAL ASSOCIATION OF COUNTY AND CITY HEALTH OFFICIALS (NACCHO), BT SITE

http://www.naccho.org

THE NATIONAL ASSOCIATION OF SOCIAL WORKERS (NASW), DISASTER STRESS

http://www.socialworkers.org/Practice/distips.htm

THE NATIONAL DOMESTIC PREPAREDNESS CONSORTIUM, ACADEMIC CONSORTIUM

http://www.emrtc.nmt.edu

THE NATIONAL DOMESTIC PREPAREDNESS OFFICE, FEDERAL BUREAU OF INVESTIGATIONS

http://www.ndpo.gov

THE NATIONAL EARTHQUAKE INFORMATION CENTER

http://neic.usgs.gov
http://neic.usgs.gov/products_and_services.html
http://neic.usgs.gov/neis/pANDs/neic_maps.html

THE NATIONAL EMERGENCY MANAGEMENT ASSOCIATION

http://www.nemaweb.org/index.cfm

THE NATIONAL EMERGENCY RESCUE AND RESPONSE TRAINING CENTER, TEXAS A&M UNIVERSITY

http://teexweb.tamu.edu/nerrtc

THE NATIONAL INSTITUTES OF HEALTH

http://www.nih.gov

THE NATIONAL INSTITUTE FOR OCCUPATIONAL SAFETY AND HEALTH

http://www.cdc.gov/niosh

NATIONAL OCEANIC AND ATMOSPHERIC ADMINISTRATION

http:// www.noaa.gov

NATIONAL ORGANIZATION FOR VICTIM ASSISTANCE (NOVA)

http://www.try-nova.org

THE NATIONAL RESPONSE CENTER, UNITED STATES COAST GUARD

http://www.nrc.uscg.mil

THE NATIONAL RESPONSE TEAM, HAZMAT & CHEMICAL SPILLS

http://www.nrt.org

NATIONAL VOLUNTARY ORGANIZATIONS ACTIVE IN DISASTER (NVOAD)

http://www.nvoad.org

THE NATIONAL WEATHER SERVICE

http://www.nws.noaa.gov

NATURAL HAZARDS CENTER, UNIVERSITY OF COLORADO

http://www.colorado.edu/hazards

THE OCCUPATIONAL SAFETY AND HEALTH ADMINISTRATION

http://www.osha.gov

THE OFFICE OF FOREIGN DISASTER ASSISTANCE

http://www.info.usaid.gov/ofda

PAN-AMERICAN HEALTH ORGANIZATION (PAHO)

http://www.paho.org

PUBLIC HEALTH LAW PROGRAM, CENTERS FOR DISEASE CONTROL AND PREVENTION

http://www.phppo.cdc.gov/phlawnet

PUBLIC HEALTH SERVICE (DHHS) OFFICE OF EMERGENCY PREPAREDNESS, THE NATIONAL DISASTER MEDICAL SYSTEM

http://ndms.dhhs.gov

REGIONAL DISASTER INFORMATION CENTER (CRID, SAN JOSE, COSTA RICA)

http://www.disaster.info.desastres/crid

RELIEFWEB

http://www.reliefweb.int

SOUTHERN CALIFORNIA EARTHQUAKE CENTER

http://www.scec.org

THE UNITED NATIONS HIGH COMMISSIONER FOR REFUGEES (UNHCR)

http://www.unhcr.ch

UNITED STATES ARMY CHEMICAL SCHOOL

http://www.wood.army.mil/usacmls

UNITED STATES ARMY MEDICAL COMMAND

http://www.armymedicine.army.mil/armymed/default2.htm

UNITED STATES ARMY MEDICAL RESEARCH INSTITUTE OF CHEMICAL DEFENSE

http://chemdef.apgea.army.mil

UNITED STATES ARMY MEDICAL RESEARCH AND MATERIAL COMMAND

http://mrmc-www.army.mil

UNITED STATES ARMY CENTER FOR HEALTH PROMOTION & PREVENTIVE MEDICINE

http://www.apgea.army.mil

UNITED STATES ARMY MEDICAL RESEARCH INSTITUTE OF INFECTIOUS DISEASES (USAMRIID)

http://www.usamriid.army.mil

UNITED STATES ARMY NATIONAL GUARD BUREAU

http://www.ngb.dtic.mil

UNITED STATES ARMY SOLDIER AND BIOLOGICAL CHEMICAL COMMAND (SBCCOM)

http://www.sbccom.apgea.army.mil

UNITED STATES ARMY SOLDIER AND BIOLOGICAL CHEMICAL COMMAND (SBCCOM), PROGRAM DIRECTOR FOR DOMESTIC PREPAREDNESS

http://dp.sbccom.army.mil

THE UNITED STATES CENSUS BUREAU

http://www.census.gov

UNITED STATES COAST GUARD, NATIONAL RESPONSE CENTER

http://www.nrc.uscg.mil

THE UNITED STATES GEOLOGICAL SURVEY

http://www.usgs.gov

THE UNITED STATES GEOLOGICAL SURVEY VOLCANO HAZARDS PROGRAM

http://volcanoes.usgs.gov
http://volcanoes.usgs.gov/educators.html

THE UNITED STATES NAVY CHEMICAL/BIOLOGICAL PROGRAM

http://www.chembiodef.navy.mil

UNIVERSITY OF WISCONSIN DISASTER MANAGEMENT CENTER

http://epdwww.engr.wisc.edu/dmc

THE WORLD HEALTH ORGANIZATION (WHO)

http://www.who.int

PERIODICALS & PUBLICATIONS:

AGENCY FOR TOXIC SUBSTANCES AND DISEASE NEWSLETTER, DHHS

http://www.atsdr.cdc.gov/HEC/hsphhome.html

AIR UNIVERSITY INDEX TO MILITARY PERIODICALS

http://www.dtic.mil/search97doc/aulimp/main.htm

THE BEACON, NATIONAL DISASTER PREPAREDNESS OFFICE, FEDERAL BUREAU OF INVESTIGATIONS

http://www.ndpo.gov/beacon.htm

BIODEFENSE QUARTERLY, CENTER FOR CIVILIAN BIODEFENSE STUDIES, JOHNS HOPKINS UNIVERSITY

http://www.hopkins-biodefense.org

CB QUARTERLY, THE UNITED STATES ARMY SOLDIERS AND BIOLOGICAL CHEMICAL COMMAND

http://www.sbccom.apgea.army.mil/RDA/ecbc/quarterly/index.htm

DISPATCH, THE CHEMICAL AND BIOLOGICAL ARMS CONTROL INSTITUTE

http://www.cbaci.org

EMERGING INFECTIOUS DISEASES, CENTERS FOR DISEASE CONTROL AND PREVENTION, NATIONAL CENTER FOR INFECTIOUS DISEASES

http://www.cdc.gov/ncidod/eid/index.htm

EMERGENCY INFORMATION INFRASTRUCTURE PARTNERSHIP NEWSLETTER

http://www.emforum.org/eiip/news.htm

EMERGENCY MEDICAL SERVICES MAGAZINE

http://www.emsmagazine.com

THE FEDERAL EMERGENCY MANAGEMENT AGENCY'S NEWS LISTING

http://www.fema.gov/fema/news.htm

MEDICINE AND GLOBAL SURVIVAL MAGAZINE

http://www.ipnw.org/MGS

MORBIDITY AND MORTALITY WEEKLY REPORT, CENTERS FOR DISEASE CONTROL AND PREVENTION

http://www.cdc.gov/mmwr

NATIONAL FIRE AND RESCUE MAGAZINE

http://www.nfrmag.com

OSHA JOB SAFETY AND HEALTH QUARTERLY MAGAZINE

http://www.osha-slc.gov/html/jshq-index.html

PROCEDURES, PROTOCOLS, INCIDENT COMMAND INFORMATION AND RESPONSE RESOURCES:

BIOTERRORISM READINESS PLAN: A TEMPLATE FOR HEALTHCARE FACILITIES, CENTERS FOR DISEASE CONTROL AND PREVENTION

http://www.cdc.gov/ncidod/hip/BIO/bio.htm

THE DEPARTMENT OF HEALTH AND HUMAN SERVICES, OFFICE OF EMERGENCY PREPAREDNESS

http://ndms.dhhs.gov/CT_Program/Response_Planning/response_planning.html

THE FEDERAL EMERGENCY MANAGEMENT AGENCY, FEDERAL RESPONSE PLAN

http://www.fema.gov/r-n-r/frp

FEDERAL EMERGENCY MANAGEMENT AGENCY REFERENCE LIBRARY

http://www.fema.gov/library

THE FEDERAL EMERGENCY MANAGEMENT AGENCY, STATE AND LOCAL GUIDE (SLG) 101: GUIDE FOR ALL-HAZARD EMERGENCY OPERATIONS PLANNING

http://www.fema.gov/pte/gaheop.htm

HOSPITAL PROCEDURES FOR WMD EVENT, JAMA ARTICLE

http://jama.ama-assn.org/issues/v283n2/full/jsc90100.html

INCIDENT COMMAND SYSTEM, FORMS AND GUIDES

http://www.uscg.mil/pacarea/pm/icsforms/ics.htm

JOINT INFORMATION CENTER GUIDE, THE NATIONAL RESPONSE TEAM, JAN 21, 2000

http:/www.nrt.org/nrt/home.nsf/Web+Pages/publications.htm/$FILE/JIC.pdf

NATIONAL FLOOD INSURANCE MANUAL

http://www.fema.gov/nfip/manual.htm

THE NATIONAL RESPONSE CENTER, CHEMICAL/HAZMAT SPILLS

http://www.nrc.uscg.mil/index.html

RAPID RESPONSE INFORMATION SYSTEM (RRIS), THE FEDERAL EMERGENCY MANAGEMENT AGENCY

http://www.rris.fema.gov

REPORT OF THE WEATHER CHANNEL FORUM: POLICY ISSUES IN HURRICANE PREPAREDNESS AND RESPONSE

http://www.ametsoc.org/ams/atmospolicy
http://www.ametsoc.org/ams/atmospolicy/forumreports/index.html

REFERENCE WEBSITES:

ANTHRAX, DEPARTMENT OF DEFENSE

http://www.anthrax.osd.mil

ATSDR TOXFAQS, MEDICAL SUMMARY SHEETS FOR HAZARDOUS MATERIAL

http://www.atsdr.cdc.gov/toxfaq.html

BIBLIOGRAPHY OF TERRORISM, THE DISASTER CENTER

http://www.disastercenter.com/terror.htm

CHEMICAL CONTAMINATION TREATMENT GUIDELINES. MEDICAL MANAGEMENT GUIDELINES FOR ACUTE CHEMICAL EXPOSURES. AGENCY FOR TOXIC SUBSTANCES AND DISEASE REGISTRY

http://www.astdr.cdc.gov/mmg.html

CNS-CHEMICAL AND BIOLOGICAL WEAPONS RESOURCE PAGE

http://cns.miis.edu/research/cbw/index.htm

THE DEPARTMENT OF DEFENSE'S SEARCH ENGINE FOR FEDERAL LAWS, REGULATIONS AND DOCUMENTS RELATING TO EMERGENCY MANAGEMENT

http://www.dtic.mil/doms/search_eadb

THE DEPARTMENT OF TRANSPORTATION, EMERGENCY RESPONSE GUIDEBOOK (FIRST RESPONDER'S GUIDE FOR HAZMAT OPERATIONS)

http://hazmat.dot.gov/erg2000/erg2000.pdf

DEVELOPING A HAZARDOUS MATERIALS EXERCISE PROGRAMS: A HANDBOOK FOR STATE AND LOCAL OFFICIALS, UNITED STATES DEPARTMENT OF TRANSPORTATION

http://www.bts.gov/smart/cat/254.html

EMERGING INFECTIOUS DISEASES, CENTERS FOR DISEASE CONTROL AND PREVENTION, NATIONAL CENTER FOR INFECTIOUS DISEASES

http://www.cdc.gov/ncidod/eid/vol5no4/pdf/v5n4.pdf

FEMA LIBRARY OF REFERENCE DOCUMENTS

http://www.fema.gov/library

FEDERAL RESPONSE EMERGENCY SUPPORT FUNCTION #8 HEALTH AND MEDICAL SERVICES PLAN, ANNEX

http://www.fema.gov/r-n-r/frp/frpesf8.htm

FIELD OPERATIONS GUIDE, OFFICE OF FOREIGN DISASTER ASSISTANCE, USAID

http://www.usaid.gov/ofda/fog/foghme.htm

FIELD OPERATING GUIDE, UNITED STATES COAST GUARD

http://www.uscg.mil/hq/g-m/mor/Articles/ICS.htm

FIRST RESPONDER HAZMAT GUIDE, UNITED STATES FIRE ADMINISTRATION, THE FEDERAL EMERGENCY MANAGEMENT AGENCY

http://www.usfa.fema.gov/hazmat/approach.htm

FOODBORNE PATHOGENIC MICROORGANISMS AND NATURAL TOXINS HANDBOOK, UNITED STATES FOOD AND DRUG ADMINISTRATION, CENTER FOR FOOD SAFETY & APPLIED NUTRITION

http://vm.cfsan.fda.gov

NATIONAL SECURITY INSTITUTE

http://nsi.org/terrorism.html

NIOSH POCKET GUIDE

http://www.cdc.gov/niosh/npg/html

ARTICLES ON TERRORISM, EMERGENCY RESPONSE AND RESEARCH INSTITUTE

http://www.emergency.com/cntrterr.htm

THE NATIONAL CENTER FOR INFECTIOUS DISEASES

http://www.cdc.gov/ncidod/publicat.htm

THE NATIONAL INSTITUTES OF HEALTH'S PERIODICAL LISTING
http://www.nih.gov/health/consumer/index.html

THE NATIONAL INSTITUTE OF OCCUPATIONAL SAFETY AND HEALTH (NIOSH) PUBLICATIONS

http://www.cdc.gov/niosh/publistd.html

THE NATIONAL LIBRARY OF MEDICINE

http://www.nlm.nih.gov

THE NATIONAL LIBRARY OF MEDICINE SEARCH SERVICE, PUBMED

http://www.ncbi.nlm.nih.gov/PubMed

NATIONAL TECHNICAL INFORMATION SERVICE HEALTH AND SAFETY

http://www.ntis.gov/health

PRO-MED MAIL PROGRAM FOR MONITORING EMERGING DISEASES, INTERNATIONAL SOCIETY FOR INFECTIOUS DISEASES

http://www.promedmail.org

RARE DISEASES, THE NATIONAL INSTITUTES OF HEALTH

http://rarediseases.info.nih.gov/ord

STRATEGIC PLAN, CENTERS FOR DISEASE CONTROL AND PREVENTION, NATIONAL CENTER FOR INFECTIOUS DISEASES

http://www.cdc.gov/ncidod/emergplan/1toc.htm

TOXNET, TOXICOLOGY DATA NETWORK, NATIONAL LIBRARY OF MEDICINE

http://toxnet.nlm.nih.gov

USA TODAY HEALTH INFORMATION/ARTICLE INDEX

http://www.usatoday.com/life/health/archive.htm

THE UNITED STATES ARMY MEDICAL DEPARTMENT INFORMATION SOURCES

http://www.armymedicine.army.mil/medcom/medlinet/virtual2.htm

THE UNITED STATES ARMY SURGEON GENERAL, NUCLEAR, BIOLOGICAL, CHEMICAL REFERENCE MATERIALS

http://www.nbc-med.org/others

FIRST AID KIT SUPPLIES

First aid supplies should be stored in a toolbox or fishing tackle box so they will be easy to carry and will be protected from water. The kit should be inspected regularly and kept freshly stocked. Important medical information and most prescriptions can be stored in the refrigerator, which also provides excellent protection from fires. In addition, copies of important papers (ie, driver's license, social security card, medical plan cards, insurance policies, personal phone book, contact information) should be secured.

FIRST AID KIT

- Drugs and Medications

- Hydrogen peroxide to wash and disinfect wounds

- Antibiotic ointment

- Individually wrapped alcohol swabs

- Aspirin and non-aspirin tablets

- Prescriptions and any long-term medications (keep prescriptions current)

- Diarrhea medicine

- Eye drops

- Dressings

- Bandage strips

- Ace bandages

- Rolled gauze

- Cotton-tipped swabs

- Adhesive tape roll

OTHER FIRST AID SUPPLIES

- First aid book

- Scissors

- Tweezers

- Thermometer

- Bar soap

- Tissues

- Sunscreen

- Paper cups

- Pocket knife

- Small plastic bags

- Safety pins

- Needle and thread

- Instant cold packs for sprains

- Sanitary napkins

- Splinting materials

SURVIVAL KIT SUPPLIES FOR THE HOME

- Tools and supplies

- Ax, shovel, broom

- Screwdriver, pliers, hammer, adjustable wrench

- Rope for towing or rescue

- Plastic sheeting and tape

ITEMS TO ENSURE SAFETY AND COMFORT

- Sturdy shoes that can provide protection from broken glass, nails, and other debris

- Gloves (rubber, heavy and durable for cleaning up debris)

- Candles

- Waterproof matches

- Change of clothing

- Knife

- Garden hose (for siphoning and fire fighting)

- Tent

- Recreational supplies for children and adults

- Blankets or sleeping bags

- Portable radio, flashlight, and extra batteries

- Essential over-the-counter medications and eyeglasses

- Fire extinguisher (multipurpose, dry chemical type)

- Food and water for pets

- Toilet tissue

- Cash

- Credit Card

SURVIVAL KIT FOR THE CAR

Assemble a survival kit for your automobile with the following list of items. Storing some of these supplies in a small bag or backpack will make them more convenient to carry if you need to walk.

- Blankets

- Bottled water

- Change of clothes

- Coins for telephone calls

- Fire extinguisher (multipurpose, dry chemical type)

- First aid kit and manual

- Emergency signal device (ie, light sticks, battery-type flasher, reflector.)

- Flashlight with fresh batteries

- Food (ie, nonperishable nutrition bars, trail mix.)

- Gloves

- Local map and a compass

- Rope for towing and rescue

- Paper and pencils

- Premoistened towelettes

- Prescription and over-the-counter medicines

- Battery-operated radio with fresh batteries

- Small mirror for signaling

- Toilet tissue

- Tools (ie, pliers, adjustable wrench, screwdriver)

- Whistle for signaling

- Jumper cables

- Duct tape

SURVIVAL KIT FOR THE WORKPLACE

- Food (ie, nonperishable nutrition bars and trail mix)

- Bottled water

- Jacket or sweatshirt

- Pair of sturdy shoes

- Flashlight with fresh batteries

- Battery-operated radio with fresh batteries

- Essential medications

- Blanket

- Small first aid kit

- Extra pair of eyeglasses and/or contact lens solution

- Whistle or other signaling device

Incident Commander's Considerations for Managing Nuclear, Biological, and Chemical Incident

ELEMENT OF COMMAND	OPERATIONAL CONSIDERATIONS	RESPONSE
Scene safety	Responder protection Secondary devices Shelter-in-place versus evacuation	Crew rotation
Command, control, and communication	Initial warning Incident Command Post location Evidence preservation and collection Airspace restriction	Apparatus approach Communication capabilities Management Transition to unified command
Medical support	Control patient's fear and modesty Casualty transport	Control patient's movement On-scene treatment
Decontamination	Casualty decontamination Water source for decontamination	Decontaminate the site Decontaminate site's run-off
Media and public information	Overwhelming response	Information control
Resource management	Available resources	Additional resources

List of Offices of the Federal Emergency Management Agency (FEMA)

FEMA
500 C Street S.W.
Washington, D.C. 20472

Office of the Director
Office of the Inspector General
Office of National Preparedness
Office of Strategic Planning & Evaluation
Office of General Counsel
Office of Equal Rights

Regional Operations
Federal Insurance & Mitigation Administration
Preparedness Training and Exercises
Response & Recovery
Public Affairs
Financial Management
Inspector General
Equal Rights

REGIONAL FEMA OFFICES

FEMA Region I
442 J.W. McCormack POCH
Boston, MA 02109-4595

Serves Maine, New Hampshire, Vermont, Rhode Island, Connecticut, and Massachusetts.

FEMA Region II
26 Federal Plaza, Room 1337
New York, NY 10278-0002

Serves New York and New Jersey as well as Puerto Rico, and the United States Virgin Islands.

FEMA Region III
615 Chestnut Street
One Independence Mall, Sixth Floor
Philadelphia, PA 19106-4404

Serves Delaware, Maryland, Pennsylvania, Virginia, West Virginia, and the District of Columbia.

FEMA Region IV
3003 Chamblee Tucker Road
Atlanta, GA 30341

Serves Alabama, Florida, Georgia, Kentucky, Mississippi, North Carolina, South Carolina, and Tennessee.

FEMA Region V
536 South Clark Street., 6th Floor
Chicago, IL 60605

Serves Illinois, Indiana, Michigan, Minnesota, Ohio, and Wisconsin.
FEMA Region VI

FRC 800 North Loop 288
Denton, TX 76201-3698
Serves Arkansas, Louisiana, New Mexico, Oklahoma, and Texas.

FEMA Region VII
2323 Grand Boulevard, Suite 900
Kansas City, MO 64108-2670

Serves Iowa, Kansas, Missouri, and Nebraska.

FEMA Region VIII
Denver Federal Center
Building 710, Box 25267
Denver, CO 80255-0267

Serves Colorado, Montana, North Dakota, South Dakota, Utah, and
Wyoming.

FEMA Region IX
Building 105
Presidio of San Francisco
San Francisco, CA 94129

Serves Arizona, California, Hawaii, and Nevada as well as American
Samoa, Guam, the Northern Mariana Islands, the Marshall Islands,
Micronesia, and Palau.

FEMA Region X
Federal Regional Center
130 228th Street, SW
Bothell, WA 98021-9796

Serves Alaska, Idaho, Oregon, and Washington.

National Emergency Training Center
16825 South Seton Avenue
Emmitsburg, MD 21727

United States Fire Administration

16825 South Seton Avenue
Emmitsburg, MD 21727

Emergency Management Institute
16825 South Seton Avenue
Emmitsburg, MD 21727

Mount Weather Emergency Assistance Center
19844 Blue Ridge Mountain Road
State Route 601
Bluemont, VA 20135

EMERGENCY MANAGEMENT STANDARDS OF THE JOINT COMMISSION ON ACCREDITATION OF HEALTHCARE ORGANIZATIONS (JCAHO)

This standard is numbered EC.1.4 in the CAMAC, CAMH, and CAMLTC, and EC.2.4 in the CAMBHC Announced June 23, 2000. Revisions become effective January 1, 2001. New language is underlined.

STANDARD EC.1.4

A plan addresses emergency management.

INTENT OF EC.1.4

The emergency management plan describes how the organization will establish and maintain a program to ensure effective response to disasters [see note 1] or emergencies affecting the environment of care. The plan should address four phases of emergency management activities: mitigation, preparedness, response, and recovery. [see note 2]

The plan provides process for

a. identifying specific procedures in response to a variety of disasters based on a hazard vulnerability analysis [see note 3] per formed by the organization;

b. initiating the plan (including a description of how, when, and by whom the plan is activated);

c. defining and, when appropriate, integrating the organization's role with community-wide emergency response agencies (including the identification of who is in charge of what activities and when they are in charge) to promote inter-operability between the health care organization and the community;

d. notifying external authorities of emergencies;

e. notifying personnel when emergency response measures are initiated;

f. identifying personnel during emergencies;

g. assigning available personnel in emergencies to cover all necessary staff positions;

h. managing the following during emergencies and disasters:

- Patient activities including scheduling and modification, discontinuation of services, control of patient information, and patient transportation;

- Staff activities (e.g., housing, transportation, and incident stress debriefing);

- Staff/family-support activities;

- Logistics of critical supplies (e.g., pharmaceuticals, medical supplies, food supplies, linen supplies, water supplies);

- Security (e.g. access, crowd control, traffic control); and

- Interaction with the news media.

i. evacuating the entire facility (both horizontally and, when applicable, vertically) when the environment cannot support adequate patient care and treatment;

j. establishing an alternative care site when the environment cannot support adequate patient care including processes that address (when appropriate)

- management of patient necessities (e.g., medications, medical records) to and from the alternative care site;

- patient tracking to and from the alternative care site;

- inter-facility communication between the organization and the alternative care site;

- transportation of patient, staff, and equipment to the alternative care site; and

k. continuing and/or re-establishing operation following a disaster

The plan identifies

l. an alternative means of meeting essential building utility needs (e.g., electricity, water, ventilation, fuel sources, and medical gas and vacuum system, etc.) when the organization is designated by its emergency preparedness plan to provide continuous service during a disaster or emergency;

m. backup internal and external communication system in the event of failure during disasters and emergencies;

n. facilities for radioactive or chemical isolation and decontamination; and

o. alternate roles and responsibilities of personnel during emergencies, including who they report to within a command structure that is consistent with that used by the local community.

The plan establishes

p. an organization and education program for personnel who participate in implementing the emergency management plan. Education addresses

    1. specific roles and responsibilities during emergencies;

    2. the information and skills required to perform duties during disasters and emergencies;

    3. the backup communication system used during disasters and emergencies and

    4. how supplies and equipment are obtained during disasters or emergencies;

q. ongoing monitoring of performance regarding actual or potential risk related to one or more of the following:

    1. Staff knowledge and skills;

    2. Level of staff participation;

    3. Monitoring and inspection activities;

    4. Emergency and incident reporting or

    5. Inspection, preventive maintenance, and testing equipment; and

r. how an annual evaluation of the emergency preparedness safety management plan's objectives, scope, performance, and effectiveness will occur.

NOTES:

1. disaster is a natural or man-made event that significantly disrupts the environment of care, such as damage to organization's building(s) and grounds due to severe wind storms, tornadoes, hurricanes, or earthquakes. Also, an event that disrupts care and treatment, such as los of utilities (power, water, telephones) due to floods, civil disturbances, accidents, or emergencies within the organization or in the surrounding community. Disasters are sometimes referred to as "potential injury creating events" (i.e., "PICE").

2. mitigation activities are those a health care organization undertakes in attempting to lessen the severity and impact a potential disaster or emergency may have on its operation while preparedness activities are those an organization undertakes to build capacity and identify resources that may be utilized should a disaster or emergency occur

3. hazard vulnerability analysis is the identification of hazards and the direct and indirect effect these hazards may have on the health care organization.

Appendix **H**

REQUIRED ELEMENTS OF HAZARD ANALYSIS

Section A-3-3.1 of the National Fire Protection Association, Inc. NFPA 1600 Standard on Disaster/Emergency Management and Business Continuity Programs 2000 Edition defines the required elements of a hazard analysis. This standard states that the hazard identification and risk assessment determine *what* can occur, *when* (how often it is likely to occur, and *how bad* the effects could be. Hazard identification should include, but is not limited to, the following types of potential hazards:

NATURAL EVENTS	**TECHNOLOGICAL EVENTS**	**HUMANS EVENTS**
Drought	Hazardous materials release	Economic failures
Fire (eg. forest, range, urban)	Explosion or fire	General strikes
Avalanche	Transportation accident	Terrorism (eg eco, cyber,
snow, ice, heail		nuclear, biological, chemical)
Tsunami	Building or structure collapse	Sabotage
Windstorm/typhoon/cyclone	Power or utility failure	Hostage situation
Hurricane/typhoon/cyclone	Extreme air pollution	Civil unrest
Biological event	Radiological accident	Enemy attack
Extreme heat or cold	Dam or levee failure	Arson
Flood or wind-driven water	Fuel or resource shortage	Mass hysteria
Earthquake or land shift	Strike	Special crowd producing events
Volcanic eruption	Business interruption	
Tornado	Financial collapse	
Landslide or mudslide	Communication disruption	
Dust or sand storm		
Lightening storm		

The methodologies and techniques for risk assessment and the resources for program administration as listed in Sec A-3-5 include, but are not limited to the following:

METHODS FOR RISK ASSESSMENT	**RESOURCES FOR ADMINISTRATION**
What if?	Inventory of equipment (eg location, quantities, accessibility, operability, maintenance)
Check list	Supplies (eg medical, personal hygiene, consumable, administrative)
Hazard operability studies	Sources of energy
Failure modes and effect analysis	Communication systems
Fault tree	Food, water, and ice
Failure logic diagrams	Technical information
Dow and bond indices	Clothing
Event tree analysis	Shelter
Human reliability analysis	Specialized personnel (eg medical, religious, emergency, utility, morticians, private contractors)
Capacity readiness for state and local governments	Volunteer groups (eg Red Cross, RACES, religious relief and charitable agencies)
	External government resources (eg Federal Response Plan, Federal Radiological Emergency Plan, National Guard)

Appendix **I**

Common Foodborne Diseases Caused by Bacteria

~~~~~~

The table on the next page will be helpful when public health professionals require a quick reference to comparative information about foodborne diseases caused by bacteria. Professionals can consult this table to review the clinical symptoms for common foodborne diseases and the typical foods associated with each disease. Finally, specific prevention and control measures are provided.

REPRINTED FROM OWEN AL, SPLETT PL, AND OWEN GM, NUTRITION IN THE COMMUNITY: THE ART AND SCIENCE OF DELIVERY SERVICES, 4TH ED., BOSTON, MA: WCB MCGRAW HILL: 1999.

Disease (causative agent)	Principal symptoms	Typical foods	Prevention and control measures
Food poisoning, diarrhea (*Bacillus cereus*)	Diarrhea, cramps, occasional vomiting	Meat products, soups, sauces, vegetables	Cook all potential food sources thoroughly, serve at correct temperature, cool rapidly.
Food poisoning, emetic (*B. cereus*)	Nausea, vomiting, sometimes diarrhea and cramps	Cooked rice and pasta	Minimize hot holding times.
Botulism: food poisoning (heat-labile toxin of *Clostridium botulinum*)	Fatigue, weakness, double vision, slurred speed, respiratory failure, sometimes death	Type A&B: Vegetables, fruits; meat, fish, and poultry products; condiments; Type E: fish and fish products	Purchase commercially processed foods, serve foods sauteed or infused in oils, promptly discard leftovers.
Botulism; food poisoning infant infection (heat-labile toxin of *C. botulinum*)	Constipation, weakness respiratory failure, sometimes death	Honey, soil	Do not feed honey to infants
Campylobacteriosis (*Campylobacter jejuni*)	Diarrhea, abdominal pain, fever, nausea, vomiting	Infected food-source animals	Cook animal foods thoroughly, cool rapidly, avoid cross-contamination, use pasteurized milk.
Food poisoning (*Clostridium perfringens*)	Diarrhea, cramps, rarely nausea and vomiting	Cooked meat and poultry	Cook animal foods thoroughly, cool rapidly, avoid cross-contamination.
Foodborne infections, enterohemorrhagic (*Escherichia coli*)	Watery, bloody diarrhea	Raw or uncooked beef, raw milk	Cook animal foods thoroughly, cool rapidly, avoid cross-contaminations.
Foodborne infections, entroinvasive (*E. coli*)	Cramps, diarrhea, fever, dysentery	Raw foods	Teach food handlers good hygiene practice, have food handlers wear gloves, minimize holding time.

Disease (organism)	Symptoms	Foods involved	Prevention
Foodborne infections, enterotoxigenic (E. coli)	Profuse watery diarrhea; sometimes cramps, vomiting	Raw foods	Teach food handlers good hygiene practice, have food handlers wear gloves, minimize holding time.
Listeriosis (Listeria monocytogenes)	Meninfoencephalitis; stillbirths; septicemia or meningitis in newborns	Raw milk, cheese, and vegetables	Use pasteurized milk, cook foods thoroughly.
Salmonellosis (Salmonella species)	Diarrhea, abdominal pain, chills, fever, vomiting, dehydration	Raw, undercooked eggs; raw milk, meat and poultry	Cook animal foods thoroughly, minimize hot holding time, chill food rapidly, avoid cross-contamination.
Shigellosis (Shigella species)	Diarrhea, fever; nausea; sometimes vomiting, cramps	Raw foods	Cook animal food thoroughly, minimize hot holding time, chill food rapidly, avoid cross-contamination.
Staphylococcal food poisoning (heat-stable enterotoxin of Staphylococcus aureus)	Nausea, vomiting, diarrhea, cramps	Ham, meat, poultry products, cream-filled pastries, whipped butter, cheese	Restrict food handlers with skin lesions or respiratory infections from handling foods.
Streptococcal foodborne infection (Streptococcus pyogenes)	Various, including sore throat, erysipelas scarlet fever	Raw milk, deviled eggs	Use pasteurized milk, teach foods handlers good hygiene practices, chill foods rapidly
Foodborne infections, (Vibrio parahaemolyticus)	Diarrhea, cramps; sometimes nausea vomiting, fever, headache	Fish and seafood	Cook fish and seafood thoroughly, minimize hot holding time.

FEDERAL COMMUNICATIONS COMMISSION RULES

SUBPART A—GENERAL PROVISIONS

§§97.3 Definitions.

(a) The definitions of terms used in Part 97 are:
(37) RACES (radio amateur civil emergency service). A radio service using amateur stations for civil defense communications during periods of local, regional, or national civil emergencies.

§§97.17 Application for new license grant.

(a) Any qualified person is eligible to apply for a new operator/ primary station, club station or military recreation station license grant. No new license grant will be issued for a RACES station.

SUBPART E—PROVIDING EMERGENCY COMMUNICATIONS

§§97.401 Operation during a disaster.

(a) When normal communication systems are overloaded, damaged, or disrupted because a disaster has occurred, or is likely to occur, in an area where the amateur service is regulated by the FCC, an amateur station may make transmissions necessary to meet essential communication needs and facilitate relief actions.

(b) When normal communication systems are overloaded, damaged, or disrupted because a natural disaster has occurred, or is likely to occur, in an area where the amateur service is not regulated by the FCC, a station assisting in meeting essential communication needs and facilitating relief actions may do so only in accord with ITU Resolution No. 640 (Geneva, 1979). The 80 m, 75 m, 40 m, 30 m, 20 m, 17 m, 15 m, 12 m, and 2 m bands may be used for these purposes.

(c) When a disaster disrupts normal communication systems in a particular area, the FCC may declare a temporary state of communication emergency. The declaration will set forth any special conditions and special rules to be observed by stations during the communication emergency. A request for a declaration of a temporary state of emergency should be directed to the EIC in the area concerned.

(d) A station in, or within 92.6 km of, Alaska may transmit emissions J3E and R3E on the channel at 5.1675 MHz for emergency communications. The channel must be shared with stations licensed in the Alaska-private fixed service. The transmitter power must not exceed 150 W.

§§97.403 Safety of life and protection of property.

No provision of these rules prevents the use by an amateur station of any means of radio communication at its disposal to provide essential communication needs in connection with the immediate safety of human life and immediate protection of property when normal communication systems are not available.

§§97.405 Station in distress.

(a) No provision of these rules prevents the use by an amateur station in distress of any means at its disposal to attract attention, make known its condition and location, and obtain assistance.

(b) No provision of these rules prevents the use by a station, in the exceptional circumstances described in paragraph (a), of any means of radio communications at its disposal to assist a station in distress.

§§97.407 Radio amateur civil emergency service.

(a) No station may transmit in RACES unless it is an FCC-licensed primary, club, or military recreation station and it is certified by a civil defense organization as registered with that organization, or it is an FCC-licensed RACES station. No person may be the control operator of a RACES station, or may be the control operator of an amateur station transmitting in RACES unless that person holds a FCC-issued amateur operator license and is certified by a civil defense organization as enrolled in that organization.

(b) The frequency bands and segments and emissions authorized to the control operator are available to stations transmitting communications in RACES on a shared basis with the amateur service. In the event of an emergency which necessitates the invoking of the President's War Emergency Powers under the provisions of Section 706 of the Communications Act of 1934, as amended, 47 U.S.C. §§606, RACES stations and amateur stations participating in RACES may only transmit on the following frequencies:

(1) The 1800-1825 kHz, 1975-2000 kHz, 3.50-3.55 MHz, 3.93-3.98 MHz, 3.984-4.000 MHz, 7.079-7.125 MHz, 7.245-7.255 MHz, 10.10-10.15 MHz, 14.047-14.053 MHz, 14.22-14.23 MHz, 14.331-14.350 MHz, 21.047-21.053 MHz, 21.228-21.267 MHz, 28.55-28.75 MHz, 29.237-29.273 MHz, 29.45-29.65 MHz, 50.35-50.75 MHz, 52-54 MHz, 144.50-145.71 MHz, 146-148 MHz, 2390-2450 MHz segments;

(2) The 1.25 m, 70 cm, and 23 cm bands; and

(3) The channels at 3.997 and 53.30 MHz may be used in emergency areas when required to make initial contact with a military unit and for communications with military stations on matters requiring coordination.

(c) A RACES station may only communicate with:

(1) Another RACES station;

(2) An amateur station registered with a civil defense organization;

(3) A United States Government station authorized by the responsible agency to communicate with RACES stations;

(4) A station in a service regulated by the FCC whenever such communication is authorized by the FCC.

(d) An amateur station registered with a civil defense organization may only communicate with:

(1) A RACES station licensed to the civil defense organization with which the amateur station is registered;

(2) The following stations upon authorization of the responsible civil defense official for the organization with which the amateur station is registered:

(i) A RACES station licensed to another civil defense organization;

(ii) An amateur station registered with the same or another civil defense organization;

(iii) A United States Government station authorized by the responsible agency to communicate with RACES stations; and

(iv) A station in a service regulated by the FCC whenever such communication is authorized by the FCC.

(e) All communications transmitted in RACES must be specifically authorized by the civil defense organization for the area served. Only civil defense communications of the following types may be transmitted:

(1) Messages concerning impending or actual conditions jeopardizing the public safety, or affecting the national defense or security during periods of local, regional, or national civil emergencies;

(2) Messages directly concerning the immediate safety of life of individuals, the immediate protection of property, maintenance of law and order, alleviation of human suffering and need, and the combating of armed attack or sabotage;

(3) Messages directly concerning the accumulation and dissemination of public information or instructions to the civilian population essential to the activities of the civil defense organization or other authorized governmental or relief agencies; and

(4) Communications for RACES training drills and tests necessary to ensure the establishment and maintenance of orderly

and efficient operation of the RACES as ordered by the responsible civil defense organization served. Such drills and tests may not exceed a total time of 1 hour per week. With the approval of the chief officer for emergency planning in the applicable State, Commonwealth, District, or territory, however, such tests and drills may be conducted for a period not to exceed 72 hours no more than twice in any calendar year.

From: Code of Federal Regulations, Title 47: Telecommunications, Chapter I — Federal Communications Commission, Subchapter D- Safety and Special Radio Services, Part 97 — Amatuer Radio Service

KEY ELEMENTS OF A PUBLIC HEALTH PREPAREDNESS PROGRAM

- Must be in place in advance of emergency (Emergency preparedness)

- Identify the type of events that might occur in your community (Hazard analysis)

- Plan emergency activities in advance to ensure a coordinated response to the consequences of a credible event (Emergency response planning)

- Build capabilities necessary to respond effectively to the consequences of those events (Emergency preparedness)

- Identify the types or nature of an event when it happens (Health surveillance, epidemiological investigation, laboratory, diagnosis)

- Implement the planned response quickly and efficiently (Consequence management)

- Recovery

Derived from The Public Health Response to Biological and Chemical Terrorism: Interim Planning Guidance for State Public Health Officials , *CDC, July, 2001 (www.bt.cdc.gov/Documents/Planning/Planning Guidance.PDF)*

Also see April 2000 MMWR Supplement and National Association of County and City Health Officers website

REFERENCES AND READINGS

BIOTERRORISM AND EMERGING DISEASES

Atlas, RM. (1998) The medical threat of biological weapons. *Critical Reviews in Microbiology*, 24:157-168

Franz, DR. Jahrling PB. Friedlander AM, et al. (1997) Clinical recognition and management of patients exposed to biological warfare agents. *J Am Med Assoc.* 278:399-411.

Journal of Public Health Management and Practice. (2000) Issue on Bioterrorism. Vol 6(4) :1-71.

Shapiro, RL. Hatheway, C. Becher, J. Swerdlow, DL. Botulism surveillance and emergency, response. *J Am Med Assoc.* 1997; 278:433-435.

Walker, DH. Barbour, AG. et al. (1996). "Emerging bacterial zoonotic and vector-borne diseases: Ecological and epidemiological factors." *Journal of the American Medical Association* 275(6): 463-469.

Woodall, J. (1998) The role of computer networking in investigating unusual disease outbreaks and allegations of biological and toxin weapons use. *Critical Reviews in Microbiology*, 24:255-272.

SMALLPOX

Henderson, DA. Inglesby, TV. Bartlett, JG,. Ascher, MS. et al. (1999) Smallpox as a biological weapon. *J Am Med Assn*, 281:2127-2137.

Henderson, DA. (1999) Smallpox: Clinical and epidemiologic features. *Em Inf Dis,* 5:537-539.
O'Toole, T. (1999) Smallpox: an attack scenario. *Em Inf Dis,* 5:540-560.

ANTHRAX

Dixon, TC. Meselson, M. Guillemin, J. Hanna, PC. (1999) Anthrax, review article. *New Eng J Med,* 341:815-826.
Inglesby,TV. Henderson, DA. Bartlett, JG. Ascher, MS. et al. (1999) Anthrax as a biological weapon. *J Am Med Assn,* 281:1735-1736.

RESPONSE

Campbell, J. Francesconi, S. Boyd, J. Worth, L. Moshier, T. (1999) Environmental air sampling to detect biological warfare agents. *Military Med,* 164:541-542.
Holloway, HC. Norwood, AE. Fullerton, CS. Engel, CC. Ursano, RJ. (1997) The threat of biological weapons. Prophylaxis and mitiga–tion of psychological and social consequences. *J Am Med Assoc,* 278:425-427.
Lederberg, J. (1997) Infectious disease and biological weapons. Prophylaxis and mitigation. *J Am Med Assoc,* 278:435-436.

LABORATORY ISSUES

Atlas, RM. Biological weapons pose challenge for microbiology com–munity. ASM News 1998;64:383-389.
Belgrader, P. Benett, W. Hadley, D. Richards, J. Stratton, P. Mariella, R. Milanovich, F. (1999) PCR detection of bacteria in seven minutes. *Science,* 284:449-450.
Engelthaler, DM. Gage, NL. Montenieri, JA. Chu, M. Carter, LG. (1999) PCR detection of Yersinia pestis in fleas: comparison with mouse inoculation. *J Clin Micro,* 37:1980-1984.
McDade, JE. (1999) Addressing the potential threat of bioterrorism-value added to an improved public health infrastructure. *Em Inf Dis,* 5;591-592.
Rowe, CA. Tender, LM. Feldstein, MJ. Golden, JP. Scrugg, SB. MacCraith, BD. Cras, JJ. Ligler, FS. (1999) Array biosensor for simultaneous identification of bacterial, viral, and protein analytes. *Analytical Chemistry,* 71:3846-3852.

CASE STUDIES

Alson, R. Alexander, D. et al. (1993). "Analysis of medical treatment at a field hospital following Hurricane Andrew, 1992." *Annals of Emergency Medicine* 22(11): 1721-1728.

Bel, N. (1993). "Triumph over tragedy: Emergency response to Hurricane Andrew." *Emergency* 25(4): 28-31, 66.

Bernstein, RS. Baxter, PJ. Falk, H. Ing, R. Foster, L. and Frost, F. (1986). "Immediate public health concerns and actions in volcanic eruptions: lessons from Mount St. Helens eruptions, May 18-October 18, 1980." *American Journal of Public Health.* 76(3 Suppl):25-37.

Brewer, RD. Morris, PD. et al. (1994). "Hurricane-related emergency department visits in an inland area: an analysis of the public health impact of Hurricane Hugo in North Carolina." *Annals of Emergency Medicine* 23(4): 731-736.

Carr, SJ. Leahy, SM.. London, S. Sidhu, S. Vogt, J. (1996). "The Public Health Response to the Los Angeles, 1994 Earthquake." *American Journal of Public Health,* 86(4):589-590.

Centers for Disease Control (1986). "Hurricanes and hospital emergency-room visits -Mississippi, Rhode Island, Connecticut." *Morbidity and Mortality Weekly Report* 34(51& 52): 765-770.

Centers for Disease Control (1991). "Tornado disaster - Illinois, 1990." *Morbidity and Mortality Weekly Report* 40(2): 33-36.

Centers for Disease Control (1992). "Rapid health needs assessment following Hurricane Andrew — Florida and Louisiana, 1992." *Morbidity and Mortality Weekly Report* 41(37): 685-688.

Center for Disease Control (1993). "Comprehensive assessment of health needs 2 months after Hurricane Andrew - Dade County, Florida." *Morbidity and Mortality Weekly Report* 42(22): 434-437.

Center for Disease Control (1993). "Injuries and illnesses related to Hurricane Andrew - Louisiana, 1992." *Morbidity and Mortality Weekly Report* 42(13): 242-251.

Centers for Disease Control (1993). "Morbidity surveillance following the Midwest Flood - Missouri, 1993." *Journal of the American Medical Association* 270(18): 2164.

Centers for Disease Control (1993). "Public health consequences of a flood disaster — Iowa, 1993." *Morbidity and Mortality Weekly Report* 42: 653-656.

Centers for Disease Control (1994). "Rapid assessment of vectorborne diseases during the Midwest Flood, United States, 1993." *Morbidity and Mortality Weekly Report* 43(26): 481-483.

Centers for Disease Control (1996). "Surveillance for injuries and ill–nesses and rapid health needs assessment following hurricanes Marilyn and Opal, September-October 1995." *Morbidity and Mortality Weekly Report* 45(4): 81-85

Centers for Disease Control and Prevention. (1998) "Community needs assessment and morbidity surveillance following an ice storm - Maine, January 1998." *MMWR Morbid Mortal Wkly Rep* 1998;47:361-364.

Centers for Disease Control and Prevention.(1996). "Surveillance for injuries and illnesses and rapid health-needs assessment following Hurricanes Marilyn and Opal, September-October 1996." *MMWR Morbid Mortal Wkly Rep* 1996;46:81-81.

Centers for Disease Control and Prevention.(1994). Rapid assessment of vectorborne diseases during the midwest flood – United States, 1993. *MMWR Morbid Mortal Wkly Rep* 1994;43:481-483.

Centers for Disease Control and Prevention.(1993). "Public health consequences of a flood disaster – Iowa, 1993." *MMWR Morbid Mortal Wkly Rep* 1993;42:663-666.

Centers for Disease Control and Prevention (1992). "Tornado disaster - Kansas 1991." MMWR - *Morbidity and Mortality Weekly Report.* 41(10):181-3, 1992 Mar 13.

Combs, DL. Parrish, RG. et al. (1996). "Deaths related to Hurricane Andrew in Florida and Louisiana, 1992." *International Journal of Epidemiology* 25(3): 537-544.

Durkin, M.E. Thiel Jr., CC. et al. (1991). "Injuries and emergency med–ical response in the Loma Prieta earthquake." *Bulletin of the Seismological Society of America* 81: 2143-2166.

Erikson, K. (1976). *Everything in Its Path: Destruction of Community in the Buffalo Creek Flood.* New York: Simon & Schuster.

Gautam, K. "Organizational problems faced by the Missouri DOH in providing disaster relief during the 1993 floods." *Journal of Public Health Management & Practice.* 4(4):79-86

Green, BL. Grace, M.C. Lindy, JD. Gleser, GC. Leonard, AC. Kramer, TL. (1990a) Buffalo Creek survivors in the second decade: Comparison with unexposed and non-litigant groups. *Journal of Applied Social Psychology, 20,* 1033-1050.

Grace, M.C. Green, BL. Lindy, JD. Leonard, AC. (1993). The Buffalo Creek disaster: A 14-year follow-up. In J.P. Wilson and B. Raphael, eds., *The International Handbook of Traumatic Stress Syndromes.* New York: Plenum Press, pp. 441-449.

Haynes, BE. Freeman, C. et al. (1992). "Medical Response to Catastrophic Events: California's Planning and the Loma Prieta

Earthquake." *Annals of Emergency Medicine* 21(4): 368-374.

Hogan, DE. Waeckerle, JF. et al. (1999). "Emergency department impact of the Oklahoma City terrorist bombing." *Annals of Emergency Medicine* 34(2): 160-167.

Jarret, JC. Hagebak, B. et al. (1995). "Lessons from the Georgia floods." *Public Health Reports* 110: 684-689.

Johnson, WP. Lanza, CV. (1993). "After hurricane Andrew: An EMS per–spective." *Prehospital and Disaster Medicine* 8(2): 169-171.

Kerns, DE. Anderson, PE. (1990). "EMS response to a major aircraft incident: Sioux City, Iowa." *Prehospital and Disaster Medicine* 5(2): 159-166.

Landesman, LY. (2001) "A Department of Health Learns about Its Role in Emergency Public Health," in L Rowitz, ed. *Public Health Leadership: Putting Principles into Practice.* Gaithersburg, MD: Aspen Publishers, pp 150-153.

McNabb, SJN. Kelso, KY. et al. (1995). "Hurricane Andrew-related injuries and illnesses, Louisiana, 1992." *Southern Medical Journal* 88: 6.

Noji, EK. Kelen, GD. Armenian, H.K., et al.(1990) "The 1988 Earthquake in Armenia: A Case Study." *Annals of Emergency Medicine.* pp 75-81.

Siders, C. Jacobson, R. (1998). "Flood disaster preparedness: a retro–spective from Grand Forks, South Dakota." *Journal of Healthcare Risk Management.*18(2):33-40.

Whitman, S. Good, G. Donoghue, ER. Benbow, N. Shou, W. and Mou, S. (1997). "Mortality in Chicago Attributed to the July 1995 Heat Wave." *American Journal of Public Health,* 87(9):1515-1518.

COMMUNICATION

Churchill, RE. Effective media relations, In Noji, EK. ed. *The Public Health Consequences of Disasters.* New York: Oxford University Press; 1997.

Ferguson, EW. et al. Telemedicine for national and international disaster response. *Journal of Medical Systems* 1995;19(2):121-123

Martchenke, J. Rusteen, J. Pointer JE (1995). "Prehospital commu–nications during the Loma Prieta earthquake." *Prehospital and Disaster Medicine.* 10(4):225-31.

Stephenson, R. Anderson, PS. Disasters and the information technolo–gy revolution. *Disasters* 1997; 21(4):305-344.

CURRICULUM

Gebbie, KM. (1999) "The Public Health Workforce: Key to Public Health Infrastructure." *American Journal of Public Health.* 89(5):660-1.

Landesman, LY. (1993). "The Availability of Disaster Preparation Courses at US Schools of Public Health." *American Journal of Public Health.* 83(10):1494-5.

Landesman, LY. (editor) (2001) Disaster Preparedness in Schools of Public Health: A Curriculum for the New Century, Association of Schools of Public Health, Public Health Foundation

Pesik, N. Keim, M. et al. (1999). "Do emergency medicine residency programs provide adequate training for bioterrorism." *Annals of Emergency Medicine* 34(2): 173-176.

CYCLONE

Friedman, E. (1994). "Coping with calamity: How well does health care disaster planning work?" *JAMA.* 272(23): 1875-1879.

Malilay, J. (1997). "Tropical cyclones." in Noji, E.K. (ed.), *The Public Health Consequences of Disasters.* pp. 287-301. New-York, Oxford: Oxford University Press.

DISASTERS, GENERAL

Dynes, RR. Tierney, KJ. eds. (1994). *Disasters, Collective Behavior, and Social Organization.* Newark: University of Delaware Press.

EARTHQUAKE

Alexander, D. (1996). "The health effects of earthquakes in the mid-1990s." *Disasters.* 20(3): 231-247.

Frankel, DH. (1994). "Public health assessment after earthquake." *Lancet.* 343: 347-348. (1994).

Freeman, C.(1990). "Casualty estimation and state medical/health response to disasters." in California Emergency Medical Services Authority (ed.), *Workshop on modelling earthquake casualties for planning and response model definition and user output requirements.* pp.18-36. Sacramento: California Emergency Medical Services Authority.

Friedman, E. (1994). "Coping with calamity: How well does health care disaster planning work?" *JAMA.* 272(23): 1875-1879.

Guha-Sapir, D. (1991) "Rapid assessment of health needs in mass emergencies: Review of current concepts and methods."

Wld.Hlth.Statist.Quart. 44(3): 171-181.

Guha-Sapir, D. (1993). "Health effects of earthquakes and volcanoes: epidemiological and policy issues." *Disasters.* 17(3): 255-262.

Noji, EK. (1997). "Earthquakes." in Noji, E.K.(ed.), *The Public Health Consequences of Disasters.* pp.135-178. New-York, Oxford: Oxford University Press.

ENVIRONMENTAL CONTROL

Esrey, S. et al. (1991). "Effects of improved water supply and sanitation on ascariasis, diarrhoea, dracunculiasis, hookwork infection, schis–tosomiasis, and trachoma." *Bull. WHO* 1991;69(5):609-21.

Hatch, D. et al. (1994). "Epidemic cholera during refugee resettlement in Malawi." *Int. J. of Epi.* 1994;22(6):1292 - 99.

Melosi, MV. (1980). *Pollution and Reform in American Cities, 1870 - 1930.* Univ. of Texas Press, Austin.

Peterson, AE. Roberts, L. Toole, M. Peterson, DE. (1998). "Soap Use Effect on Diarrhea: Nyamithuthu Refugee Camp." *Int. J. of Epi.* 1998;27:520-524.

EPIDEMIC

Manderson, L. Aaby, P. (1992). "An epidemic in the field? Rapid assess–ment procedures and health research." *Soc.Sci.Med.* 35(7): 839-850.

Mohamed, J. (1999). "Epidemics and public health in early colonial Somaliland." *Soc.Sci.Med.* 48: 507-521.

Perrin, P. (1996). *War and public health: Handbook on war and public health.* Geneva: International Committee of the Red Cross.

Toole, MJ. (1994). "The rapid assessment of health problems in refugee and displaced populations." *Med.Glob.Surv.* 1(4): 200-207.

Toole, MJ. (1997). "Communicable diseases and disease control." in Noji, E.K.(ed.), *The Public Health Consequences of Disasters.* pp.79-100 New York, Oxford: Oxford University Press.

Toole, MJ. Waldman, R. (1993). "Refugees and displaced persons: War, hunger, and public health." *JAMA.* 270(5): 600-605.

World Health Organization. (1999). *Rapid health assessment protocols for emergencies.* World Health Organization. Geneva: WHO.

EVALUATION METHODS APPLIED TO EMERGENCIES AND DISASTERS

Bissell, R. Pretto, E. Angus, D. et al (1994). "Post Preparedness Medical Disaster Response In Costa Rica." *Prehospital and Disaster Medicine*, 9(2).

Cayton, C. Herrmann, N. Cole, L. et al. (1978). "Assessing the validity of EMS data." *Journal of the American College of Emergency Physicians* 7:11.

Cayton, C. Murphy, J. (1986). "Evaluation." *In* Schwartz G, Safar P, Stone I, et al: *Principles and Practices of Emergency Medicine*, ed 2. Philadelphia, WB Saunders, p. 634

De Boer, J. (1997) Tools for evaluating disasters: preliminary results of some hundreds of disasters. *European Journal of Emergency Medicine* 4:107-110.

Donabedian, A. (1980) *The Definition of Quality and Approaches to Its Assessment.* Ann Arbor, MI, Health Administration Press

Eisenberg, M. Bergner, J (1979) "Paramedic programs and cardiac mortality: Description of a controlled experiment." *Public Health Reports* 94(1): 80-84

Klain, M. Ricci, E. Safar, P. et al. (1989) "Disaster reanimatology potentials: A structured interview study in Armenia, I: Methodology and preliminary results." *Pre-hospital and Disaster Medicine* 4(2):135-154

Manni, C. Magalini, S. (1989). "Disaster Medicine: A new discipline or a new approach?" *Pre-hospital and Disaster Medicine* 4(2): 167-70

Noji, EK. (1987) "Evaluation of the efficacy of disaster response." *United National Disaster Relief Organization News*, July/August, 1987, pp 11-13

Ricci, E. (1985) "A model for evaluation of disaster management." *Prehospital and Disaster Medicine* (Suppl 1), 1985

Roy, A. Looney, G. Anderson, G. (1979). "Prospective vs. retrospective data for evaluating emergency care: A research methodology." *JACEP* 8:141, 1979

Succo, W. Champion, H. Stega, M. (1984) *Trauma Care Evaluation.* Baltimore, University Park Press.

FAMINE

Seaman, J. (1994). "Population, food supply, and famines: An ecological or an economic dilemna?" in Cartledge, B. (ed.), *Health and the environment.* pp.29-45. Oxford: Oxford University Press.

Sen, A. (1981). *Poverty and famines: an essay on entitlement and deprivation,* Oxford: Clarendon Press.

Toole, MJ.(1992). "Famine-affected, refugee, and displaced popula–tions: Recommendations for public health issues." *MMWR.* 41(RR-13): 1-366.

Toole, MJ. Waldman, R.(1993). "Refugees and displaced persons: War, hunger, and public health." *JAMA.* 270(5): 600-605.

Yip, R. (1997). "Famine." in Noji, E.K.(ed.), *The Public Health Consequences of Disasters.* pp.305-335. New-York, Oxford: Oxford University Press.

Young, H. (1992). *Food scarcity and famine: Assessment and response.* Oxford: Oxfam.

Zaman, MS.(1991). "Famine: causes and health consequences." in World Health Organization and United Nations Institute for Training and Research (ed.), *The challenge of African disasters.* pp.77-107. New York: UNITAR.

FLOOD

Ali, HM. and Homeida, MMA. (1991). "Flood disaster impact on health and nutritional status of the population - Khartoum, Sudan." in Abu Sin, M.E., *Disaster prevention and management in Sudan.* pp.82-104. Khartoum: University of Khartoum.

Malilay, J. (1997). "Floods." in Noji, E.K.(ed.), *The Public Health Cnse –quences of Disasters.* pp.287-301. New-York, Oxford: Oxford University Press.

HOSPITAL PREPAREDNESS

Landesman, LY. (ed). (1997). *Emergency Preparedness in the Healthcare Environment.* Joint Commission of Healthcare Organizations, Oakbrook, Ill.

Landesman, LY. Markowitz SB, and Rosenberg SN (1994). "Hospital preparedness for chemical accidents: the effect of environmental legislation on health care services." *Prehospital and Disaster Medicine.* 9(3):154-9, 1994 Jul-Sept.

Landesman, LY. (1994). *"Hospital Preparedness for Chemical Accidents"* Plant, Technology & Safety Management Series, The Joint Commission on Accreditation of Healthcare Organizations, Oakbrook, Ill. Number 3:39-44.

Landesman, LY. Leonard, R. (1993) SARA Three Years Later: Physician Knowledge and Actions in Hospital Preparedness. *The Intl Journal of Prehospital and Disaster Medicine* Jan-Mar 39-44.

Lewis, CP. Aghababiam, R. (1996)Disaster planning, part 1: Overview of hospital and emergency department planning for internal and external disasters. *Disaster Medicine,* 14(2):439-452.

Peters, MS. (1996). "Hospitals respond to water loss during the Midwest floods of 1993: preparedness and improvisation." *Journal of Emergency Medicine.* 14(3):34-50.

Salinas, C. Kurata, J. (1998). "The effects of the Northridge earthquake on the pattern of emergency department care." *American Journal of Emergency Medicine.*16(3): 254-6.

Simon, HK. Stegelman, M. Button, T. (1998). "A prospective evaluation of pediatric emergency care during the 1996 Summer Olympic Games in Atlanta, Georgia." *Pediatric Emergency Care.* 14(1):1-3.

INFORMATION SYSTEMS

Butler, DL. Anderson, PS. (1992) "The use of wide area computer networks in disaster management and the implications for hospital/medical networks." *Annals of the New York Academy of Sciences.* 670:202-10, 1992 Dec 17

O'Carroll, PW. Friede, A. Noji, EK. Lillibridge, SR. Fries, DJ. Atchison, CG. (1995). "The rapid implementation of a statewide emergency health information system during the 1993 Iowa flood." *American Journal of Public Health.* 85(4):564-7.

van Bemmel, JH. Musen, MA. eds. (1997). *Handbook of medical informatics.* Houten, the Netherlands: Bohn Stafleu Van Loghum.

LEGAL

Gostin, L. (2000) Public Health Law: Power, Duty, Restraint. U of California Press. Berkeley. Milbank Memorial Fund

Public Assistance Applicant Handbook (1999) Federal Emergency Managment Agency. FEMA 323

Public Assistance Guide (1999) Federal Emergency Managment Agency. FEMA 322

Public Assistance Policy Digest (1998) Federal Emergency Managment Agency. FEMA 321

MANAGEMENT

Bouzarth, W. Mariano, J. Smith, J. (1986) "Disaster preparedness." *In* Schwartz G, Safar P, Stone I, et al: *Principles and Practice of Emergency Medicine,* ed 2. Philadelphia, WB Saunders.

Carter, WN. (1992). *Disaster Management.* Manila, Philippines: Asian Development Bank, 1992.

Dove, D. Del Guerico, L. Stahl, W. et al. (1982). "A metropolitan air–port disaster plan–Coordination of a multi-hospital response to provide on-site resuscitation and stabilization before evacuation." *J. Trauma* 22:550.

Drabek, TE. (1991): *Emergency Management: Principles and Practice for Local Government.* International City Management Association, Washington, pp. 213-218.

de Ville de Goyet, C. (1993). " Post disaster relief: The supply - man–agement challenge." *Disasters* 17(2): 169-176.

Drabek, TE. (1991). *Emergency Management: Principles and Practice for Local Government.* Washington, DC, International City Management Association.

Federal Emergency Management Agency (1999). *The Federal Response Plan.* Washington, DC: Federal Emergency Management Agency. April. FEMA 9230.1-PL

Heath, SE. et al. Integration of veterinarians into the official response to disasters (1997). *Journal of the American Veterinarian Medical Association* 210 (February 1).

Henderson, AK. Lillibridge, SR. et al. (1994). "Disaster medical assis–tance teams: Providing health care to a community struck by Hurricane Iniki." *Annals of Emergency Medicine* 23(4): 726-730.

Landesman, LY. Malilay, J. Bissell, RA. Becker, SM. Roberts, L. Ascher, M. (2001) Roles and Responsibilities of Public Health in Disaster Preparedness and Response in Novick, LF. and Mays, GP. (eds.) *Public Health Administration: Principles for Population-Based Management,* (646-708), Gaithersburg, Maryland, Aspen Publishers.

Leaning, J. Briggs, SM. Chen, LC. eds. (1999). *Humanitarian Crises: The Medical and Public Health Response.* Cambridge, MA: Harvard University Press.

Leviton, LC. Needleman, CE. Shapiro, MA. (1998). *Confronting Public Health Risks: A Decision Maker's Guide.* Thousand Oaks, CA: Sage Publications.

Logue, JN (1996). Disasters, the environment, and public health: Improving our response. *American Journal of Public Health,* 86(9):1207-1210.

Noji, EK. (1995). 26. Natural disaster management. *Management of Wilderness and Environmental Emergencies.* P. S. Auerbach. St. Louis, Mosby-Yearbook: 644-663.

Pan American Health Organization (2000). *Natural Disasters: Protecting the Public's Health.* Scientific Publication No. 575, Washington, DC, Pan American Health Organization.

Phreaner, D. Jacoby, I. et al. (1994). "Disaster preparedness of home health care agencies in San Diego County." *Journal of Emergency Medicine* 12(6): 811-818.

Sadler, A. Sadler, B. Webb, J. (1997) *Emergency Medical Care: The Neglected Public Service* Cambridge, MA, Ballinger Publishing Co.

Schultz, CH. Koenig, KL. Noji, E. (1996) A medical disaster response to reduce immediate mortality after an earthquake. *The New England Journal of Medicine.* 334(7):438-444.

Schwartz, L. (1986). Field intervention medicine. *In* Schwartz G, Safar P, Stone I, et al: *Principles and Practices of Emergency Medicine.* ed 2. Philadelphia, WB Saunders, p. 593

MENTAL HEALTH

American Psychiatric Association (1994). *Diagnostic and Statistical Manual of Mental Disorders.* Fourth Edition (DSM-IV). Washington, DC: American Psychiatric Association.

American Psychiatric Association (1988). *Post-traumatic stress disorder (brochure).* Washington, DC: APA Joint Commission on Public Affairs and the Division of Public Affairs.

Austin, LS. ed. (1992). *Responding to Disaster: A Guide for Mental Health Professionals.* Washington, DC: American Psychiatric Press.

Baum, A. Fleming, R. Davidson, LM. (1983). Natural disaster and tech–nological catastrophe. *Environment and Behavior,* 15(3):333-354.

Black, D. Newman, M. Harris-Hendriks, J. Mezey, G. eds. (1997). *Psychological Trauma: A Developmental Approach.* London: Royal College of Psychiatrists.

Bracht, N. ed. (1990). *Health Promotion at the Community Level.* Newbury Park, CA: Sage.

Carll, EK. ed. (1996). *Developing a Comprehensive Disaster and Crisis Response Program for Mental Health: Guidelines and Procedures.* Albany, NY: New York State Psychological Association (NYSPA) Disaster/Crisis Network.

DeGirolamo, G. McFarlane, AC. (1996). The epidemiology of PTSD: A comprehensive review of the international literature. In AJ. Marsella, MJ. Friedman, ET. Gerrity & RM. Scurfield, eds. *Ethnocultural Aspects of Post-traumatic Stress Disorder: Issues, Research, and Clinical Applications.* Washington, DC: American Psychological Association, pp. 33-85.

Erikson, K. (1995). *A New Species of Trouble: The Human Experience of Modern Disasters.* New York: W.W. Norton.

Everly, Jr. GS. Mitchell, JT. (1997). *Critical Incident Stress Management: A New Era and Standard of Care in Crisis Intervention.* Ellicott City, MD: Chevron Publishing Corporation.

Farberow, NL. Gordon, NS. (1981, 1995). *Manual for Child Health Workers in Major Disasters.* Washington, DC: Center for Mental Health Services, Substance Abuse and Mental Health Services Administration, U.S. Public Health Service.

Field Manual for Human Service Workers in Major Disasters (1978, 1990). Rockville, MD: National Institute of Mental Health.

Friedman, MJ. Marsella, AJ. (1996). Post-traumatic stress disorder: An overview of the concept. In AJ. Marsella, MJ. Friedman, ET. Gerrity & RM. Scurfield, eds. *Ethnocultural Aspects of Post-traumatic Stress Disorder: Issues, Research, and Clinical Applications.* Washington, DC: American Psychological Association, pp. 11-32.

Fritz, CE. (1996). *Disasters and Mental Health: Therapeutic Principles Drawn from Disaster Studies.* (Historical and Comparative Disaster Series #10). Newark, DE: Disaster Research Center, University of Delaware.

Fullerton, CS. Ursano, RJ. (1997a). Post-traumatic responses in spouse/significant others of disaster workers. In C.S. Fullerton & R.J. Ursano, eds., *Post-traumatic Stress Disorder: Acute and Long-Term Responses to Trauma and Disaster.* Washington, DC: American Psychiatric Press, pp. 59-75.

Fullerton, CS., Ursano, RJ. (1997b). The other side of chaos: Understanding the patterns of post-traumatic responses. In C.S. Fullerton & R.J. Ursano, eds., *Post-traumatic Stress Disorder: Acute and Long-Term Responses to Trauma and Disaster.* Washington, DC: American Psychiatric Press, pp. 3-18.

Gerrity, ET. Flynn, BW. (1997). Mental health consequences of disas–ters. In E.K. Noji, ed., *Public Health Consequences of Disasters.* Oxford: Oxford University Press, pp. 101-121.

Gerrity, ET. Steinglass, P. (1994). Relocation stress following natural disasters. In R.J. Ursano, BG. McCaughey & CS. Fullerton, eds., *Individual and Community Responses to Trauma and Disaster: The Structure of Human Chaos.* Cambridge: Cambridge University Press, pp. 220-247.

Girolamo, Giovani De, McFarlane, Alexander, C. (1996) In Ethnographic aspects of posttraumatic stress disorder." Edited by Anthony J. Marsella, Matthew J. Friedman, Ellen T. Gerrity and Raymond Scurfield. American Psychological Association, 1996.

Green, BL. (1996). Cross-national and ethnocultural issues in disaster research. In A.J. Marsella, MJ. Friedman, ET. Gerrity & RM. Scurfield, eds. *Ethnocultural Aspects of Post-traumatic Stress Disorder: Issues, Research, and Clinical applications.* Washington, DC: American Psychological Association, pp. 341-361.

Green, BL. Solomon, SD. (1995). The mental health impact of natural and technological disasters. In J.R. Freedy & S.E. Hobfoll, eds., *Traumatic Stress: From Theory to Practice.* New York: Plenum Press, pp. 163-180.

Gusman, FD. Stewart, J. Young, BH. Riney, SJ. Abueg, FR., Blake, DD. (1996). A multicultural approach and developmental framework for treating trauma. In AJ. Marsella, MJ. Friedman, ET. Gerrity & RM. Scurfield, eds. *Ethnocultural Aspects of Post-traumatic Stress Disorder: Issues, Research, and Clinical applications.* Washington, DC: American Psychological Association, pp. 439-457.

Hartsough, DM. Myers, DG. (1985, 1995). *Disaster Work and Mental Health: Prevention and Control of Stress Among Workers.* Washington, DC: Center for Mental Health Services, Substance Abuse and Mental Health Services Administration, U.S. Public Health Service.

Hodgkinson, PE. Stewart, M. (1998). *Coping with Catastrophe: A Handbook of Post-Disaster Psychosocial Aftercare.* Second edition. London: Routledge.

Hoffman, KJ. Sasaki, JE. (1997). Comorbidity of substance abuse and PTSD. In CS. Fullerton & RJ. Ursano, eds., *Post-traumatic Stress Disorder: Acute and Long-Term Responses to Trauma and Disaster.* Washington, DC: American Psychiatric Press, pp. 159-174.

Kasperson, RE. Kasperson, JX. (1996). The social amplification and attenuation of risk. *The Annals of the American Academy of Political and Social Science,* 545, 95-105.

Kleber, RJ. Brom, D. (1992). *Coping with Trauma: Theory, Prevention and Treatment.* Amsterdam: Swets & Zeitlinger.

Kliman, J. Kern, R. Kliman, A. (1982). Natural and human-made disas–ters: Some therapeutic and epidemiological implications for crisis intervention. In U. Reuveni, RV. Speck & JL. Speck, eds., *Therapeutic Intervention: Healing Strategies for Human Systems.* New York: Human Sciences Press.

Lystad, M. ed. (1988). *Mental Health Response to Mass Emergencies: Theory and Practice.* New York: Brunner/Mazel Publishers.

Marsella, AJ. Friedman, MJ. Gerrity, ET. & Scurfield, RM. eds. (1996). *Ethnocultural Aspects of Post-traumatic Stress Disorder: Issues, Research, and Clinical applications.* Washington, DC: American Psychological Association.

McFarlane, AC. (1995). Helping the victims of disasters. In J.R. Freedy & S.E. Hobfoll, eds., *Traumatic Stress: From Theory to Practice.* New York: Plenum Press, pp. 287-314.

McKnight, JL. Kretzmann, JP. (1990). *Mapping Community Capacity.* Evanston, IL: Center for Urban Affairs and Policy Research, Northwestern University.

Mega, LT. McCammon, SL. (1992). Tornado in Eastern North Carolina: Outreach to school and community. In LS. Austin, ed., *Responding to Disaster: A Guide for Mental Health Professionals.* Washington, DC: American Psychiatric Press, pp. 211-230.

Mitchell, JT. Everly, Jr. GS. (1997). *Critical Incident Stress Debriefing: An Operations Manual for the Prevention of Traumatic Stress Among Emergency Service and Disaster Workers (Second Edition, Revised).* Ellicott City, MD: Chevron Publishing Corporation.

Myers, D. (1994). *Disaster Response and Recovery: A Handbook for Mental Health Professionals.* Rockville, MD, U.S. Department of Health and Human Services, Public Health Service, Substance Abuse and Mental Health Services Administration, Center for Mental Health Services.

Norris, FH. Thompson, MP. (1995). Applying community psychology to the prevention of trauma and traumatic life events. In J.R. Freedy & S.E. Hobfoll, eds., *Traumatic Stress: From Theory to Practice.* New York: Plenum Press, pp. 49-71.

O'Brien, LS. (1998). *Traumatic Events and Mental Health.* Cambridge: Cambridge University Press.

Quarantelli, EL. ed. (1998). *What is a Disaster? Perspectives on the Question.* London: Routledge.

Raphael, B. Wilson, JP. (1993). Theoretical and intervention consider–ations in working with victims of disaster. In J.P. Wilson and B. Raphael, eds., *International Handbook of Traumatic Stress Syndromes.* New York: Plenum Press.

Responding to the Needs of People with Serious and Persistent Mental Illness in Times of Disaster (1996). Washington, DC: Emergency Services and Disaster Relief Branch, Center for Mental Health Services, Substance Abuse and Mental Health Services Administration.

Shrivastava, P. (1996). Long-term recovery from the Bhopal crisis. In J.K. Mitchell, ed., *The Long Road to Recovery: Community Responses to Industrial Disaster.* Tokyo: United Nations University Press, pp. 121-147.

Streeter, CL. Murty, SA. eds. (1996). *Research on Social Work and Disasters.* New York: The Haworth Press.

Terr, LC. (1992). Large-group preventive techniques for use after disaster. In LS. Austin, ed. *Responding to Disaster: A Guide for Mental Health Professionals.* Washington, DC: American Psychiatric Press, pp. 81-99.

Training Manual for Human Service Workers in Major Disasters (1978, 1996). Center for Mental Health Services, Substance Abuse and Mental Health Services Administration, U.S. Department of Health and Human Services.

Ursano, RJ. McCaughey, BG. Fullerton, CS. eds. (1994). *Individual and Community Responses to Trauma and Disaster: The Structure of Human Chaos.* Cambridge: Cambridge University Press.

Van der Kolk, BA. McFarlane, AC. Weisaeth, L. eds. (1996). *Traumatic Stress: The Effects of Overwhelming Experience on Mind, Body, and Society.* New York: The Guilford Press.

Weisaeth, L. (1993). Disasters: Psychological and psychiatric aspects. In L. Goldberger and S. Breznitz, eds., *Handbook of Stress: Theoretical and Clinical Aspects.* Second edition. New York: The Free Press.

Yehuda, R. ed. (1998). *Psychological Trauma.* Washington, DC: American Psychiatric Press.

Young, BH. Ford, JD. Ruzek, JI. Friedman, MJ. Gusman, FD. (1998). *Disaster Mental Health Services: A Guidebook for Clinicians and Administrators.* Menlo Park, CA: National Center for Post-Traumatic Stress Disorder.

MEDICAL CARE DELIVERY

Pointer, JE. Michaelis, J. et al. (1992). "The 1989 Loma Prieta earthquake: Impact on hospital patient care." *Annals of Emergency Medicine* 21(10): 1228-1233.

Quinn, B. Baker, R. et al. (1994). "Hurricane Andrew and a pediatric emergency department." *Annals of Emergency Medicine* 23(4): 737-741.

Sabatino, F. (1992). "Hurricane Andrew: South Florida hospitals shared resources and energy to cope with the storm's devastation." *Hospitals, JAHA*: 26-30.

Scott, S. Constantine, LM. (1990). "When natural disaster strikes: With careful planning pharmacists can continue to provide essential services to survivors in the aftermath of a disaster." *American Pharmacy* NS30(11): 27-31.

MORBIDITY AND MORTALITY

Burkle, FM. (ed).(1984). *Disaster Medicine*. New Hyde Park, NY: Medical Examination Publishing.

McNabb, SJ. Kelso, KY. Wilson, SA. McFarland, L. Farley, TA. (1995). "Hurricane Andrew-related injuries and illnesses, Louisiana 1992." *Southern Medical Journal* 88(6):615-8.

Noji, EK. (1993). "Analysis of medical needs during disasters caused by tropical cyclones: anticipated injury pattens." *Journals of Tropical Medicine and Hygiene* 96: 370-376.

Noji, EK. Armenian, HK. et al. (1993). "Issues of rescue and medical care following the 1988 Armenian earthquake." *International Journal of Epidemiology* 22(6): 1070-1076.

Saylor, LF. Gordon, JE. (1957). "The medical component of natural dis–asters." *A. J.Med Sci.* 1957;234:342-362.

NATURAL HAZARDS

White, GF. (1974). *Natural hazards: Local, national, global*. New York, Oxford, London, Toronto: Oxford University Press.

White, GF. and Haas, JE. (1975). *Assessment of research on natural hazards*. Cambridge, Massachusetts, London: The MIT Press.

Zebrowski, Jr. E. (1997) *Perils of a Restless Planet: Scientific Perspectives on Natural Disasters*. Cambridge, England: Cambridge University Press

PLANNING

Auf der Heide, E. (1996): Disaster planning, Part II: Disaster problems, issues, and challenges identified in the research literature. *Emerg. Med. Clin. North Am.* 14(2, May), 453-480.

Auf der Heide, E. (1994). "Designing a disaster plan: Important ques–tions." *Plant, Technology & Safety Management Series (Joint Commission on Accreditation of Healthcare Organizations)* 3 (Special Issue: Disaster Preparedness: Facing the real crisis): 7-18.

Auf der Heide E. (1996). *Community Medical Disaster Planning and Evaluation Guide*. American College of Emergency Physicians, Dallas Centers for Disease Control and Prevention, (1999)

"Public Health Performance Assessment - Emergency Preparedness," OctoberCenters for Disease Control, "Pandemic Influenza: A Planning Guide for State and Local Officials (Draft 2.1)

Dynes, RR. (1994). "Community Emergency Planning: False Assumptions and Inappropriate Analogies." *International Journal of Mass Emergencies and Disasters* 12(2 August): 141-158.

Fong, F. Schrader, DC. (1996). "Radiation disasters and emergency department preparedness." *Emergency Medicine Clinics of North America* 14(2): 349-370.

Gibbs, M. Lachenmeyer, JR. et al. (1996). "Effects of the AVIANCA air crash on disaster workers." *International Journal of Mass Emergencies and Disasters* 14(1): 23-32.

Lindell, MK. Perry, RW. (1992). *Behavioral Foundations of Community Emergency Planning.* Hemisphere Publishing Corporation, Philadelphia. pp. 34-36.

Quarantelli, EL. (1991). *Converting Disaster Scholarship into Effective Disaster Planning and Managing: Possibilities and Limitations.* Newark, DE, Disaster Research Center, University of Delaware

Waeckerle, JF. (1991). "Review Article: Disaster planning and response." *New England Journal of Medicine* 324(12): 815-821.

PUBLIC HEALTH

Lechat, MF. (1979). "Disasters and public health." *Bulletin of the World Health Organization* 57(1): 11-17.

Lillibridge, SR. Sharp, TW (1998) "Public Health Issues Associated with Disasters." In Maxcy Wallace. RB, Doebbeling. BN, and Last. TM, eds. Makey-Rosenau – Last Public Health and Preventive Medicine. Connecticut: Appleton 9 Lange 1998: 1169-1173.

Noji, E. (ed) (1997). *The Public Health Consequences of Disaster.* Oxford University Press, New York

Rosen, G. (1993). *A History of Public Health.* Johns Hopkins Univ. Press, 1993

RAPID NEEDS ASSESSMENT

Guha-Sapir, D. (1991). "Rapid assessment of health needs in mass emergencies: Review of current concepts and methods." *World Health Statistics Quarterly* 44:171-181.

Hlady, WG. Quenemoen, LG. et al. (1994). "Use of a modified cluster sampling method to perform rapid needs assessment after Hurricane Andrew." *Annals of Emergency Medicine* 24(4): 719-725.

Lillibridge, SR. Noji, EK.et al. (1993). "Disaster assessment: The emer–gency health evaluation of a population affected by a disaster." *Annals of Emergency Medicine* 22(11): 1715-1720.

International Federation of the Red Cross and Red Crescent Societies. (1993). *"Vulnerability and capacity assessment."* Geneva: International Federation of Red Cross and Red Crescent Societies.

International Federation of the Red Cross and Red Crescent Societies. (1993). *"Vulnerability and capacity assessment."* Geneva: International Federation of Red Cross and Red Crescent Societies.

Malilay, J. Flanders, WD. Brogan, D.(1996). "A modified cluster-sampling method for post-disaster rapid assessment of needs." *Bull World Hlth Org* 74:399-406.

World Health Organization. (1999). *Rapid Health Assessment Protocols for Emergencies.* Geneva, WHO.

Yahmed, SB. Koob, P. (1996). "Health sector approach to vulnerability reduction and emergency preparedness." *World Health Statistics Quarterly* 49:172-178.

RECOVERY

Ball, N. (1997) "Demobilizing and Reintegrating Soldiers: Lessons from Africa," pp. 85-105, in *Rebuilding Societies After Civil War. Critical Roles for International Assistance,* ed. Krishna Kumar, Boulder and London: Lynne Rienner Publishers.

Berke, PR. Kartez, J. Wenger, D. (1993) "Recovery after Disaster: Achieving sustainable development, mitigation and equity." *Disasters,* 17 (3): 93-109.

Cohen, R. (1995) *Refugee and internally displaced women: A development perspective.* The Brookings Institution-Refugee Policy Group Project on Internal Displacement.

Cuny, F. (1983) *Disasters and Development.* Oxford University Press.

Eadie, C. (1996) "Kobe Eight Months After: Images of the "Interim City"." *Earthquake Engineering Research Institute Special Report.*

Krug, EG. Kresnow, MJ. Peddicord ,JP. Dahlberg, LL. Powell, KE. Crosby, AE. Annest, JL. (1998) "Suicide after natural disasters." *NEJM,* 338 (6):373-8.

McDonnell, S. Troiano, RP. Barker, N. Noji, E. Hlady, GW. Hopkins, R. (1995) "Evaluation of long-term community recovery from Hurricane Andrew: Sources of assistance received by population sub-groups." *Disasters,* 19(4): 338-347.

Operations Evaluation Department. (1994) "Financing disaster reconstruction: The Popayan earthquake." *OED Precis,* #68.

Tokyo Guidelines for Trauma and Reconstruction: Draft conclusions and recommendations. Newsletter of The Japan Foundation Center for Global Partnership (CGP), Winter 1998; vol. 18.

www.cgp.org/cgplink/vol16/articlesvol16a.html
Wickramanayake, E. Shook, GA. (1995) "Rehabilitation planning for
flood affected areas of Thailand: Experience from Phipun District."
Disasters; 19 (4): 348-355.

RISK ASSESSMENT

Malilay, J. Henderson, A. McGeehin, M. Flanders, WD. (1997).
"Estimating health risks from natural hazards using risk assessment
and epidemiology." *Risk Analysis* 17:363-368.

SURVEILLANCE

Disaster surveillance

Glass, RI. Noji, EK. (1992). "Epidemiologic surveillance following dis–
asters." In: Halperin, W. Baker, EL. eds. Public health surveillance.
New York: Van Nostrand Reinhold, 195-205.
Lechat, MF. "Accident and disaster epidemiology." *Public Health
Reviews.* 21(3-4):243-53, 1993-4
Lee, LE. Fonseca, V. Brett, KM. et al.(1993). "Active morbidity surveil–
lance after Hurricane Andrew, Florida, 1992." JAMA 1993;270:591-
594.
Legome, E. Robbins, A. et al. (1995). " Injuries associated with floods:
The need for an international reporting scheme." *Disasters* 19(1):
50-54.
Lore, EL. Fonseca, V.et al. (1993). "Active morbidity surveillance after
Hurricane Andrew-Florida, 1992." *Journal of the American Medical
Association* 270(5): 591-594.
Noji, EK. (1997). "The use of epidemiologic methods in disasters." in
Noji EK (ed): *The Public Health Consequences of Disasters.* New York:
Oxford University Press, 21-36.
Western, KA. (1982). *Epidemiologic surveillance after natural disasters.*
Washington, D.C.: Pan American Health Organization,
1982:(scietific publication no. 420).
Wetterhall, SF. Noji, EK. (1997). "Surveillance and epidemiology." In:
Noji EK, ed. *The Public Health Consequences of Disasters.* New York:
Oxford University Press, 1997:37-64.

General surveillance

Halperin, W. Baker, EL. Monson, RR. eds.(1992). *Public health surveil–
lance.* New York: Van Nostrand Reinhold. 238 pp.

Klauke, DN. Buehler, JW. Thacker, SB. et al. (1988). "Guidelines for evaluating surveillance systems." MMWR 37(S-5):1-18.

Langmuir, AD. (1971). "Evolution of the concept of surveillance in the United States." *Proc Roy Soc Med* 64:9-12.

Thacker, SB. Berkelman, RL. (1988). "Public health surveillance in the United States." Epidemiol Rev 1988;10:164-190.

Thacker, SB. Berkelman, RL. Stroup, DF. (1989). "The science of public health surveillance." *J Public Health Policy* 10:187-203.

Thacker, SB. Choi, K. Brachman, PS. (1983). "The surveillance of infectious diseases." *JAMA* 249:1181-1185.

Environmental public health surveillance

Deutsch, PV. Adler, J. Richter, ED. (1992). "Sentinel markers for industrial disasters." *Israel Journal of Medical Sciences.* 28(8-9):526-33.

Thacker, SB. Stroup, DF. (1994). "Future directions of comprehensive public health surveillance and health information systems in the United States." *Am J Epidemiol,* 140:1-15.

Thacker, SB. Stroup, DF. Parrish, RG. Anderson, HA. (1996). "Surveillance in environmental public health: issues, systems, and sources." *Am J Public Health,* 86:633-638.

Surveillance after specific disasters

Centers for Disease Control and Prevention. (1996). "Deaths associated with Hurricanes Marilyn and Opal United States, September-October 1995." MMWR Morb Mortal Wkly Rep, 45:32-38.

Centers for Disease Control and Prevention. (1996). "Surveillance for injuries and illnesses and rapid health-needs assessment following Hurricanes Marilyn and Opal, September-October 1995." MMWR Morb Mortal Wkly Rep, 45:81-85.

Centers for Disease Control and Prevention.(1997)., "Tornado associated fatalities Arkansas, 1997." MMWR Morb Mortal Wkly Rep, 46:412-416.

Centers for Disease Control and Prevention.(1994). "Coccidioidomycosis following the Northridge earthquake California, 1994." MMWR Morb Mortal Wkly Rep, 43:194-195.

Centers for Disease Control and Prevention.(1990). "Surveillance of shelters after Hurricane Hugo." MMWR Morb Mortal Wkly Rep, 39:41-47.

Centers for Disease Control and Prevention.(1998). "Community needs assessment and morbidity surveillance following an ice storm Maine, January 1998." MMWR Morb Mortal Wkly Rep, 47:351-354.

Centers for Disease Control and Prevention. (1993) "Rapid assessment of vectorborne diseases during the Midwest flood- United States." MMWR - *Morbidity and Mortality Weekly Report* 43(26):481-3, 1994 Jul 8.

Centers for Disease Control and Prevention. MMWR - (1992) "Rapid assessment following Hurricane Andrew Florida and Louisiana, 1992". *Morbidity and Mortality Weekly Report.* 41(38):719, Sep 25.

Malilay, J. Guido, MR. Ramirez, AV. Noji, E. Sinks, T. (1996). "Public health surveillance after a volcanic eruption: lessons from Cerro Negro, Nicaragua, 1992." *Bulletin of PAHO,* 30(3):218-226.

Ocarroll, PW. Friede, A. Noji, EK. Lillibridge, SR. Fries, DJ. Atchison, CG. (1995). "The rapid implementation of a statewide emergency health information system during the 1993 Iowa flood." *Am J Public Health,* 85:564-567.

TECHNOLOGICAL DISASTERS

Baum, A. (1987). Toxins, technology, disasters. In G.R. VandenBos and B.K. Bryant, eds., *Cataclysms, Crises, and Catastrophes: Psychology in Action.* Washington, DC: American Psychological Association.

Becker, SM. (1997). Psychosocial assistance after environmental acci–dents: A policy perspective. *Environmental Health Perspectives,* 105(S6):1557-1563.

Bromet, EJ. Parkinson, DK., Dunn, LO. (1990). Long-term mental health consequences of the accident at Three Mile Island. *International Journal of Mental Health,* 19, 48-60.

Cuthbertson, BH. Nigg, JM. (1987). Technological disaster and the nontherapeutic community: A question of true victimization. *Environment and Behavior,* 19(4):462-483.

Edelstein, MR. (1988). *Contaminated Communities: The Social and Psychological Impacts of Residential Toxic Exposure.* Boulder, CO: Westview.

Edelstein, MR. Wandersman, A. (1987). Community dynamics in cop–ing with toxic contaminants. In I. Altman and A. Wandersman, eds., *Neighborhood and Community Environments,* Volume 9 in the Series Human Behavior and Environment: Advances in Theory and Research. New York: Plenum Press.

Haavenaar, JM. Rumyantzeva, GM. van den Brink, W. Poelijoe, NW. van den Bout, J. van Engeland, H. Koeter, MWJ. (1997). Long-term mental healths effects of the Chernobyl disaster: An epidemiologic survey of two former Soviet regions. *American Journal of Psychiatry,* 154, 1605-1607.

FRC (1996). Annex III: The role of the Red Cross and Red Crescent Societies in response to technological disasters. *International Review of the Red Cross*, 310, 55-130.

Leonard, RB.(1993). "Hazardous materials accidents: Initial scene assessment and patient care." *Aviation, Space and Environmental Medicine* June, 1993:646-661.

Levitin, HW. Siegelson, HJ. (1996). "Hazardous materials: Disaster medical planning and response." *Emergency Medicine Clinics of North America* 14(2): 327-348.

Levy, K. Hirsch, EF. Aghababian, RV. Segall, A. Vanderschmidt, H. (1999). "Radiation Accident Preparedness: report of a Training Program Involving the United States, Eastern Europe, and the Newly Independent States." *American Journal of Public Health* 89(7):115-6.

Kroll-Smith, JS. Couch, SR. (1993). Technological hazards: Social responses as traumatic stressors. In JP. Wilson and B. Raphael, eds. (1993). *The International Handbook of Traumatic Stress Syndromes.* New York: Plenum Press, pp. 79-91.

Lillibridge, SR. (1997). *Industrial Disasters.* In EK. Noji, ed., *The Public Health Consequences of Disasters.* New York: Oxford University Press, pp. 354-372.

Quarantelli, EL. (1993). The environmental disasters of the future will be more and worse but the prospect is not hopeless. *Disaster Prevention and Management*, 2, 11-25.

ABOUT THE AUTHOR

Dr. Linda Landesman, a native of Michigan, has over 25 years of experience in social services, health care and emergency preparedness. She earned Bachelors of Arts and Masters of Social Work degrees from the University of Michigan. Dr. Landesman practiced clinical social work for 10 years before pursuing a DrPH in health policy and management from the Columbia School of Public Health. Her doctoral dissertation focused on hospital preparedness for chemical accidents and won the Doctoral Dissertation Award from the Health Services Improvement Fund in 1990.

Dr. Landesman is currently an assistant vice president at the New York City Health and Hospitals Corporation where she is responsible for over $500 million in programmatic contracts. She has promoted an increased public health role in disaster preparedness and response since 1982, through the development of national EMS response standards and national APHA policy, conducting research, organizing meetings, teaching, and consulting. She is an Assistant Clinical Professor and investigator with the Center for Public Health Preparedness at the Mailman School of Public Health, Columbia University. Dr. Landesman led the CDC - ASPH sponsored effort to develop a national curriculum in the public health management of disasters. Her course is now being used nationwide.